AN INDIAN PIONEER OF SCIENCE

THE LIFE AND WORK OF SIR JAGADIS C. BOSE

Yours Sincerely
J.C. Bose

AN INDIAN PIONEER OF SCIENCE

THE LIFE AND WORK OF SIR JAGADIS C. BOSE

PATRICK GEDDES

WITH PORTRAITS AND ILLUSTRATIONS

GYAN

Published by

GYAN

Gyan Publishing House
5, Ansari Road
Daryaganj, New Delhi-110002
Phone: 011-47034999, 9811692060
E-mail: books@gyanbooks.com

Distribution Network
gyanbooks.com
India, USA, Canada, UK, Australia, France

ISBN : 978-81-212-3617-1 (PB)
First Published, London, 1920

2nd Impression 2020

Printed at: Gyan Press, Delhi.

The Life and Work of Sir Jagadis C. Bose
Author: Patrick Geddes

AN INDIAN PIONEER OF SCIENCE

THE LIFE AND WORK OF SIR JAGADIS C. BOSE

M.A., D.Sc., LL.D., F.R.S., C.I.E., C.S.I.

EMERITUS PROFESSOR, PRESIDENCY COLLEGE, CALCUTTA
DIRECTOR OF THE BOSE RESEARCH INSTITUTE

BY

PATRICK GEDDES

LATE PROFESSOR OF BOTANY (UNIV. COLL., DUNDEE)
ST. ANDREWS UNIVERSITY, AND PROFESSOR OF SOCIOLOGY
AND CIVICS, UNIVERSITY OF BOMBAY

WITH PORTRAITS
AND
ILLUSTRATIONS

LONGMANS, GREEN, AND CO.
39 PATERNOSTER ROW, LONDON, E.C. 4
FOURTH AVENUE & 30TH STREET, NEW YORK
BOMBAY, CALCUTTA, AND MADRAS

1920

PREFACE

I AM asked whether the title of this book means especially a pioneer in science, who happens to be an Indian, or a pioneer of science in and for India. The answer is—Both. For on one hand Bose is the first Indian of modern times who has done distinguished work in science, and his life-story is thus at once of interest to his scientific contemporaries in other countries and of encouragement and impulse to his countrymen. But it will also be seen, in the general world of science, independent of race, nationality and language, which looks only to positive results, that here is much of pioneering work, and this upon levels rarely attained, with intercrossing tracks still commonly held and treated as distinct—in physics, in physiology, both vegetable and animal, and even in psychology. Pioneering too in all these fields, not in virtue of mere variety of interests, of mental versatility, and of inventive faculty of the rarest kind, though all these are present, but also as guided, inspired, even impassioned, by an endowment more than usually deep and strong of that faith in cosmic order and unity which is the fundamental concept of each and all the sciences. So it has come to pass that we have in this single and long solitary worker 'a mind working in long sweeps—and attracted alike by gulfs which separate, and by borderlands which unite,' and successful to a high and rare degree in such high intellectual adventures. Hence his contributions are from their very outset towards the unification of whole groups of phenomena hitherto explored separately. But here is not simply a physicist of fine experimental skill, and of full subtlety, but also a naturalist of the keenest interest in life-processes and life-movements, and these among the most perplexing and intricate. His special and characteristic lines of pioneering have thereby arisen. With this dual outlook and equipment, as physicist he brings to the physiologist his intellectual and experimental resources with fruitful results to knowledge, and henceforth with transformation of laboratories of physiology and their standards of observation and research by the refinement of his new methods and appliances. Rarer still, he has not only divined in matter, as sometimes did physicists before him, 'the promise and potency of life,' but has experimentally demonstrated, as in seeming inert metals, not only a strangely life-like passivity to environment, but a yet more life-like reactivity to it as well.

Here, then, is offered some account of pioneerings in discovery, and of the type and personality of the pioneer also. In science we need more and more of both, in the East no doubt, but in the West likewise. Hence the present outline of main scientific results and biographic sketch together.

And though alike in scientific summary and in biography the less the writer obtrudes himself the better, a few words of personal explanation are permissible, even customary in any preface. Though primarily of biological interests and trainings, I felt in student days the wonder and call of the physical sciences, and realised something of their bearings on physiology. As for some forty years a teacher and investigator in botany and more of physiological and evolutionary interests than of traditional ones, I have constantly felt my limitations in vegetable physiology in general, and with regard to plant-movements in particular; and thus to some extent realised the interest of Bose's work when I first met him nearly twenty years ago, and when later I read a volume he sent me. But in the press of other work and without actual acquaintance with his new and strange devices and apparatus, the impression gradually faded. And only in the last two or three years, in Calcutta and at Darjeeling, have I gradually come to know more and more of Bose and of his researches, of his Institute, and of its aims.

All the sciences and all their scientific men are social products, and must be studied as such in the sociological way. This book, though originally planned in its simplest and most direct aspect and purpose—as an exposition of a life-work—is thus something of a sociological study also; and as such, one of its purposes—that of incentive to encouragement and emancipation of the student, of science in general, and in India in particular—may be more clear. For here is, at any rate, no conventional rhapsody on a 'genius,' but an endeavour to see what may be the conditions favourable to life and conducive to full mental stature and productivity; and what the adverse conditions which may arrest, yet may also provoke to, their surmounting. And it is this latter which I wished to make specially clear from the study of Bose's life, so that others also may be encouraged to face their difficulties, and to overcome them as far as may be, towards something greater than merely individual end.

Enough then of preface. Any dedication should be to those in memory or still with us, who as we shall find have best helped the hero of this tale upon his life's adventure. Nor should we forget his old teachers, his friends and fellow-workers in science, nor yet his assistants and pupils, by whom his work has also henceforth increasingly to be continued; nor that active youth of the Indian Universities to whom it is so largely addressed.

P. G.

JERUSALEM, 1920.

CONTENTS

ILLUSTRATIONS

PLATES

ILLUSTRATIONS IN THE TEXT

THE LIFE AND WORK
OF
SIR JAGADIS C. BOSE

CHAPTER I

CHILDHOOD AND EARLY EDUCATION

'THE boy is father of the man.' Hence the writers of biographies have always sought to learn and tell all they could of the early environment of their subjects; for these formative influences, and the response of childhood and youth to them, are often seen to throw lights on characters as brought out in later years, and so on their achievements. Thus Auguste Comte—as yet the most comprehensive and appreciative of biographers, since most clearly setting before himself and his successors the appreciation of the main contributors to civilisation—was wont to quote two lines of de Vigny's: 'What is a great life? It is a thought of youth wrought out in ripening years.' And as psychology progresses, we are learning more and more fully not only how fundamental is ancestral and parental influence, how influential are early conditions, but also how significant are childish feelings and fancies, dreamings and doings; how important too are the boy's thoughts and endeavours; and how deeply determinative those of the adolescent, as he looks onwards towards his life, and makes his choices among its oft-dividing ways.

Vikrampur is a large area west of Dacca, the capital of Eastern Bengal. It is a region of fair fertility, but even now outside that of jute cultivation, so that its old character may still be seen. The Mahommedan population is considerable; but for Hindus it is interesting as rich in traditional culture, even in sacred associations; and of course fifty years ago it was much more so. Vikrampur is included in the Dacca district; and the village of Rarikhal in Vikrampur is the family home of the Boses, this being about 35 miles west of Dacca city. Jagadis Chunder Bose was born on November 30, 1858, and his early childhood was mainly spent at Faridpur, which is the centre of the next district, 35 miles farther west again. These distances are as the crow flies; to get from one place to another the communication was by river and thus circuitous.

Vikrampur has from very ancient times been famous as a seat of learning. From surrounding districts, even from distant provinces of India, youths were wont to come to the 'Tols'—Sanskrit schools kept by Brahmins of the old type and learning: in fact we may think of Vikrampur as till lately a University centre of the type of bygone ages. Of this a good deal was surviving fifty years ago, and something lingers to this day. Tradition is extant of there being a *Man Mandir* or astronomical observatory where transit of stars and planets were observed. Why this localisation? As so commonly throughout India, definite historic records are lacking, though oral traditions of saints and sages used to be rife. Moreover the evidence of surrounding monuments, and yet more numerous ruins, proves Vikrampur to have been a peculiarly rich and active centre of Buddhist culture: hence it is but natural that the Hindu revival which followed this should have been active here, and so strike deep and firm roots in its turn.

These ancient cultures, then, have their influence in producing a population interested in education, affected by ideas and ideals: hence it is not solely for Bose's individual sake that a new and ambitious school is at present being founded in his ancestral village to bear his name, but also as an expression of the old cultural interest, here as elsewhere feeling its way towards readjustment to the times. Mahommedans here, too, as nearly always tinged by their Hindu surroundings, are moving along with them.

But East Bengal people are by no means all a gentle peasant folk, responsive to religion and education. The great rivers introduce strong elements of movement and enterprise, of fishery and transport ; in various ways stimulating, adventurous, unsettling, even to the peasant villages. The contrast, the mingling and the clashing of peasant and fisher populations, so deeply formative throughout the history of Mediterranean and Western Europe, have long been here in evidence, though of course on the smaller scale of a river system as compared with seas and coasts, and thus operative on the small scale instead of the great. Peasant prosperity was advanced by easy transports, and vigour and wellbeing improved by fish diet. The villagers were also relieved of their more restive young spirits by the call of the rivers, with their long perspectives promising freer and more adventurous careers.

But beside the elements of sport and luck which give charm to the fisher life, and the more ambitious lure of gain, even comparative fortune, through transports and commerce, these rivers have an old and evil reputation for dacoity ; for such robberies they notably facilitate, since their numberless creeks and adjacent jungles afford sally-ports and refuges by turns. Here then we have the conditions at once for agricultural and riverine villages in prosperity, but also for a vigorous lawless class, who find these villages worth robbing. Yet the robbers never became strong enough to dominate their district: for even apart from the vigilance and repression of governments, the water-thief and pirate cannot venture far from his boat. Thus his depredations were but sufficient only to produce watchfulness in the villages, with frequent and ready defence and resistance, attack and pursuit, in turn. In short, such villagers tend to be roused beyond the plodding life of the peasant, which is too readily acceptant of life's ills ; and they develop more or less of that type of people described by an old traveller as 'difficult and dangerous to deal with; for when you attack them they defend themselves.' Modern government, with its magistracy and police, has long abated this defensive necessity; yet its best instruments for maintaining security are obviously the picked local men who in earlier times were such village defenders; while the best of local magistrates is the man who would have been their leader, at once by natural and acquired qualities.

Here then in this Faridpur district we see, though in too scanty outline, other main factors, besides those of Vikrampur, in the child Jagadis' early surroundings and upbringing. These factors were operative in eliciting that note of strenuous and persistent courage in facing dangers and adversities, and of untiring combativeness against every difficulty, which we shall find throughout his youthful and maturing years.

For Bose's father—Bhagaban Chunder Bose, Deputy Magistrate of Faridpur—was the active defender, not only of the townlet, but of the scores of villages around as well. The modern magistrate is mainly settled between his court-house and his home; but here in those days a man was needed, picked not only for judicial capacity, intelligence and local knowledge, but for active initiative and courage, and thus prepared at any moment to assume command of his own police and his people as well, and be ready even to raid the raiders. Of this readiness various stories might be told. As a single example, hearing of a gang of dacoits in his neighbourhood, Mr. Bose mounted an elephant and, with the very few police available, rode straight into the very heart of the dacoits' camp. Taken by surprise, they broke and scattered; the ready magistrate dropped down, captured the leader with his own hands, and took him back for trial.

Such vigour of action, with total freedom from those elements of tacit compromise between police and crime which had sometimes existed before (and are said even now not to be unknown in India), could not but exasperate the dacoits; and their fiercer spirits repeatedly organised attempts at revenge. One group, whom he had tried and sentenced, turned on him as they were being led away with the threat that 'when we get out, we will make the red horse fly.' Three or four years later they kept their word. One midnight the thatch of Mr. Bose's bungalow was set on fire from three or four corners, and the outhouses also were ablaze. Suddenly aroused from sleep by the crackling and smoke, the household could but rush out into the compound, without time to remove anything. The immediate neighbours, who as it happened were mostly Mahommedans, hastened to the rescue. One of them saw in the burning house a small figure, which in the smoke and firelight he mistook; he ran back to Mr. Bose, saying, 'You would not like us to touch your idol, but I think it can be saved.' 'Idol! I have no idol,—let me see!'—and here was the little daughter (afterwards Mrs. M. M. Bose), then aged only three, who in the scattered confusion of the family had not been missed, but was sitting on her bed, fascinated rather than terrified by the scene. The father rushed in, and carried the child out; and a moment after the roof fell in. Everything was lost; when the strong-box was extricated from the ruins, ornaments and money, gold, silver and copper were fused into a mass; and the horses and cows in the outhouses had perished. But one neighbour lent a part of his house, others lent clothing and cooking-vessels, and so the family encamped as best it could for a month or more, until a fresh house—this time prudently of substantial construction—was secured. The burned house had been Mr. Bose's own, so this severe loss was a beginning of the many misfortunes of his later career.

A year or two later, when the boy Jagadis was five or six, he recalls from a 'Mela' or popular fair, a wrestling match among the policemen, mostly big stalwart fellows from the North-Western Provinces, who practised much among themselves. A fine performance, though it was said afterwards not without previous arrangement of who was to win. A peasant onlooker remarked that if he were allowed to take part he would wrestle the champion. So Mr. Bose took him at his word, and started the pair. Sure enough the peasant made good his boast; but the policeman, indignant at his defeat, suddenly threw his legs round his victor's neck before he could rise. The peasant was plainly choking; the spectators shouted for fair play; but the angry man would not let go, not even for Mr. Bose's orders; so he had to strike him sharply on the feet till he relaxed, leaving his unlucky victor half-strangled. The fellow was revengeful as well as angry; and at a quiet corner of the road he lay in wait for Mr. Bose, as he would come to the *Jatra*, the old form of Indian drama, to be played that evening. He missed his intended victim; so outside the big tent where the play was held, he egged on his fellow-policemen, who were also feeling humiliated before the peasants, to annoy and hinder them as they came to the performance, and keep them out of the tent, even with blows. Mr. Bose, hearing a scuffle, came up; and seeing the policemen were bullying, and without cause, demanded their sticks from them, and took up an armful. The ex-champion refused: Bose pulled the bamboo from his hands, and a sword fell out. With his criminal intent thus publicly exposed, the man fell down at Mr. Bose's feet, and confessed his intention to murder him. Then and there he was forgiven: 'Get up; go back to your duty.' He was a decent man ever afterwards.

Another story of the same type—of mercy following justice, instead of superseding it—is of a notorious dacoit to whom he had given a long sentence. After his years of jail were served, he came to Mr. Bose and said, 'What am I to do? I can get no honest employment: I have no chance as a released convict.' Said Mr. Bose, I will take you into my service: this little boy has to begin school; carry him there, and bring him back every day.'

So this young Jagadis, mounted on the dacoit's side, had a glorious half-hour or more each way, his infant mind being fed with all the stories of his new guardian's adventures —one for each of the spear-thrusts and arrow-wounds from the old fights of his wild days, which had covered his breast and arms with scars. Tales of the assembling dacoits and of their attacks on a village, with suddenly lighted torches and loud war-cries, to scare the people and take them unawares. Yet tales also of the courage of the defenders, now of their defeat and robbery, or again of their successful resistance; tales of his own narrow escapes and of the death of companions, or their capture, and finally of his own: all these tales and more were vividly told again and again to the wondering child. So here at first-hand was that romantic arousal to the dangers and adventures of life, for which most youngsters have to depend on books alone, as of Red Indians for modern Western boys, or of highwaymen or pirates in their grandfathers' time. After a year of this companionship, young Jagadis was given a pony; and this became a part of the charge of the dacoit, who was always as honest and faithful a servant as could be. Once indeed he had a special opportunity of proving himself true to his salt. On one of the family's visits to the old family home at Vikrampur, on Mr. Bose's annual vacation-leave, a long boat journey, a suspicious-looking boat, with many rowers, dashed out of a creek, and made after them: plainly dacoits, from whom there seemed no escape. But now our tamed dacoit rose to the occasion: he jumped up on the boat roof and, standing erect to be recognised, gave a long and peculiar call. It was at once understood and accepted, for the pursuers straightway turned round and disappeared. This man remained with the family for four or five years in all, until Mr. Bose's promotion to Burdwan, when he returned to his native village, armed with the respectable record of a magistrate's old servant, behind which no one need inquire. Are criminals often thus kindly and wisely treated? If not, have not the world's magistratures, nowadays so regularised and formalised in their procedure, something to learn from such old-fashioned predecessors—of whom there have always been a few, but too few in every land?

The innate gentleness of this vigorous magistrate becomes increasingly manifested throughout our too scanty records of a career which plainly in itself might have made a volume. For despite unusually active duties, he found time alike for advancing material interests and cultural ones; and these both separately and together. Thus year by year he organised one of the Melas which were even then beginning to fall into desuetude, but which he effectively revived. He encouraged their old elements of religious festivals, public holiday, and fair, with dramatic and athletic performances; and he was wont to organise along with them an exhibition of local manufactures and agricultural products—much, in fact, as if in European villages we could revive the old 'Holy Fair' with its sports and miracle plays, arranging along with them an exhibition of home industries and an agricultural and horticultural show.

One of his son's vivid recollections is of the joys of a Mela to which his father had brought an excellent troupe of *Jatra* players, whose performance was as great and amazing a joy to the Bose children as to the people. This appreciation is evidenced not only by an enduring memory of the vivid scenes, the breathless and crowded audience, but by a quaint and pleasing recollection of the English chief magistrate who was in the audience, and who not only emptied his pocket of the substantial handful of rupees he had brought for the players after their performance, but—stirred and shaken altogether out of usual official decorum and reserve—bade them wait while he ran hastily back to his house for more; and with many added compliments, sent the delighted players on their homeward way.

In 1869 (when Jagadis was ten years old) his father became Assistant-Commissioner of Burdwan, where he remained four or five years, till 1874. Here the duties were more of the ordinary kind ; but a new emergency soon arose to call out his powers. Burdwan had long enjoyed a peculiarly good reputation for health ; so much so indeed as to be a frequent holiday centre for Calcutta people, who described it as a veritable sanatorium on their return. Malaria had been almost unknown ; but suddenly in 1870 there was an outbreak, which is still remembered as among the severest in the recent tragic records of Bengal. Thousands perished, leaving a multitude of orphans. The Assistant-Commissioner, after energetic work during the epidemic, took their case actively in hand—not only giving, collecting, and administering relief, but establishing industries, whereby the boys might be trained to self-supporting usefulness. No building was available, so he gave up a great part of his own large house and compound ; and there he opened workshops in carpentry, in metal turning, in general metal-work, and even a foundry. From this there survives a big and noble brass vessel still in daily use in the Bose household in Calcutta—an heirloom which will long survive to show the quality of the foundry's products. Here too the little Jagadis begged from his mother some old brass vessels, and persuaded the foundryman to cast them into quite a good-sized brass cannon, which was fired off in season and out of season accordingly, and is still looked back to with an affection even exceeding that for the scientific toys of his later life, more elaborate but less noisy and formidable.

In 1875 Mr. Bose became Executive Officer in charge of the Cutwa Sub-division, and here he came to the severest emergency of his career—the terrible famine of 1880. Though now past his prime, he faced this disaster with fuller energy than ever, organising relief throughout his district. But after the famine was ended, the nervous wear and tear, as well as the physical strain of such work, told heavily on him. With heroic asceticism, he could not bear to eat well while the people starved ; and so went out day by day to the starving villagers, with long rides out and home, and painful overwork between, with only a few handfuls of powdered wheat, taken with water as chance allowed. With broken health—apparently a slight stroke of paralysis—he was thus compelled to take two years of medical leave, which he spent mainly in Calcutta, where his son was by this time at College. Here too his busy brain could not rest. He had always seen the need of promoting Indian agriculture and industry: and as for such a man thought is inseparable from action, he more and more invested in active enterprise the considerable savings of his career, supplemented as these were from home property and by family inheritance. He acquired land in the Terai and set about clearing and stock farming; but despite the excellence of some of the produce, it lay too far from markets, and the land was unhealthy as well. The enterprise therefore ended with loss. Tea-planting was also then beginning: he saw its possibilities and argued—If Scotsmen can face such enterprises and such climate, why should not Indians do the same? So he acquired a couple of thousand acres in Assam. Large expenditure was needed for clearing and planting, and this again in unhealthy conditions; additional capital had to be borrowed at high interest, far more than the slowly beginning returns of tea could meet: thus anxieties, losses, disappointments, year after year. At length, though unhappily not in his time, this pioneering has prospered, and the plantation has for a good many years been increasingly successful; first in the hands of an Indian manager, and now of sons of his daughters, effective in their turn.

The final disaster was that of a weaving company in Bombay which Mr. Bose had been persuaded by high and patriotic promises, anticipating those of the later Swadeshi movement, to support with his remaining capital. With this the directors then absconded, leaving no trace.

Still the sufferer was not embittered by his disasters; and at the expiry of his long sick leave he resumed his official duties, this time at Pabna, where he worked on for four or five years longer, till the age of retirement. We may now return to earlier and happier years, and to the father's virile initiation and guidance of his son's education.

A father so exceptionally active in public duties—and these beyond ordinary routine and with external interests as well, in these days generally leaves the care of his children's education to others. But not so in the Bose household, where the father all along was felt not only as authority, but as guide and friend. Philosopher too for the child Jagadis, to whom the father, discerning nascent powers, wisely gave all the time he could spare, especially during those earliest years of a child's development and awakening, perhaps the most marvellous of all the many wonders of mental evolution, and correspondingly important for the educator. Tired after his long day, the father used to lie down beside the child after the evening meal, to encourage and patiently answer the flood of questions which the eager little observer had been gathering for him throughout the day, and which he had to go through before he could be induced to settle down to sleep. 'I saw so-and-so to-day: why was that?'—was a standard type of question, and always patiently answered when possible; yet often—perhaps most important and educative of all for the future investigator—with a candid confession of ignorance, and never any of the evasion, or pretence of knowledge beyond a child's, which is so common a discouragement to children from parents less frank and wise. 'I don't know, my son: we cannot tell; we know so little about nature!' was thus a frequent reply: but instead of lowering the child's respect, as foolish parents and teachers fear, this only aroused further wonder, and kept curiosity and observation alive. In such ways it is that the questioning child later becomes the scientific man: and what scientific man worth the name in history is more than such a child of larger growth? The 'advancement of Science' is no such easy matter as founders of its schools and departments suppose. It requires a corresponding supply of men of science; these again are not the mere products of specialist training. Scientific training can only be of real service to the few survivors amidst the too common home and family indifference to knowledge. That is only advanced by those who, when children, were encouraged to observe and question, and were not silenced and dulled for life, like their elders before them, with 'Don't ask silly questions!' or evaded with 'I have no time!'

A quaint memory of this intensity of questioning of the father survives—that of the good grandmother pretending to frighten the little Jagadis with a big stick—and really a little angry: 'Boy, why don't you let my son sleep? Don't you know he is tired out? You will be the death of him!'

Here is a flash of child-insight. 'Father, before coming in I saw a bush on fire! I went to it, and saw it was all full of flies—flies all on fire! What was this? What did it mean? Why did they do this?' Then the candid answer, which even naturalists had not then got beyond. 'I cannot tell: we know too little!' 'Father, is not beauty enough?' So the writer has seen his own little boy too fascinated by some outdoor sight to come in to food; and then, when at last reluctantly brought in, and asked, 'What kept you—why did you not come?'—reply, 'Beauty is better than hunger!' (meaning of course the satisfaction of it). Such incidents show that the philosophy of beauty—of which so many thinkers have had glimpses, as well as the poets and artists their fuller vision—is natural to childhood; so Croce or Baldwin, as main exponents of this philosophy to-day in the West and in America, are plainly also children who have kept this early and natural vision of the world.

Here is another quaint reminiscence of child and grandmother. A devout soul, often in prayer, she was wont daily to model in clay, to concentrate her devotions, an image of Shiva: and this, after worship and offering of flowers, was thrown back to the earth—an evidence, we may note in passing, that 'idolatry' is not so idolatrous as we are often told, but may be purely symbolic. This well-kneaded clay was valued by the children for their less spiritual efforts; and the little Jagadis was wont to wait patiently until worship was over, and he could claim the image, no longer sacred, for modelling of playthings. But one day the devotions were unusually long-continued, and the child could restrain himself no longer and so ran off with the image, while in use. The grandmother's shock was great when she realised the sacrilege; and though the offender was gently dealt with, Brahmins and poor folks were fed, and other expiatory rites performed.

As said before, the Bose family lands were at Rarikhal, a Vikrampur village 35 miles east from Faridpur, so that the old home was visited at most hardly once a year; and the main environment for the children's years was that of the Faridpur official residence—a fairly spacious dwelling, with good-sized compound and garden, beside the main road and separated only by this and a large meadow from a branch of the Padma river: one not of great size, as the main East Bengal rivers go, but strong and turbulent in flood-time.

The roadside stream too then ran strong, and especially where narrowed by the little bridge leading to the house: so there the child would watch the river—' Water moving! —Moving water!'—with an intensity, a strong fascination still vividly remembered by the ageing man. Here plainly was one of those deep and elemental child-experiences of matter and motion which were needed to make the physicist later; to whom 'kinetic energy,' 'wave-motion,' and the like, were never the mere book-terms of the crammed student, but expressed and defined real imagery from early experience. Thus the man's scientific and speculative thoughts find ready store of early and vivid images to attach themselves to—images at once concrete and beautiful, fascinating and mysterious. And does not the electrician's mental conception owe such clearness as it has been acquiring for the last century not a little to the imageries of water in movement, as from 'current' onwards?

Besides such subconscious preparation of the future physicist, the boy had from the first a strong interest in animal life, which might well have made him a zoologist. The fish and fish-trap of the little home-bridge over the road-stream, the water-snake he captured, to the alarm of his elder sister, are to this day vivid memories. So too are the varied insects, so often beautiful or strange, in which India abounds. But above all the kindly creatures, which could be made pets of, attracted him; and this taste was wisely encouraged from the first.

From his fifth year he was given a pony, and soon learned to stick on—indeed so well and pluckily that at the Faridpur races some of the spectators in fun said to the child, 'Go on; you are to race too!' Taking them at their word, the child stirred on his pony, which rose fully to the occasion, and carried him for his first gallop round the course after the big horses. The rough saddle-girths, which he had to grip with his short legs, and with all his might—he had no stirrups—scratched and tore his skin so deeply that it still bears the marks; but he felt the joy of the race, stuck to his purpose, finished the round, and came in duly last, to receive hearty praise, as of victory. He said nothing of his wounds, till the blood betrayed them, and he was sent home for repairs. Thus early in childhood does the man's character appear. Again, just before beginning school, little Jagadis had seen a man brought in mauled by a tiger, and watched the village surgery of his wounds. Some days after, being reproved by his mother, he made off into the sugar-cane plantation, where the tiger had seized his victim, there to offer himself up in his turn—and thus make mother repent her hard words! But deep among the rustling canes, his courage failed him; and he returned with wailings, which soon brought him maternal consolation and renewed peace.

But in these modern days of earlier and earlier schooling even then beginning, a boy's home freedom soon ends; and even with his fifth year Jagadis was sent to school. There were two schools in Faridpur: one vernacular, established by Mr. Bose for the children of the people; the other the Government school with its instruction in English; and to this practically all destined for a more advanced education were sent from their earliest years. But here Mr. Bose, defying the local public opinion and the shocked remonstrances of his friends, and even of his own clerks, whose sons were at the English school, insisted on sending his boy to the vernacular one. And this with outspoken expression of his two reasons, educational and social—that a child should know his own mother tongue before beginning English; and further, that he should first know his own people, and not be kept apart by that false pride which nowadays in India tends to separate the prosperous classes from their less fortunate brethren—here following the disastrous example set by England, which for two generations has been so deeply influenced by 'Tom Brown's Schooldays,' yet has missed their earliest and perhaps most truly educative prologue, telling of Tom in the little village school before going to the great public one. Jagadis' companions were the sons of fisher-folk and peasants, and a natural comrade to and from school was the son of his father's orderly. So to this day, though the formal teaching of the school has long faded from memory, there survive many lively impressions of the peasant-life, and with enduring sympathy, perhaps most vividly of all, the stories of the fisher-boys, of their fathers' experience of the river, with its incidents and dangers. All these the boy eagerly wove into his imaginative world of the wonders of nature and the romance of man; moreover, these went well with the dacoit servant's adventures already mentioned. This little Faridpur school — essentially of the 'Three R's'—seems to have been already moving into that well-conventionalised dullness which has been so characteristic of those of the past generation in East and West alike, and from which both are too slowly escaping. Indeed in those days games—which in later years have become so popular, at length even in many schools compulsory, were still contraband. The master strongly disapproved of cricket, even in the boys' free afternoon hours, as 'a waste of time,' which should be given for the preparation of lessons. But the boys—there as everywhere spontaneously carrying out this needed scholastic revolution—were too clever for their pedagogue. They got the village carpenter to shape them rough bats and stumps; and from the juice of an india-rubber tree, slowly rolling and modelling it, they managed a pretty fair ball. For a field they chose a broad road-crossing, at a quiet place well off the main way between village and school: they posted a scout at each of the approaches from these, and so played with fearful joy; till sometimes the alarm was given of the suspicious master's coming. But the boys were ready for him: the stumps were pulled, and all dived into the nulla-bed, where they had already collected a store of dry leaves; among these they lay concealed till the danger had passed, and, happier than 'the babes in the wood,' they could come out to resume their game.

The schoolbooks too were already more or less acquiring the European standard, their cram-trade type, and so could be of little interest to the children: still, although more slowly, the young Jagadis did really learn to read for himself at home. Thanks to the good early start given by the *Jatras*, the old popular plays mentioned above, he grew more and more interested in the stories of the 'Mahabharata' and 'Ramayana.' In the latter the character of Rama, and still more the soldierly devotion of his brother Lakshmana, impressed him; but 'the characters were mostly too good, too perfect.' It was the old warriors of the 'Mahabharata,' more rudely virile and strenuous, with their defects and qualities, at once human and superhuman, who made more appeal to the imagination of the boy, and who have thus made more impression upon his character and outlook on life. Above all, and most characteristically, it was Karna who became the boy's hero; and this from ten years old onwards, up to the formative years of puberty —indeed so deeply that it might still be put on his garden-stage to-day and the part vividly played by him, despite grey hairs and science! Indeed it should be so; for hear him talk: 'Karna! Karna! the greatest of all the heroes! Eldest of the Pandavas, he should have been the king; but he was more—the son of a great god. Floated away by his mother, he was found and brought up by the wife of a charioteer, who trained him to be the great warrior he was. From his low caste came rejections, came every disadvantage; but he always played and fought fair! So his life, though a series of disappointments and defeats to the very end—his slaying by Arjuna—appealed to me as a boy as the greatest of triumphs. I still think of the tournament where Arjuna had been victor, and then of Karna coming as a stranger to challenge him. Questioned of name and birth, he replies, "I am my own ancestor! You do not ask the mighty Ganges from which of its many springs it comes: its own flow justifies itself, so shall my deeds me!" Then later, when before the great battle his mother reveals to him the secret of his birth, and tells him that if he will refrain from this contest with her sons—whom he now for the first time knows to be his younger brothers—she will answer for it that he shall be their chief, and reign as Emperor; he says "No! Those who brought me up are my true mother and father, poor though they be; and it is Duryadhana, King of the Kauravas, who has been my chief through life. I cannot change sides now. But this I promise you: on your other sons, my brothers, I will not lay a hand, save only on Arjuna; but him I must fight to the end!" And then their battle! At Arjuna he aims his arrow, and would have slain him; but a defending god shakes the earth under his feet as he lets the arrow fly, and so it misses his enemy by a hairbreadth. Now the arrow was magical, though Karna knew it not; so it flew back into his hand and spoke to him: "I was made to kill Arjuna; with my winged sharpness and your aim we are invincible: aim me once more." But Karna threw it away, saying, "I will have no advantage; I fight but in my own strength!" And so he took again another arrow. But this time the unfriendly god suddenly opened an earth-crack which swallowed Karna's chariot-wheel; he leapt down to lift it out, and as he stooped Arjuna cut him down with his great sword; and so he fell, still defiant of his fate!

'This too was the hero I loved to identify with my own father—always in struggle for the uplift of the people, yet with so little success, such frequent failures, that to most he seemed a failure. All this too gave me a lower and lower idea of all ordinary worldly success—how small its so-called victories are!—and with this a higher and higher idea of conflict and defeat; and of the true success born of defeat. In such ways I have come to feel one with the highest spirit of my race; with every fibre thrilling with the emotion of the past. That is its noblest teaching—that the only real and spiritual advantage and victory is to fight fair, never to take crooked ways, but keep to the straight path, whatever be in the way!'

Again—and still in his own words—'I feel how necessary it is to keep alive the great traditions of the heroic age of India through travelling *Jatra* players and the reciters of the epics. It is through them that the highest national culture has been kept alive among the people. They are fast disappearing, and we must either revive the institution or have its modern equivalent. Last night I was thinking of your Edinburgh and London Masques of Learning, with our Indian students presenting our traditions. Why not do the same here, on the full Indian scale, from the old Aryan forefathers onwards, and with all races, all castes, with their heroes and their sages? And the cities too, from the early days of old Pataliputra, and holy Benares! Yes, and on to modern Bombay.

And the people too ; from our old primitive folk to modern Bengal, and to Calcutta, with its poets, artists, thinkers ! Why cannot this be done ? It should be ! It must be ! Then and then only shall we fully realise the true India, where all peoples with their traditions became unified by the spirit of their land, and where even elements seemingly discordant may yield factors of individuality and strength. It is these which have kept India rejuvenescent and ever evolving ; and which will save her from that palsy of death which has extinguished so many of her ancient contemporaries !'

To all this the writer cannot but warmly agree ; since for him, among all the many advances of education, amid which he has worked experimentally throughout life, there is none in his experience which has more fully justified its value than does dramatisation ; and this from the earliest childish make-believe and its small home scenes, and through village and family plays, up to the largest culture-pageanting which University has yet made for City. So let him recall from one of these Masques its scene of highest dramatic and literary commemoration for the English tongue—that of the Mermaid Tavern, with Ben Jonson in its chair, and Shakespeare making his farewell to him and all his old companions. Among them high place was given to three whose names are seldom remembered, yet who were none the less the virtual professoriate of that illustrious group of dramatists and poets. For one was the chronicler who gave Shakespeare his plot for 'Macbeth,' and for his English historical plays ; another the translator of Plutarch's ' Lives ' of the great Greeks and Romans, without which we should lack Mark Antony, and more ; and the third was the translator of Montaigne, whose kindly wisdom suffused Shakespeare's thought, and kindled Bacon to his scarcely less immortal Essays. Such a scene is thus no mere past revival, but an affirmation too, of a long-lost yet now returning secret—that of the permeation of the Theatre with the great heritage of the university. For by this union the one may be redeemed from its too common triviality, or worse : the other from its too common dullness, and worse ; and thus may come, through these together, the needed renewal of popular culture as well.

Return from such forecasts of the coming education of the next generation to the early days of our elder one, fifty years ago ; and so start with young Jagadis at his next school. At this time his father was transferred to Western Bengal, as the Assistant-Commissioner of Burdwan. By nine years old his vernacular grounding, on which his father had so wisely insisted, was secure enough to justify his sending him now to a higher English school ; and so, after three months at the Hare School in Calcutta, he was sent to the more strictly English teaching of St. Xavier's. Even then it was introducing that high educational tradition of the Jesuits which, despite Protestant and other ill will, has made their teaching respected in all lands. Still, we scientific men cannot but plead for further progress into that fuller life of all studies with which the Jesuits, and more or less all other Western schools, so vividly began. Hence, as indeed for most of us in East or West, the boy's real and inward education was largely left in his own hands, and in those of external circumstances, and these were not without their painful sides. The school was almost exclusively of English boys, themselves but little acquainted with Bengali, and that not of the best ; so little Jagadis's situation was perplexing, with only a beginning of English, enough to puzzle out sentence by sentence, but not really to read, much less to talk. Moreover, while the other boys were at home in the great city, the newcomer was completely a country boy, with no previous town experience at all, and with his familiar world suddenly left behind, and of little avail, save as a solace of memory. After the teasings and baitings which new boys have so often to suffer, there came the compulsory fight ; in this case—quite normally as boys' stories go—with a substantially bigger fellow, the class champion, not to say bully, who had already had frequent experience in the use of his fists, while the little Jagadis had never yet clenched his fist at all. Heavily pounded accordingly, with bleeding nose and dazed and watery eyes he seemed defeated and the fight practically at an end; but then came a burst of war-fury, a memory perhaps of the old heroes, at any rate an onslaught so furious as to surprise the other, and knock him down, wellnigh stunned, and unwilling or unable to rise at call. So the youngster was hailed victor, and acquired full rights of freemanship; yet hardly of comradeship, for the respective backgrounds of town and country, of East Bengal and England, remained too different. A further disadvantage was that Jagadis had been placed in a hostel in which the others were not schoolboys, but students of different colleges, who took little or no notice of the little chap, and whose world was also too far away. Though not wholly isolated from games of his schoolfellows, he found his main interest through return to his home pursuits. His pocket money was spent on animal pets, and to their housing and tending his spare time was devoted. In the corner of the compound too he laid out a little garden and spent much ingenuity upon its water-supply, winding about some pipes which he managed to lay hands on, and making a little stream with a little bridge, evidently based on those of home. It is amusing to note the renewal of this piping and stream in later years in Bose's Darjeeling garden, and to find stream, bridge and all in the little garden of his Calcutta home, next the Bose Institute. Indeed the writer, as veracious chronicler and would-be interpretative critic, cannot but see in this old child-interest the explanation of an otherwise unintelligibly strong, even emphatic, longing for a stream and bridge in the recent lay-out of his enlarged garden at the Bose Institute last year. The writer's argument of impracticability, joined to those of the architect, at the time discouraged them; yet we see that the mature Director of the Bose Institute may still be constrained, by his inmost and subconscious self, to introduce them, despite all our arguments! For not simply is the boy the father of the man: the boy is the man; and the happiest man is he who most truly remains the boy.

In such ways the man's happiest recollections are of the bi-annual vacation at Burdwan and later at Cutwa—and plainly the most truly educational experience also. Returning from school laden with new pets—rabbits, pigeons, a long-tailed lamb, and others—he found occupation in building houses for them, with willing co-operation of admiring and rejoicing sisters. There too he had his riding horse, faithfully kept for him. And the father's wisdom, the mother's love, the grandmother's kindness and piety, renewed the old atmosphere and encouraged fuller growth.

CHAPTER II

COLLEGE DAYS AT CALCUTTA AND IN ENGLAND

AT sixteen Jagadis passed from school to St. Xavier's College; and there—while doing the ordinary work, in a more or less ordinarily respectable way, but as yet without marked interest or distinction—he fell under the influence which plainly determined his turning to Physics, rather than to the natural history of his own more prominent tastes. All the pupils of Father Lafont, so long Professor of Physics in that college, recall his teaching and influence as truly educative. His wealth of experiments and vivid clearness of exposition of them, made his class the most interesting in the whole college; and his patient skill, his subtlety, as well as brilliance of experimentation, were appreciated by this young student above all. Here was Bose's first discipline towards that combination of intellectual lucidity with wealth of experimental device and resource by which he has all the more fully represented and honoured his old master by surpassing him.

But, as is common to youth, with its vague ferment of ideas, its perplexity among ambitions, his career was not at all clearly in sight. Finding that he could pass examinations, and not without distinction, his first idea, beyond taking his B.A., was to visit England for higher training. At this time, as indicated in the preceding chapter, Mr. Bose's schemes and investments had not only mostly failed, but had burdened him with debts, of which the high interests were swallowing all he could spare and save.

Jagadis keenly realised that his first duty was to take the burden off his father, and by his own earnings to pay off the debt. The most promising career for this was to win a place in the Indian Civil Service. But Bose's father, though himself successful and even distinguished in the Government service, vetoed his son's proposals. He strongly felt the position of an administrator as one too much above and aloof from the fortunes and struggles of the people; and he did not wish his son to repeat this authoritative experience, but to take a more ordinary part among his fellow-men. He was willing to see him a scholar or utilising his scientific aptitudes and training for the advancement of Indian agriculture.

Young Bose then turned his attention towards medicine, apparently the only avenue and means of support for the career of natural science. This he still hoped to study in some English University, and so thought of London. But the great cost of a stay in England had to be reckoned with; and at this time his father was on his two years' medical leave on reduced pay, and uncertain whether his health would admit of return to duty, and its larger income. It was clearly inexpedient for Jagadis to undertake the expensive educational stay in England in circumstances so uncertain.

A further complication, and for an affectionate son the most serious of all, was his mother's dread of separation—her fear not only of the strange unknown Western world on which her boy's heart was set, but also that terror of the sea which is so common in India, though so strange to us Western folk with seafaring in our blood. Is not this perhaps a survival, with old folk-lore exaggeration, of the dangers of the Indian coasts?—above all, perhaps, of the perils of the days of Indian maritime enterprise towards the West, and of voyaging to China with its typhoons, of colonisation of Java and Cambodia, doubtless all with disasters, which, like so much of Indian history generally, have lapsed from record and even oral tradition, but survive in the national mind,

Dr. J. C. Bose's Parents.

and pre-eminently in the minds of the mothers, and in feelings intensified by vagueness ?

The mother had lost her second son, aged ten, when Jagadis was seventeen, and she continued long to mourn deeply; but now concentrated her highest hopes and tenderest caresses on her remaining son, as an Indian mother so intensely does. Her nerves were thus doubly shaken, since after her sorrow there came new and increasing fears for Jagadis' wanderings. The father's affairs went on from bad to worse, so a family council was held, and it decided, for every reason, that Jagadis must not go. To do him justice, he was also ending his own struggle with similar conclusion; he loyally admitted that under the circumstances it would be selfish of him to press further. In short, he renounced his projects, and promised to settle down to do his best in India.

But when all seemed settled, the mother's strength of character came out, and to the full. She thought the whole matter out afresh for herself, and rallied from her fears—her all but nervous breakdown. So coming to Jagadis' bedside one evening, and taking his head in her lap as if he were still the child she felt him, she said: 'My son, I cannot understand much of this going to Europe, but I see your heart's desire is to educate yourself to the utmost; and so I have made up my mind. You shall have your heart's desire. Though nothing is left of your father's fortune, I have my jewels; I have even some money of my own. Between these I can manage it. Go you shall!'

With the mother thus decided, there was naturally no more of family council in opposition, nor of father in hesitation. After all, his veto had only been for the Civil Service, and for the Law. He welcomed the idea of his able son's doing well in medicine; for science as a career was then practically unthought of. His own health improved, and he went back to his duties (now at Pubna), which meant an increase of income. Hence the jewels were not sold, and the mother was induced to keep her money for Jagadis' return from Europe, though the family economies were henceforth doubtless stricter than ever for their student's sake as well as for relief of the father's burden.

To follow our student's changing fortunes more clearly, we must look beyond his educational routine and its anxious vicissitudes, and into the less conventional elements which were meantime also part of his preparation for life. The love of nature, of pets, of horses, readily develops in youth towards sport and adventure in the wild. With the advent of vigorous boyhood had come the joy of taking risks, even in chancing narrow escapes; and these were forthcoming. Thus, when under fifteen, fording a doubtful river on horseback, which the flood had cut deep, the horse slipped into a hole, and turned over under water, leaving its rider to disentangle himself, swim from under the struggling animal, and land himself and it, little the worse. This fine horse thereafter would tolerate no other rider, not even his father, and so was idle during the long terms of absence in Calcutta. His attendant, now an old Rajput Sepoy, taught the boy shooting; whence hunting expeditions as often as might be. A college vacation at nineteen culminated in a month in the Terai, with first experience of big game, and vivid impressions of jungle and forest. Then six months later came a fascinating invitation to a hunting holiday in Assam, from a friendly zemindar—a crack shot and distinguished hunter; and with not only wild buffalo in his forest, but rhinoceros. Arriving at the nearest railway station in the evening, a palanquin was waiting for a night journey of twenty-one miles. Then he was out for an active day's sport, but in the evening came an alarming attack of fever, of an unprecedented violence. It was agreed he should return at once before it grew worse. But the palanquin was not now available. Anxious to be off, he asked, 'Can you not spare me a horse?' 'The only horse available is too dangerous for you—a fine racer, but a brute with every vice, who nearly killed his last rider, and whom no one has mounted since.' 'Let me see him!' Out came the horse from his stable; but at the first advance it reared, to fall on him with his forefeet, and to bite as well. Dodging this attack, he jumped on its back, whereupon the furious creature instantly bolted with him; and so, without a moment for farewell, much less for preparation for a more decorous start, the headlong gallop went on without possibility of restraint. On the way appeared a river previously crossed when asleep in the palanquin, and with the road apparently making clear for its bridge; but with a path breaking off alongside some way ahead. With the hunter's instinct and quick decision, he forced the horse aside; and the next moment saw the justification of his action in avoiding the bridge broken by the flood, into which horse and he, but for this change, must have plunged together. In another moment the path led to a light bamboo footbridge extemporised to replace the broken one, and this the wild creature took in a few bounds, cracking it nearly to breaking. Only after fourteen miles was it exhausted, and so the final seven miles it went quietly. The fever patient, exhausted still more, started on the long railway journey to Calcutta. The fever resisted quinine and all other treatment, and made frequent and exhausting returns; so that the University degree was taken under difficulties. Nor did the brief home holiday before sailing to England relieve it either.

With the sea-voyage, the fever grew worse, not better. One day of extreme paroxysms, in making for the surgery, he collapsed at the door, and was carried to his berth in the doctor's arms. Treatment and nursing failed, as in Calcutta; and the patient overheard people saying, 'That poor boy will never see England.' His one pleasurable recollection of the whole long journey is of two ladies on the railway journey from Southampton, who spoke to him kindly and gave him their illustrated papers;

and so gave a touch of life and cheerfulness to lighten his depression.

Arrived at London, his B.A. diploma served him for matriculation, and he started the usual first-year work of the medical student. The physics and chemistry were much what he had done before, but the zoology course, under Ray Lankester, was interesting and wholly new; for even to this day Calcutta University excludes zoological science. Botany too, in the summer term, was congenial, so that the preliminary scientific examination was passed without difficulty. With the following autumn term began the first year of medical studies proper, with anatomy. But the fever was still as bad as ever, with even more frequent attacks, which were brought on intensely by the odours of the dissecting-room. Hence the anatomist advised young Bose to give up his medical course as hopeless. Dr. Ringer, then the most distinguished physician of the Hospital, as well as one of the best and kindliest of professors, who had already been treating him with arsenical and other injections, but all without success, concurred in this advice. Thus thrown into new perplexity, Bose decided on leaving London and taking to science at Cambridge. The fever determined his course afresh, and for life. First came a dreary struggle to cram Latin, etc., enough for the entrance examination (in which Sanskrit was accepted in lieu of Greek); but of all this little recollection remains, save a lifelong ill will to Paley! A natural science scholarship was won at Christ's College, and he entered in January 1881. A very different life was thus begun, more congenial, though only very slowly curative; for this old metropolis of the Fens was for an ague patient one of the worst of climates to be found in Britain—indeed north of the Mediterranean. Abandoning all drugs, young Bose took to boating, with daily perspiration accordingly, and general strengthening as well. But the fever persisted, and at one time became so severe as to alarm the college authorities. An upset in the icy water of the Cam was a setback. The attacks continued, first weekly, then fortnightly ; and not until well on in the second year did ordinary health return, and working powers get their fair chance. After this Bose seems to have become immune to malaria ; but insomnia, whether as accessory or as an acquired habit, lingered for six or seven years, and at times of overwork this has ever since more or less threatened to return.

Nowadays recalling symptoms, kindred cases very largely fatal, the place of origin, and other circumstances, it seems probable that this illness was no ordinary fever, but 'Kala-azar,' still a serious and recurrent pest, of Assam especially, though nowadays becoming amenable to treatment, and happily still more to prevention.

The first batch of students who called on the new-comer were a rather fast set, and Bose was gently lectured by his tutor, who advised him as a stranger to drop these acquaintances, and for good. After this came a period of shyness and solitude ; but with the second year, with returning strength, the merry company of hall dinners, and what not, the enjoyment of college life and companionship really began ; and a wide circle of acquaintances was formed, and a few friendships. His range of contacts was widened beyond the college through a natural science club, with active meetings for papers and discussions, and abundant comradeship and gaiety. Though after nearly forty years most old acquaintances have vanished or been forgotten, a few cordial recollections survive, as notably of Theodore Beck, afterwards Principal of Aligarh College, and of D'Arcy Thompson, since at Dundee and St. Andrews. Of Shipley too (now head of Christ's), though senior to him, he has warm memories, and of a few others now scattered through the professions, and mostly lost sight of. Among other friends were Fitzpatrick, afterwards an active physicist and master of Emmanuel College, and Reynolds Green the botanist.

The first summer vacation was spent in the Isle of

Wight, in the main pleasantly. But on too adventurous a solitary rowing outside Shanklin Bay he got caught in a squall, and had a very hard three hours' struggle to return, with constant risk of upset; hence a new increment of fever, though happily with a kindly landlady to nurse him. The next summer included a couple of months as one of a small college party tramping in the Highlands, of which the Trossachs are best remembered; while the last long vacation was spent in degree work at Cambridge.

At the outset of these Cambridge studies Bose was still perplexed as to his course, and uncertain of his aptitudes, and he adopted the plan of going as fully as possible to the courses of science lectures—'a perfect orgie of lectures'—and with these to as many laboratories as possible. And with good results; what better teacher could he have had for Physiology than Michael Foster, or for the Embryology than Francis Balfour, then at the very height of his brilliant powers. Geology too had its interest, both from Professor Hughes and his kindly and hospitable wife; and so on. But after the middle of the second year, he settled down to regular work in Physics, Chemistry and Botany. Of Professor Liveing's chemical course, the stimulus to spectroscopy is specially remembered. Vines' lectures and laboratory of Botany were also much appreciated, and Francis Darwin's first course of Vegetable Physiology was given before he left. But most educative and decisive for the future physicist was the teaching of Lord Rayleigh, whose admirably patient and careful experimentation, to the most scrupulous accuracy, with every factor of disturbance allowed for or compensated, and all with correspondingly clear and careful explanation, produced a profound impression, which has been lifelong. Coming after Father Lafont's experimentation, which had been so brilliant and illuminating, and thus the best of introductions to physical science, was this complemental instruction needed by the more advanced student—that of the minutest painstaking, so necessary when dealing with large problems, and ensuing discovery. And though our student's own original powers had not yet appeared, as indeed seldom happens so early in life, his work satisfied his teachers: as was evidenced first by his Cambridge degree in the Natural Science Tripos, and that of B.Sc. taken at London about the same time and without further work. In later life Bose's friendly contacts developed, with cordial subsequent encouragement of his investigations, as these began to appear in later years; and of these old teachers Lord Rayleigh and Professor Vines have been actively appreciative of his researches in Physics and Vegetable Physiology respectively, throughout their long series, and sponsors for their presentation to the Royal and Linnean Societies. With Francis Darwin, too, cordial relations have been maintained; and now and then an old acquaintanceship is revived.

CHAPTER III

EARLY STRUGGLES

THRICE armed with good degrees, from Cambridge and London in addition to the initial Calcutta one, young Bose felt it time to return to India, towards which not only family ties and homesickness, but increasing family cares as well, had long been straining him. Four years is a long exile, in youth especially; and now, at nearly twenty-five, we have the almost grown man ready and eager for a career. Fortunately for him, Professor Fawcett the economist, then Postmaster-General, who had kept up an old acquaintance with Bose's much senior brother-in-law—the late Mr. A. M. Bose, afterwards a Calcutta barrister, and a man of much note and a leader of public opinion in his day, still warmly remembered—wrote spontaneously, inviting him to call. After this Fawcett asked his colleague, Lord Kimberley, then Secretary for State for India, if he knew of any appointment in the Education Department; but none was then intimated, so he could only advise him to go home to India and see. Fawcett gave young Bose an introduction to Lord Ripon, then Governor-General, and this he presented at Simla on his journey home. The reception was of the kindest, and the Viceroy promised to nominate him for the Educational Service. Yet in course of the conversation he suddenly broke out, in full bitterness of disappointment: 'My life here has been a failure: I wanted to serve India, and to give Indians more responsibilities. At first all seemed promising, but then came this

Ilbert affair! I never thought our English liberal tradition could be thus abandoned!'

On reaching Calcutta Bose called on the Director of Public Instruction, who had already received, through the Government of Bengal, a letter from Lord Ripon recommending him t them for an appointment. The Director was none too pleased, and blurted out, 'I am usually approached from below, not from above. There is no higher-class appointment at present available in the Imperial Educational Service. I can only offer you a place in the Provincial Service, from which you may be promoted.' Bose declined this offer. Noticing that Bose's appointment had not been gazetted, the Viceroy wrote to the Government of Bengal for an explanation of the delay. This pressure from above highly irritated the Director. When Bose saw him in answer to his letter, he told him that his hand had been forced, and he would offer him an appointment in the higher service, but that it would be only an officiating appointment giving no claim for permanence. If Bose satisfied the test of service, he would then consider the question of making his appointment permanent.

There was also a strong doubt, not to say prejudice, against the capacity of an Indian to take any important position in science. Intellectual acuteness in Metaphysics and Languages had always been frankly acknowledged, but it was assumed that India had no aptitude for the exact methods of science. For science, therefore, India must look to the West for her teachers. This view was accepted by the Government, and so strongly maintained in the Education Department that when Bose was appointed Officiating Professor of Physics in the Presidency College, its Principal protested against this appointment on the above grounds.

Thus opens a chapter of Bose's life in which the writer's condition of personal freedom has most definitely decided him to disregard the reticence of his sitter, who would fain let bygones be bygones—right and proper on personal grounds though that be, and at an age when even the sharpest wounds of battle have healed. But the writer is interested in his subject on more than personal grounds, and has so undertaken it; in fact, at every point on general grounds also, and equally as regards Bose's constructive work in science, his attitude in education, and his linking of Eastern with Western thought and culture. For these reasons, and in this spirit, old difficulties, otherwise too controversial and personal, have here to be noted and frankly discussed.

To understand not only the immediate situation, but much that follows, the writer may explain that he writes peculiarly on his own responsibility, as a lifelong student of Universities, and with more than five years' acquaintance with Indian ones. To begin with, the non-Indian reader must understand that while the Indian Civil Service is open to any Indian who can win his place by examination in it, and who thereafter is on the same scale of status and pay as his English colleagues, the Higher Education Service is accessible only by nomination; and these posts, with extraordinarily rare exceptions, had not been given to Indians, even of the highest European qualifications. In general, the Indian professors, though of the very same duties and responsibilities, formed the 'Provincial Service,' with much lower pay. Promotion from this service to the higher branch is nominally possible to all distinguished members of the Provincial Service, but it is practically extremely rare. So much has this been the case that even the chemist who is now at the head of his subject in India, as Bose in physics—although coming back to India with his Doctorate in Chemistry, won with high distinction, showing the promise he has since amply fulfilled, and appointed to the Presidency College—was never promoted to the full position. Yet for many years he did the teaching and examining work without European colleagues, and has besides won European reputation by his discoveries. In the writer's opinion, it is to this unfortunate system that the lower general level of individual studies and of original productivity, in comparison with the staffs of other Universities in the world, which of all things in India has most surprised and disappointed him, is plainly not a little due. In the Civil Service, at the Bar, or on the Bench, European and Indian must and do work together ; yet in every University and its colleges, where unity of working is the daily necessity, and should be far easier of attainment, they are practically segregated into two distinct racial camps, and thus with deterioration of the one and depression of the other, and with diminished values to both and diminished respect from their students, who are too much dissociated from both camps accordingly. If and when real efficiency of higher education, with corporate spirit and active intellectual life, are to be adequately realised in India, this system will have not only to be abandoned in its working but transformed in its spirit. Indeed, one very real reason for the writer's undertaking this biography, beyond the great contributions Bose has made to the advancement of science, is found in his efforts towards raising and maintaining the professorial standard and ideal above and beyond racial difference altogether. And while this chapter is being completed, the writer is gratified to find that this invidious distinction has been officially removed—thanks, in great measure, to the life-work of Bose, not simply as a man of science, but as an educationist with fearless advocacy of this and other needed improvements in higher education—as recently demonstrated before the Indian Services Commission.

To return to Bose. Young educational officers used to be sent out to the provincial colleges ; and it was after experience and approved services that they were brought to the Presidency College, which has long been reckoned the premier educational institution in India. The students of this college were anything but tame. They were indeed highly critical of the teaching power of their professors. They had earned for themselves the reputation of an independence which had been too readily interpreted as a spirit of insubordination, and thus were sometimes driven towards it An unfortunate altercation had occurred between two English professors and their students, and had gone to such a length as to force the Government to appoint a Commission of Inquiry. Strong feeling had been engendered; and no more difficult test could have been imposed than to hold the wilder spirits in check and discipline. The conditions which confronted Bose in the beginning of his career might well have daunted the most resolute. We shall see later that on these were superposed others, against which he had to struggle for many years to come.

When Bose joined the service, an Indian professor's income, even if in the Imperial Service, was two-thirds that of a European's. (Bose succeeded later in getting this distinction abolished.) After entering on his duties, Bose found that this two-thirds pay was to be further reduced by one half, since his appointment was only officiating. In other words, he was to get one-third of the pay normally attached to the office hitherto. From the first he was very clear as to his course—that of performing all that could be asked from him and more; but at the same time he resolved to do all in his power throughout his career towards raising the status of Indian professors. With this combination of personal pride with loyalty to his countrymen and colleagues, he decided on a new form of protest, and maintained it with unprecedented definiteness and pertinacity. As his protest was disregarded, he resolved never to touch the cheque received by him monthly as his pay; and continued this for three years, with what privations accordingly need not now be entered into, save with a word of appreciation for his wife's brave acceptance of them.

Bose was confronted with other difficulties. The family fortune was now at its lowest ebb. Of the many projects started by his father some turned out to be highly successful from the beginning: among these may be mentioned the People's Bank, which was the forerunner of the later Co-operative Societies. He had taken many shares in this Bank, as became its active founder. The shares of the Bank rose high before many years, and it is now one of the most successful concerns in its line. Had he kept those shares, he and his family would have been permanently provided for; but, always generous to a fault, he gave away his shares to poorer friends. The burden of other industrial and agricultural ventures which were not immediately successful fell on him. Moreover, he stood as security for others who had started kindred enterprises, and ultimately the responsibility of these fell on Mr. Bose; and thus young Bose more and more realised that he must put his whole mind and effort to extricate his father from this heavy burden of debts. He took matters personally into his hands and, going straight to his ancestral home, parted with all the property which the family possessed. None but an Indian can realise the shock to the family honour of parting with ancestral property that has been hallowed by the memories of forefathers; for in India this is a general feeling, and not simply that of aristocratic tradition. All the relations came to dissuade him from this humiliation, but Bose was adamant in his resolve. All the landed properties were sold, and their proceeds paid to the creditors. This cleared off 50 per cent. of the debt. Then he appealed to his mother; for according to Hindu law a wife's property is held sacred, and the husband, or his creditors, can on no account estrange it. She had held this aside for her son's return, but when that son wished to face the future undaunted, the mother became no less heroic in her sacrifice. Her personal property was disposed of; and the total clearance was now 75 per cent. of the principal and accumulated interest. The creditors, touched by this determination of the family to do their very utmost, expressed themselves fully satisfied, and accepted the unexpected instalments as payment in full. But young Bose had a different view on the subject, which he kept to himself. For the next nine years he struggled; until, out of his own earnings, the balance of the 25 per cent. which the creditors had renounced was paid them in full.

As regards Bose's work at the Presidency College, where his capacity for teaching and maintaining discipline was to be tested, his influence over the students became established from the first day. The usual device of taking daily roll to enforce regular attendance at the classes was found superfluous; and so interested did the students become in his lectures that there used to be a struggle for securing front seats for better view of the experiments. The cram books, formerly used for memorising purposes, were soon discarded as unnecessary. His old students, even those who in later life have taken up other professions, still recall with delight, as the writer can testify, the permanent impression made on them by his direct and vivid method of teaching.

After three years' work in this temporary post, both the Principal (Mr. C. H. Tawney) and the Director of Public Instruction (Sir Alfred Croft) came fully to realise the value of Bose's professorial work, and to understand his character, and they became henceforth his staunchest friends. The Director had found that Bose could be inflexible when questions of principle were concerned. Bose on his part also realised more fully than ever that the best way to get on with an Englishman is to stand up to him. The same man, when firmly stood up to by the Indian, may not only become his personal friend, but be substantially improved thereafter in his ideas and manner. This matter is important; and we may later note one or two other instances of it among the many which have arisen in Bose's career.

In consequence of this change of view of the Director, Bose's appointment, by help of a special order from the Government, was not only made permanent, but this with retrospective effect. He therefore received his full pay for the last three years in a lump sum, which was promptly made over to his father's creditors. The balance was gradually cleared off in the course of the next six years.

After the discharge of the debt, his father survived only for a year, and his mother for two years more. They did not live to see their son's scientific success. Many years later, the people of Faridpur asked Bose to speak at the fiftieth anniversary of the Exhibition and Mela founded by his father. His address was on 'A Failure that was Great.' It told the story of his father's efforts and initiatives, and the too frequent unsuccess of his sowings. Here are the concluding words:

> A failure? Yes, but not ignoble nor altogether futile. And through witnessing this struggle, the son learned to look on success or failure as one, and to realise that some defeat may be greater than victory. To me his life has been one of blessing, and daily thanksgiving. Nevertheless everyone had said that he had wrecked his life, which was meant for greater things. Few realise that out of the skeletons of myriad lives have been built vast continents. And it is on the wreck of a life like his, and of many such lives, that will be built the greater India yet to be. We do not know why it should be so; but we do know that the Earth-Mother is always calling for sacrifice.

The memory of those whose love had filled his life has thus been a lifelong inspiration. But his future struggles were to be not for professional survival nor for family honour; and on his thirty-fifth birthday, November 30, 1894, he fully resolved that his life henceforth was to be above all dedicated to the pursuit of new knowledge. Within three months of this resolve, with no laboratory to speak of, and with the help of an untrained tinsmith, he was able to devise and construct new apparatus for his first research on some of the most difficult problems of electric radiation. Success was immediate: and in the course of a year the Royal Society undertook the publication of his investigations, and offered help from their parliamentary grant for their continuation. In recognition of the value of his researches the University of London conferred on him its Doctorate of Science without examination. Lord Kelvin wrote to him in 1896 that he was 'literally filled with wonder and admiration: allow me to ask you to accept my congratulations for so much success in the difficult and novel experimental problems which you have attacked.' M. Cornu, the former President of the French Academy of Sciences, and a veteran leader in this field of physics, also wrote him early in 1897, saying that 'the very first results of your researches testify to your power of furthering the progress of science. For my own part, I hope to take full advantage of the perfection to which you have brought your apparatus, for the benefit of the Ecole Polytechnique and for the sake of further researches I wish to complete.'

Scientific success had come unexpectedly to him: how was he to accept it? Not in a spirit of mere personal gratification; but as encouragement to incessant work, which should win for his countrymen recognition of their capacity for science, and stir them to like effectiveness. The dream of establishing an Institute of Science came to him at this time, with its hope that others might by it be saved from the harassing difficulties that had so long confronted him. But he was too proud to ask help towards realising his vision, which appeared to others as a mere dream. What could be done must be done by himself, and at his own risk. He and his wife therefore once more accepted the continuance of their life of economy, almost of privation, so that he might some day be able to help on the needed modern revival of the ancient scientific tradition of India. From these days, and for the next quarter of a century, that has been the goal on which his mind has been concentrated; and the many papers and books he has produced are best understood as steps towards the creation of the Research Institute he has at last fully initiated.

A word now of the conditions under which research had to be carried out. The feeling of the Education Department had long been unfavourable; the two friends he had at length made, the Principal and the Director, were retiring from the service ; and now Bose's success kindled hostility which more or less persisted. The departmental view was that the teaching of classes was the whole duty of a professor, and that research must therefore involve neglect of his proper function : even this in spite of his giving, with characteristic thoroughness and pride, twenty-six hours of weekly lectures and demonstrations in the College, although the average performed by his colleagues was very much less. Hence the only time to carry on investigations was after the long day's teaching and preparation work were over. No grant was available for research ; Bose, from his own slender income, had to find means for the construction of his apparatus and the payment for assistance.

But hopefully for Bose, the interest of his work, and its high appreciation by leading Western men of science, attracted the notice of the Lieutenant-Governor of Bengal. He understood the higher function of a University : that it was not mere routine teaching—which in India especially had too much become the encouragement of cram for the passing of examinations—but the training of students in clear and constructive thinking, and towards the advancement of knowledge. He realised the difficulties under which Bose was labouring, and therefore arranged for the creation of a new post with higher emoluments, with more initiative, and with reasonable leisure for research. The duties of this post were to be the organisation and development of laboratories in the many and widespread colleges under the Government, and the personal training of advanced students for original investigations. The scheme was sanctioned, and Bose was informed that he would receive the formal letter of appointment in the course of a few days.

But at this very time a matter came up which nullified all these hopes. Bose was a Fellow of the Calcutta University, which, though supported by the Government, is so far an independent body. Bose had formed very definite views with regard to the duties he owed to his

College under Government, and those which he owed to the University in his independent capacity as one of its fellows. While his new appointment was waiting final sanction, a question came up before the University, in which the majority of officials under Government held very pronounced views. Bose was present at the University meeting, and in his vote he did not follow the lead of his official chief. The new appointment proposed for him was immediately cancelled.

On a subsequent occasion he was informed by a Government Secretary that there was a matter before the University in which some of the members of the Government were especially interested. Bose could not attend on the day on which the matter was decided, and he was requested to submit an explanation. In reply, Bose wrote inquiring whether, in attending any meeting of the University, the Government expected him to vote on the particular side of a question which might be advanced by his official superiors, irrespective of any opinion which he might form as a result of the discussion. If, in following an independent course, the Government thought that he was not properly discharging his duties as a Fellow of the University, he begged permission to resign his Fellowship.

The Lieutenant-Governor, to whom the matter was referred, appreciated Bose's point of view, but could not overcome the opposition of the Education Department in giving sanction to the new appointment. He, however, thought it just that Bose should be recouped for the great expense he had incurred in course of investigations which had redounded to the credit of the Indian Government. An official communication reached him that the Government was willing to pay the expenses he had incurred in pursuit of his research; but Bose, while expressing gratitude for this consideration, declined to accept any remuneration for his past work. The Government then sanctioned an annual grant of Rs. 2500 (£166) towards the outlay for his future research carried on at the Presidency College.

But all this did not mitigate the pressure of his daily routine work; and the concession which Bose most needed for research was some relaxation from the excessive hours of teaching above mentioned. It had been a great disappointment that, after recognising the value of his services, the new appointment that was contemplated should be withdrawn because he could not always obediently follow the particular views of his official superior in regard to affairs of the University. He had passed through years of severe overwork and strain, and the hostile attitude of the Department had chilled the freshness and spontaneity needed for all initiative work. He therefore waited on the Lieutenant-Governor, and preferred a request that he should be allowed the year's furlough which was his due, to enable him to visit Europe and come in touch with other scientific men and their work. The Lieutenant-Governor, who, as we have seen, entertained a personal regard for Bose, was fully sympathetic; but knowing the slenderness of his means, asked if it was not injudicious for him to venture on a costly foreign visit, even though conducive to his scientific work. Bose, with sudden impulse, inquired whether, in these circumstances, the Government could not send him to England on a scientific 'deputation.' The Governor answered that the Imperial Government would never sanction a deputation on a matter which was merely educational. The Education Board at Simla had lately issued a resolution expressing regret that India had never taken to scientific pursuits, in spite of the efforts of the Government, and Bose had naturally felt the injustice of this ignoring of the scientific work he had been carrying on at the Presidency College, which had had such wide publicity in India since its appreciation in Europe. He could not help expressing his bitter disappointment at the contrast between such professions of desire for scientific study and research by Indians and the real apathy of the Education Board. The Lieutenant-Governor seemed irritated by such plain speaking, and turned the conversation;

so the interview was closed without definite result. Bose had gone up to Darjeeling for the interview and was returning next day to Calcutta. But as he was stepping into the train a messenger brought him a letter from the Director of Public Instruction, informing him that the Governor had on his own responsibility decided to send him to England on a scientific deputation for six months; and that he could therefore start for Europe any day that suited him. The Lieutenant-Governor would telegraphically communicate with the Government of India and the Secretary of State in London.

The despatch which followed included the following statement from the Director of Public Instruction, now aroused to full support:

> Dr. Bose's work is not merely the education of candidates for University degrees, but the promotion of physical science in a line which he has made peculiarly his own. To help him in that is to promote the cause of science all over the world; and this, I assume, falls within the functions of the Government.

To this the Lieutenant-Governor added his own recommendation that—

> he had done what he could to encourage and advance Dr. Bose's researches, as he thinks it the duty of a great Government to do, when it has a man of such exceptional qualifications on its staff; and he attaches much importance to Professor Bose's visiting Europe and conferring with the leaders of scientific inquiry there.

By sheer persistence of work, and by his personality, Bose had thus won from Government a measure of recognition and practical support for scientific work which was then unique, and remains everywhere too rare. And the successes which he has once and again achieved, even against departmental difficulties, in winning appreciation and support from his own Government, are so many points gained for the cause of science all over the world towards its more adequate recognition.

CHAPTER IV

FIRST RESEARCHES IN PHYSICS

Electric Waves

Now an outline of Bose's first researches. Towards some new age the progress of science and its applications has been tending ever since the dawn of civilisation; and to-day, it may be, more than ever. In the past its growth has been too often like that of a coral reef—storm-beaten and broken, even subsiding: but now its workers hope they are city-building for all time—helping to erect the ideal city of knowledge which should grow indefinitely, though it can never be completely realised. Each of its busy workers is searching and quarrying out, shaping or laying his stone; and at some point, and for its moment, it rests on the highest edge of the rising wall. But on this stone, so soon as accepted, others may speedily follow; and thus each sound and solid piece of work is overbuilt, and so far surpassed. Each stone commonly bears its own mason's mark, but the world cares little for that: its brief glance of interest is naturally enough on the handling of the new blocks as they are lifted and laid on the wall-edge against the sky. At most there can survive in history but a few individual names, whose memory is preserved by the mighty columns they have wrought; while these again stand on earlier foundations laid by toilers long forgotten, giants though they must have been. Still the old masons know, and at times recall, the significance of past work; they review it and its doers from the standpoint of permanent contribution, underlying present superstructure and future alike. Hence, though every science seems and so far is in continual change—and this often of style and aspect with each new group and mood of workers—its growth has yet a substantial unity.

In this way appreciation, such as the present, of a notable living worker involves some brief mention of such work of past years as is now fully taken into the general structure, to support later work by successors; before we come to the growing edge where he is actively employed. Indeed, lower than these two levels we may sometimes find a third, that of portions of wall with stones long laid, where their worker has been interrupted, and where no one has yet continued his task.

In this comparison much of Bose's earlier physical investigation naturally belongs to the first of these categories, that of accepted and established science, now fully incorporated and utilised. His later work, that centering around the Response to Stimulus of the Living and Non-Living, is of the second category: where the builder is conspicuously busy with his assistants on the growing edge of science. To this we shall come in a later chapter; but there are also elements of his physical researches belonging to the third category—those still awaiting continuance, whether by himself or others. For the moment then we may look to the first and last-named of these categories, leaving the second for later treatment.

From the previous chapter we see how little time for fresh thought or experiment remained after long days of three or four lectures, with usually more hours of apparatus-making, and experiment-preparing, of lecture syllabus-writing, paper-correcting, and so on; and with evening leisure disturbed too often by the various struggles of academic existence above briefly indicated, and too long fretted also by the struggle of paying off the debt of honour from an income peculiarly modest. It was not until 1894, as already mentioned, when reaching his thirty-fifth year, that Bose felt free enough definitely to start regular work as an investigator; indeed on that birthday, Indian fashion, he made to himself that vow. And, as we have seen, he was well prepared, not only in physical knowledge and experimental skill, but also in character, his initial adventurous courage and strenuousness now matured and strengthened by life.

In these years the most conspicuously interesting movement in physics centred round the work of Hertz, the brilliant and too short-lived experimentalist who produced the electric waves which Clerk Maxwell, building in his turn on the experimental work of Faraday, had predicted mathematically, twenty years before, in his magnificent correlation of light-waves with electro-magnetic disturbance. So in the formative years of our investigator, as older readers will remember, the Hertzian waves were the wonder of their time, just as later the X-rays of Röntgen, and a little later the magical radium of Madame Curie, and the later developments of that still branching investigation.

First, then, a word of explanation is needed before we come to Hertz and his problem, much less to Bose's development of it. In the previous generation Fresnel had cleared the wave-theory of light, and enabled us to visualise it, in terms of vibrations of the ether: but these not in longitudinal pulsations like sound-waves in air, but transversal, like the up and down movements which take place in the waves of the sea, which travel fast and far without corresponding movement of the water itself until it breaks upon the beach. Throw a stone into a standing pool; and watch the surface rising and falling as the wave-circles extend to the bank; watch too how this reflects these wave-circles back into the pond, and at angles varying with those of their incidence; and thus, in the minor infinities of intersecting ripples which arise, we have a simple introduction to those intricate yet orderly wave-motions of the ether which the physicist has to assume as filling space, in order to realise the manifold phenomena which appear in course of his study of light, and which he can thus not only experiment upon, but explain with mathematical clearness.

Contemporary with Fresnel, as mathematician of light, was Ampère, the mathematician of electricity. He worked out the laws of those mutual actions of currents which had been discovered by the succession of brilliant experimentalists up to Faraday. In thus rising from the experimental and empirical level, and establishing Electro-dynamics as a rational science, he naturally enough suggested that the ether which carries the waves of light must also be the vehicle of electric disturbances. But the testing of this attractive hypothesis by experiment—no easy matter—was next accomplished by Clerk Maxwell, who was rewarded by the discovery that electrical disturbances travelled with the same velocity as that of light—a result concordant with previous independent calculation of the speed of a current through a perfectly conducting wire. That some intimate correspondence must exist between electricity and light could thus no longer be doubted. Maxwell's next step was to reinterpret the familiar contrast of conductors and non-conductors ; and now, instead of thinking the latter inert, as scientific men had hitherto done (so that the reader may be pardoned for perhaps still doing so), he reinterpreted both together. The familiar copper wire is not a perfect conductor, but has an appreciable resistance, of which Ohm had already determined the simple law ; with progressive loss of energy accordingly, which appears in the wire as heating ; this raised to white heat gives us light as in an electric lamp. The process of electric loss in production of heat, Maxwell compared to what he observed when water is forced through pipes, with friction and heat increasing as these are narrowed ; and it is evident that since fluids are all more or less imperfect (indeed water being a viscous fluid compared with many others), the movement of the fluid must sooner or later come to a stop, and all its energy converted into heat. In short, then, the electrical resistance of conductors can be thought of as a viscous resistance.

What now of that of non-conductors ? This term is also relative, since these differ among themselves ; and hence at first they were thought of as but extremely bad conductors. But here Maxwell had a fresh idea, that of their non-conductivity as by no means comparable to an exaggerated viscosity, but of a contrasted nature, like the resistance offered by elastic springs, which do not waste the kinetic energy expended on them into friction and heat, but store it as potential, in their coils, as far as the structure of these allows ; and then give it out anew, as the pressure upon them is reduced or withdrawn. Thus while the familiar current of conduction along a wire goes on as long as its electro-motive force continues, the currents of displacement, which Maxwell's speculative eye discovered in the non-conducting body (answering to the metal springs of his mechanical image above), can but have a short duration, for their distortion soon comes to an equilibrium, of electrostatic energy. Now imagine the coiled springs to break, or burst free ; there is a sudden and complete discharge of their energy—a process obviously sharply contrasted with that dissipation into heat which we find in conductors carrying a current.

Thus Maxwell escaped from the old and merely negative view of the non-conductor as a passive obstacle ; and saw it thrilling with its own internal currents of displacement, like the rapid oscillations of a mass of springs. But ordinary currents manifest themselves (1) by being wasted into heat by the resistance due to the imperfections of the conductor, (2) by their action on the magnet, so conveniently shown by introducing a galvanometer into the circuit, and also (3) by their induction of currents in conductors in their neighbourhood. So if Maxwell's hypothetical currents in non-conductors really exist, they must have these properties ; but so rapid are their oscillations, and so brief is their duration, that no ordinary experiment can detect them. Still, with the reasoned certitude of his mathematical treatment, Maxwell stuck to it that the currents are none the less there; and so framed his electro-magnetic theory of light. For now, from this point of view, the light-waves of the ether, already lucidly—but separately—visualised and measured by Fresnel and others, may be interpreted as the product of rapidly alternating currents set up in the dielectric ether (and as it were the oscillations of the elastic springs) and thus carried through space. The mathematical mind was impressed by Maxwell's theory and its calculations; but neither physicist nor plain man could be satisfied without concrete proof, through experimental demonstration. But how reach experimental mastery and understanding of alternating currents and oscillating discharges of such high frequency as is required by the known velocity of light—about 300,000 kilometres (186,000 miles) per second? And with the numberless waves in that second, when even the longest visible red rays are pouring upon our retina every second at the rate of at least 25,000 crowded into every inch of that vast distance; and those which affect the photographic plate are more than twice as many in the same time? The difficulty of experiment is here obvious. Still, experimenters set to work; and Feddersen, working with the Leyden jar, photographed its long-known spark, by help of a rapidly revolving mirror. Now if this discharge be a continuous one, the photograph would be that of a luminous streak, like that of a star slowly photographed while the earth turns round. But the photographs showed successive firefly-like flashes, proving the intermittency of the discharge, and the photographs of sparks showed these as not homogeneous, but as symmetrically contrasted, the bright points at one end corresponding to dark points at the other, and conversely. Here, then, was clear ocular demonstration that the discharge, which to our eye seems but a single and instantaneous spark, is really a succession of sparks, in oscillation between positive and negative. This oscillation was next lucidly imaged by Kelvin, as the swing of 'the electric pendulum.' But is the energy of these electric oscillations simply dissipated through resistance, and into heat, as in the incandescent particles of the spark we see? Maxwell had predicted that there must also be some such radiation for electric waves; so here arises an experimental test between his theory and preceding ones, by which no such phenomenon had been imagined, or is even possible.

Here then is where at length Hertz came in, soon with decisive experiments. First he had to devise a fresh apparatus for exciting the oscillating discharges more steadily and more rapidly (a shortened electric pendulum, as it were), and with the discharges more fully under observation and control. In this he succeeded, but not without great difficulties, traced especially to the uncertain and irregular behaviour of the brass balls between which the oscillating discharge took place. But next, how was he to know whether the electric waves, which Maxwell had foreseen, and which he was seeking for, were really being projected into space from his radiator's oscillating discharge, or no? Here, obviously, he needed some kind of receiver for the anticipated rays; and to contrive it was a new and perplexing experimental problem. His method was to place in the path of the expected rays an exploring apparatus—a pair of closely approximated metallic rods, in which the rays should induce an electric tension; which should then, when strong enough, give minute sparks between its adjacent poles. Alas! no spark could be observed; yet Hertz was not discouraged. Realising that such induced currents must needs be extremely small, he had recourse to the microscope. The poles could thus be brought to within a minute distance; and then he had the joy of success, for a minute but unmistakable spark now appeared with every impulse from the exciting apparatus at some distance off. Here, then, in this tiny spark was at once the success of the primary experiment so long needed for the demonstration of Clerk Maxwell's theory, and the corresponding justification of the young experimenter's labours; at once raising him from the level of the many dreamers and inventors whom most men despise or ridicule before they succeed, to that pinnacle of success which compels respect and arouses admiration.

Turn now from experimental process and details to appreciate the magnitude of Hertz's result, his proof of the real and objective existence of this new range of ethereal vibrations. Not simply as a joy for the mathematicians, whose vigorous method, in Maxwell's powerful hands—that of imaged conception, strongly guided and boldly driven—had thus triumphed, as dramatically as ever of old, say for the first verified prediction of an eclipse, or in later days by the telescopic finding of a new planet in the very place where calculation foretold its presence. Yet the main wonder remained the physical one. For here on one side is light, on which our intellectual life, no less than our practical life, so intimately depends, and as to which, moreover, we have the fullest and longest, the most varied yet also most exact, knowledge of any of the forces of nature. But there on the other hand are the phenomena of electricity and magnetism, so potent and yet so subtle, so varied and complex, so paradoxical, so obscure and even mysterious; and so long defying ordinary representation and visualisation wellnigh altogether. Heat too is organically familiar to us; and its measurement and observation have been increasingly in progress for centuries. The identification of radiant heat with light, as but a continued spectrum of ultra-red rays, had been in its time, and not so long before, one of the great advances of discovery—one readily and essentially connected too with the all-embracing doctrines of energy, so far in its conservation, but especially in its dissipation. The small visible spectrum into which Newton's prism spread out a beam of white light, though ranging through the whole pageant of colour, from red to violet, had been shown to be but a single octave of a vaster spectrum, of cosmic radiation; witness the additional octaves of shorter and shorter ultra-violet (photographic) rays, and corresponding octaves of heat-waves longer than the lowest visible red. But now far below these heat-rays of the great spectrum, large by comparison with those of light (which range from 60,000 to 25,000 to the inch), Hertz had experimentally produced new rays altogether, whose existence, and to some extent therefore their light-wave-like behaviour, had indeed been foreseen by Maxwell; yet with strange and varied properties he had not foreseen, and soon capable of applications which would have surprised and delighted him as much as any. To realise the enormous magnitude of Hertz's waves, as compared with those of the longest heat-rays known, we must leave their scale, that of known ether-waves hitherto, and compare them with the big waves of sound, slow-moving through our atmosphere, a heavy and viscous fluid unlike the imponderable and elastic ether. Taking, then, the ordinary velocity of sound in warm weather at 1200 feet per second, and the range of audible vibrations at from 16 per second for deepest note and 30,000 for highest—a wide range of no less than 11 octaves—we have about 70 feet for the largest and lowest appreciable sound-waves, and say 4 inches for the shortest and highest. But, even Hertz's shortest waves when measured turned out to be about 4 yards, and his longest waves ranged to hundreds of yards, while evidence was soon forthcoming that this immense electric spectrum could be extended in both directions, not only shortening towards the heat spectrum, but lengthening also to an unknown immensity of magnitude.

But Hertz, while thus triumphantly vindicating Maxwell's main life-labour, was still only at the opening of the full verification necessary. Given these electric waves, even with their enormously longer wave-length than light, must they not behave like light? If so, one would expect them, in the first place, to be variously transmissible—i.e. some bodies should be transparent to them, some absorbent and opaque, and some midway—translucent, as it were. Experiment immediately justified these anticipations, although, as a physicist would be prepared to expect, with different media than for ordinary light. Thus a sheet of water is opaque to the electric waves, while glass and pitch turned out alike to be transparent to them.

The next question is naturally—Can these waves be reflected, like light? With big plane mirrors, sheets of zinc and other metal, reflection was found to take place; but not with the precision of optical phenomena, in which the angle of reflection is exactly equal to the angle of incidence, whereas here the reflection was spread out. But this too was only what was to be expected from the large size of waves. Indeed, though light is propagated rectilinearly, a certain curl of its waves inwards on passing an obstacle has long been known to take place; and this 'diffraction' has been beautifully investigated, experimentally and mathematically. On the great scale of Hertz's waves, comparable to those of sound—indeed far surpassing these, since ranging from several metres, the shortest he produced, up to two hundred yards, or thence again to even a mile—it was natural that their rectilinear propagation should be but relative, and that they should curl round corners, just as sound-waves do.

Hertz next tested whether Newton's classic experiment—the refraction of light by the prism—could be repeated with his new rays. But for their immense and spreading magnitude, a correspondingly large prism was needed, on a scale beyond that of glass-casting. Still, Hertz rose to the occasion, and cast a gigantic prism with some two tons of pitch. Experiment rewarded him: the electric rays were unmistakably bent towards the base; and though his measurements with such long and curling waves were naturally but a first and rough appproximation, the great thing was proved—the expected refraction did take place, and that very appreciably. Thus encouraged, Hertz set to testing whether his electric rays could not also be polarised, like those of light. For the polariser and analyser of the optician, he employed grids of metal, each a row of parallel wires, and found that electric vibrations parallel to these were absorbed, while those at right angles to the wires could pass through. When the two gratings were parallel, the electric beam passed through ; but when placed at right angles to each other, it was completely stopped, just as for light with the crossing of Nicol's prisms. Broadly then, Hertz's comparison of the new electric rays with light was so far complete, and the confirmation of Maxwell's theory accordingly.

There remained of course much to be done : both as regards the improvement of the whole range of apparatus in detail, and the increased precision of research towards bringing in other considerations which hold good in the case of light, not to speak of unknown developments. There can be no doubt that Hertz would have gone further in such directions ; but at this stage his weak health—doubtless overstrained by those years of intense thought and labour, aggravated more or less by neglect—gave way ; and he died—of an ailment even then rarely fatal, and now easily treated by the surgeon—the consequence of a mere nasal catarrh. The regret throughout the scientific world for this early loss has rarely been paralleled—the only fully analogous case within the writer's memory being that of Francis Balfour, the embryologist of Cambridge, in an Alpine accident now some thirty-five years ago. But, as Hertz had wished, the path was opened ; and able physicists entered on it, first to test and verify, then to extend the investigation in new directions. The first defect to be grappled with was the uncertain behaviour and irregularity of discharge of the balls between which the oscillating discharge took place. Hence to improve this portion of the apparatus to ensure 'good' sparks without 'bad,' has been a main endeavour for subsequent investigators. Here Lodge and Bose were specially successful: the first by introducing an intermediate ball, which served as a regulator of the discharge, and the second by the use of platinum-covered surfaces, from and to which the alternating sparks could pass without roughening or oxidation. Bose's radiators, instead of being disordered by specks of dust, as previous workers had found, continued to emit their sparks, and these their waves, so steadily as to be uninterrupted even when a jet of air mingled with street-dust was turned upon it. Bose also used for his radiator a sphere surrounded by two hollow hemispheres. This device increased the energy of radiation.

Further advance of the determination of the optical properties of electric radiation by quantitative measurements have been retarded, since on account of the large size of the waves their strictly linear propagation could not be secured. Bose was able to produce extremely short waves, which largely filled up the gap between the infra-red rays and Hertz's long electric waves.

For this purpose, the whole of the radiating part of the apparatus was enclosed within double metal walls to cut off stray radiation: the outer of copper to prevent the escape of the electric rays, and the inner of soft iron as a shield to cut off the magnetic disturbance.

The next problem before experimenters was to improve upon Hertz's receiver. Here the initiative was afforded by Professor Branly, of the Catholic University College of Paris, whose 'radio-conductor' has since become so well known. In principle it is merely a slender tube containing metal filings, in which, although themselves good conductors, there is yet considerable resistance, since their contacts are comparatively few, and these variably imperfect. But Branly found that the Hertzian waves, which could not but produce considerable induction in the filings, enormously reduced their resistance, sometimes even to a millionth. Hence it followed that the apparatus could be used as the needed improved receiver, since detecting the electric rays more finely and more clearly than did the first receiver of Hertz. After the filings have thus acted, a tap suffices to shake them back to their former irregularity, and the apparatus is ready for the next experiment.

Lodge made able use of this simple expedient ; he also offered an interpretation of its action, as due to fusing or soldering of the minute points of contact of the filings by the inductive effect produced in them through the incidence of the Hertzian waves, and for this reason he renamed it a 'Coherer.' Branly, however, maintains the original name, with his explanation that the Hertzian waves merely modify in some ways the non-conducting film upon the surface of the filings. Bose's receiver—a great advance on that of Branly and Lodge, of which the sensibility is variable, sometimes even seeming capricious—replaced the irregular filings by fine wire spiral springs, adjusted with a thousand regular contacts or thereabouts, and fixed in ebonite, and under control by a screw. A weak current is passed through this, to which the spirals offer a very appreciable resistance. The current is enormously reduced, as with Branly's apparatus, but now even more sensitively and more regularly when the instrument is placed in the path of the electric waves ; the more since the electric beam of Bose's generator is not only sharp and well defined, but better regulated. The sensibility of this apparatus, says M. Poincaré (to whose clear treatise the writer is much indebted), 'is exquisite : it responds to all the radiations in the interval of an octave. One makes it sensitive to different kinds of radiations, by varying the electromotive force which engenders the current which traverses the receiver.' Bose also was successful in inventing other types of receivers which recovered automatically without any tapping. It is also well worth notice that the whole apparatus has thus not only been improved by Bose and perfected in all details, but condensed from the enormous dimensions of Hertz's original devices, and the still very considerable magnitude of those of Lodge and other investigators, to a small and compact set of appliances, which stands conveniently upon one end of a writing-table, and may be packed into a suit-case, and thus carried and exhibited to any audience.

Bose had now made himself the best equipped among physicists in this field of investigation. For with the most perfect production of rays, and these under the fullest control, it was possible to work towards shorter and shorter waves, less dispersive in their diffraction, and producible as a definite beam of half-inch section. Furthermore, his receiver not only surpassed previous ones in that sensibility which is so great in all forms, but—what is more important—in its certainty and uniformity of action. His problem thus admitted of fuller and clearer statement, and came substantially to this: Hertz's study of the electric waves, and still more his comparisons of their behaviour with optical phenomena, were more or less qualitative. But 'science is measurement': it must have quantitative precision; and for this purpose more regular waves must be produced, and as near those of heat and light as may be—i.e. as short as possible. With the perfected apparatus Bose carried out his extended investigations on the optical properties of the electric rays. The scheme adopted was as follows:—

(*a*) Verification of the Laws of Reflection (plane mirror, curved mirror).
(*b*) Phenomena of Refraction (prisms, total reflection, opacity caused by multiple refraction and reflection; determination of the indices of refraction).
(*c*) Selective Absorption (electrically coloured media).
(*d*) Phenomena of Interference (determination of wave-length).
(*e*) Double Refraction and Polarisation (polarising gratings, polarising crystal, double refraction produced by crystals, by other substances, and by strain; circular polarisation; electro-polari-

Professor J. C. Bose's Friday Evening Discourse on 'Electric Waves' before the Royal Institution (1896).

scope and polarimeter; rotation of plane of polarisation.

Fully to summarise the results of this comprehensive experimental inquiry is here impossible: enough to borrow from a recent retrospect of it by an eminent American physicist, Dr. Kunz of Illinois University:

Bose showed that these short electrical waves have the same properties as a beam of light, exhibiting reflection, refraction, even total reflection, double refraction, polarisation and rotation of the plane of polarisation. The thinnest film of air is sufficient to produce total reflection of visible light with its extremely short wave-lengths; but with Bose's short electric waves, the critical thickness of the air-space was determined by the refracting power of the prism, and by the wave-length of the electric oscillations. He found a special crystal, Nemalite, which exhibits the polarisation of electric waves in the very same manner as a beam of light is polarised by selective absorption in crystals like Tourmaline, which Bose found to be due to their different electric conductivity in two directions. The rotation of the plane of polarisation was demonstrated by means of a contrivance twisted like a rope, and the rotation could be produced to left or right, just as different sorts of sugar rotate the plane of polarisation of ordinary light towards one direction or the other. The index of refraction of these electrical waves was determined for different materials; and a difficulty was eliminated which presented itself in Maxwell's theory, as to the relation between the index of refraction of light and the dielectric constant of insulators. Bose also measured the wave-length of the various oscillations. In order to produce the short electrical oscillations, to detect them and to study their optical properties, he had to invent a large number of new apparatus and instruments; and he has indeed enriched physics by a number of apparatus distinguished by simplicity, directness, and ingenuity.

So far the American physicist. But for the conclusion of this chapter we may best quote one of Bose's own passages, which better unveils the spirit which lies behind research: in fact the part of the scientific imagination which ever unifies reason and experiment alike.

Imagine a large electric organ, provided with an infinite number of stops, each giving rise to a particular ether note. Imagine the lowest stop producing one vibration in a second. We should then get a gigantic ether wave 186,000 miles long. Let the next stop give rise to two vibrations in a second, and let each succeeding stop produce higher and higher notes. What an infinite number of stops there would be! Imagine an unseen hand pressing the different stops in rapid succession, producing higher and higher notes. The ether note will thus rise in frequency from one vibration in a second, to tens, to hundreds, to thousands, to hundreds of thousands, to millions, to millions of millions. While the ethereal sea in which we are immersed is being thus agitated by these multitudinous waves, we shall remain entirely unaffected, for we possess no organs of perception to respond to these waves. As the ether note rises still higher in pitch, we shall for a brief moment perceive a sensation of warmth. This will be the case when the ether vibration reaches a frequency of several billions of times in a second. As the note rises still higher, our eyes will begin to be affected, a red glimmer of light would be the first to make its appearance. From this point the few colours we see are comprised within a single octave of vibration—from 400 to 800 billions in one second. As the frequency of vibration rises still higher, our organs of perception fail us completely; a great gap in our consciousness obliterates the rest. The brief flash of light is succeeded by unbroken darkness.

How blind we are! How circumscribed is our knowledge! The little we can see is nothing compared to what actually is!

But things which are dark now will one day be made clear. Knowledge grows little by little, slowly but surely. Many wonderful things have recently been discovered. We have already caught broken glimpses of invisible lights; some day, perhaps not very distant, we shall be able to see light-gleams, visible or invisible, merging one into the other, in unbroken sequence.

CHAPTER V

FURTHER PHYSICAL RESEARCH AND ITS APPRECIATION

Bose's scientific results, given in the last chapter, passed rapidly into current science, and its text-books, English and Continental, through a series of papers communicated to the Royal Society by Lord Rayleigh, whose constant sympathy was the best of encouragements for the young investigator. A reprint of Bose's collected Physical Papers may some day be published, and lead to further development of some of their inquiries, whether by Bose, his pupils, or others.

The main results of all these papers were also popularised in the standard way through various lectures, concluding with one of that series of Friday Evening Discourses at the Royal Institution, which has so long given one of the very best of platforms for the announcement of fresh investigation.

The invitation to deliver this discourse so impressed the India Office that they granted Bose three months' extra deputation leave, which admitted of its preparation and delivery. Its reception was fully appreciative. The scientific public had been fully prepared to be interested in the work, not only by the Royal Society papers, and the publication of full abstracts and appreciative articles in the *Electrician* and other technical journals, but from Bose's first appearance in England at the Liverpool meeting of the British Association. After Bose's paper there, Lord Kelvin not only broke into the warmest praise, but limped upstairs into the ladies' gallery and shook Mrs. Bose by both hands, with glowing congratulations on her husband's brilliant work. Moreover, the general press and the public were struck by him as the first Indian to win distinction through investigation in science—in the most strictly Western of all its departments, and at that time also the most progressive.

The preceding generation had handed on many recollections of the achievements of applied physics, beginning with the laying of the first transatlantic cable, which had brought Sir William Thomson (afterwards Lord Kelvin) into fame, after which came successive marvels, such as electric light, the telephone, the phonograph, Röntgen rays, and more. Now a new marvel was silently preparing to break upon the world — the application of Hertz's waves to wireless telegraphy, towards which Hertz seemed to have some premonition and various later investigators were feeling their way, as notably Lodge, and above all Marconi. Bose himself had as early as 1895, in a public lecture in Calcutta, demonstrated the ability of the electric rays to travel from the lecture-room, and through an intervening room and passage, to a third room 75 feet distant from the radiator, thus passing through three solid walls on the way, as well as the body of the chairman (who happened to be the Lieutenant-Governor). The receiver at this distance still had energy enough to make a contact which set a bell ringing, discharged a pistol, and exploded a miniature mine. To get this result from his small radiator, Bose set up an apparatus which curiously anticipated the lofty 'antennae' of modern wireless telegraphy—a circular metal plate at the top of a 20-foot pole being put in connection with the radiator and a similar one with the receiving apparatus. Encouraged by this success, our inventor not only went on signalling through the College but planned to fix one of these poles on the roof of his house and the other on the Presidency College a mile away; but he left for England before effecting this.

On the publication of Bose's papers on Electric Waves, *The Electrician*, in its review (December 1895), drew attention to the practicability of devising—

> a practicable system of electro-magnetic 'light'-houses, the receiver on board ship being some electric equivalent of the human eye. The evolution of a suitable generating apparatus would, we thought, present little difficulty; that of a suitable receiver, on the other hand, seemed likely to give considerable trouble. In this connection we would draw attention to the substantial and workmanlike form of 'Coherer' devised by Professor Bose, and described by him at the end of his paper 'On a new Electro-Polariscope.' The sensibility and range of this type of 'Coherer' would appear to leave little to be desired, and it is certainly more likely to withstand, with equanimity, the thousand and one shocks that the flesh is heir to at sea, than any of the forms hitherto brought about.

And subsequently, after Bose's Friday Evening Discourses at the Royal Institution, *The Electric Engineer* expressed 'surprise that no secret was at any time made as to its construction, so that it has been open to all the world to adopt it for practical and possibly money-making purposes.'

Bose has sometimes, and not unnaturally, been criticised as unpractical for making no profit from his inventions. But as to this he was determined from the first. His child-memory had been impressed by the pure white flowers offered in Indian worship; and it came early to him that whatever offerings his life could make should be untainted by any considerations of personal advantage. Moreover, he was painfully impressed by what seemed to him symptoms of deterioration, even in scientific men, by the temptation of gain; and so at this time he made the resolve to seek for no personal advantage from his inventions.

In 1901 one of the great manufacturers of wireless apparatus proposed to Bose, just before his Royal Institution lecture of that year, to sign a remunerative agreement as to his new type of receiver; but to the business man's frank surprise, not to say disgust, he declined the offer.

An American friend, indignant with what seemed such unpractical quixotism, forthwith patented the invention in his name in America, but Bose would not use his rights, and allowed the patent to lapse. As a consequence, his improved coherer came into use till a fresh device was adopted in its stead.

It may be frankly admitted—even in some cases maintained—that under present industrial and economic conditions it may be practically impossible to organise and apply certain useful and desirable inventions without conforming to the customary rules of the game. After full recognition of the prevalent economic situation, it has been necessary to explain Bose's position as that of no mere quixotist. Simply stated, it is the position of the old rishis of India, of whom he is increasingly recognised by his countrymen as a renewed type, and whose best teaching was ever open to all willing to accept it. It also concurs with that of the modern pilgrim of a later chapter and of the boy growing up in the enthusiasm of the antique poetry and chivalry of the past, whose acquaintance we made at the beginning.

Towards the close of Bose's stay in England in 1897, he was invited to explain his results in Paris by prominent members of its Physical Society, and also by the leading physicists of Berlin. At the Société de Physique the chair was taken by M. Cornu, who had been President of the Academy of Sciences, a veteran investigator in optics and electricity, whose generous appreciation remains one of Bose's most valued reminiscences. Lippmann, already famous through his inventions in colour-photography, Cailletet, who had made one of the first successes in the liquefaction of gases, and others of foremost rank were present. Lippmann and others were so enthusiastic as to insist upon a later demonstration in the Sorbonne; and soon afterwards Bose was made an honorary member of the Société de Physique.

In Berlin his discourse was to the Academy of Sciences, which printed his comprehensive experimental summary. To this discourse not only the Berlin physicists turned out, but some from a much greater distance: thus old Professor Quincke of Heidelberg, who had been greatly interested in the subject and had endeavoured to construct Bose's apparatus, came all the way expressly to hear him, and to invite him to visit his laboratory. At Berlin, Helmholtz's successor, Professor Warburg, told another investigator who was asking his advice about taking up electric waves: 'Bose has left you practically nothing to do: better try something else.' A visit to Kiel to lecture before the University and to meet Ebert, a notable worker in Electro-magnetism, and next a pleasant stay in Heidelberg to visit Quincke, Lenard and others, completed this tour; and Bose then started homewards from Marseilles.

From the above account of the success of Bose's scientific deputation to Europe, it will be seen that the long-standing prejudice which the West had entertained regarding the incapacity of Indians to do advanced scientific work was removed. Bose was in fact here the pioneer who succeeded in breaking through what had so long seemed a closed door, and thus opened the highway into active and productive science for his countrymen.

Referring to Bose's work, Sir Henry Roscoe, the Vice-Chancellor of the University of London, acknowledged that the Eastern mind was equally capable of making great scientific discoveries and producing experimentalists as eminent as those of the West. And Lord Reay, the former Governor of Bombay, representing the statesman's point of view, drew attention to the importance of India's contribution to science: 'For science was absolutely international, and any result obtained by Dr. Bose in India could at once be annexed by us without protest.'

Not only were scientific men impressed by the importance

of such collaboration of the East in the advance of science, but enthusiasm was aroused in the most unexpected quarters. The London *Spectator* had consistently maintained a critical attitude towards Indian aspirations; but its editor was drawn by curiosity to attend Bose's discourses at the Royal Institution; and in the following week a long leading article appeared, from which the following is an extract:

There is however, to our thinking, something of rare interest in the spectacle there presented, of a Bengalee of the purest descent lecturing in London to an audience of appreciative European savants upon one of the most recondite branches of modern physical science. It suggests at least the possibility that we may one day see an invaluable addition to the great army of those who are trying by acute observation and patient experiment to wring from Nature some of her most jealously guarded secrets. The people of the East have just the burning imagination which could extort a truth out of a mass of apparently disconnected facts; a habit of meditation without allowing the mind to dissipate itself, such as has belonged to the greatest mathematicians and engineers; and a power of persistence—it is something a little different from patience—such as hardly belongs to any European. We do not know Professor Bose; but we venture to say that if he caught with his scientific imagination a glimpse of a wonder-working 'ray' as yet unknown to man but always penetrating ether, and believed that experiment would reveal its properties and potentialities, he would go on experimenting ceaselessly through a long life, and, dying, hand on his task to some successor, be it son or be it disciple. Nothing would seem laborious to him in his inquiry, nothing insignificant, nothing painful, any more than it would seem to the true Sanyasi in the pursuit of his inquiry into the ultimate relation of his own spirit to that of the Divine. Just think what kind of addition to the means of investigation would be made by the arrival within that sphere of inquiry of a thousand men with the Sanyasi mind, the mind which utterly controls the body and can meditate and inquire endlessly while life remains, never for a moment losing sight of the object, never for a moment letting it be obscured by any terrestrial temptation.

We can see no reason whatever why the Asiatic mind, turning from its absorption in insoluble problems, should not betake itself ardently, thirstily, hungrily, to the research into Nature which can never end, yet is always yielding results, often evil as well as good, upon which yet deeper inquiries can be based. If that happened—and Professor Bose is at all events a living evidence that it can happen—that would be the greatest addition ever made to the sum of the mental force of mankind.

And more briefly *The Times* wrote :

The originality of the achievement is enhanced by the fact that Dr. Bose had to do the work in addition to his incessant duties as Professor of Physical Science in Calcutta, and with apparatus and appliances which in this country would be deemed altogether inadequate. He had to construct himself his instruments as he went along. His work forms the outcome of his twofold lines of labour—construction and research.

Many of the leading scientific men wished to show their appreciation of the value of Bose's work in a practical way. Their natural spokesman, Lord Kelvin, strongly realised the all but impossible conditions under which that work had hitherto been carried out ; and he wrote to Lord George Hamilton, then Secretary of State for India :

It would be conducive to the credit of India and the scientific education in Calcutta, if a well-equipped Physical Laboratory is added to the resources of the University of Calcutta in connection with the Professorship held by Dr. Bose.

Following on this letter a memorial was sent, drawing the Secretary of State's attention—

to the great importance which we attach to the establishment in the Indian Empire of a Central Laboratory for advanced teaching and research in connection with the Presidency College, Calcutta. We believe that it would be not only beneficial in respect to higher education, but also that it would largely promote the material interest of the country ; and we venture to urge on you the desirability of establishing in India a Physical Laboratory worthy of that great Empire.

Among the memorialists were Lord Lister, then President of the Royal Society, Lord Kelvin, Professor Clifton, Professor Fitzgerald, Dr. Gladstone, Professor Poynting, Sir William Ramsay, Sir Gabriel Stokes, Professor Silvanus Thompson, Sir William Rücker, and others.

Impressed by all this, the Secretary of State sent a dispatch (May 1897) to the Government of India enclosing the memorial, and supporting it—'being of opinion that the question of establishing an institution of the kind mentioned is deserving of consideration by Your Excellency in Council.'

Lord Elgin, then Viceroy, told Bose that the Government was interested in his project, and would communicate with the Government of Bengal. This came filtering through departmental channels, with the appended note that though the scheme was important, yet it might be postponed to a future date. Bose understood what this really meant. He had succeeded in making the India Office and the Government recognise the claims of science; but he also realised that the Government working machinery could be effectively delayed by departmental cogwheels. His friends in England were anxious to hasten matters at headquarters, if he would let them know what was causing delay. But that would have meant dropping his work of research for an indefinite period; so he made up his mind to face the old difficulties as best he could, and be independent of facilities that the Government might offer, but by which there seemed little chance of his benefiting. It is worthy of remark that the cogwheels suddenly became mobile when Bose had neared the period of retirement from Government service. Then the scheme for which he had striven for many years resulted in the recent foundation (1914) of a fully equipped Physical Laboratory. Though this came too late to be of much advantage for himself, he had the consolation that he had been able to leave the Presidency College better than he found it. Pupils whom he had trained were now in charge of Physical Departments with Laboratories in different colleges. His efforts had not altogether been in vain.

Bose's attitude of detachment appeared quixotic and unpractical to many, as other resolves had done previously. Though he seems never to have evaded any fight for principles, he was the more indifferent to personal advantage. He answered the criticisms of his friends by saying that he had long ago made up his mind to choose not the easier but the more difficult path; that appeared to him the true scope for manhood.

But, although abandoning the advantage derived from general recognition of his work towards securing facilities for his own research, he continued his dream of securing these for his successors; and thenceforth was more resolved than ever to establish a Research Institute, as far as might be through his own savings and efforts. Again he and his wife curtailed their expenses, and religiously put aside a portion of pay and other earnings, from University examinations and from the proceeds of books and lectures. These he invested in securities which fortunately for him trebled in value after twenty years. A windfall also came, and in an unexpected way. By seniority, and by the distinction of his service, the highest appointment in the Educational Service, the Directorship of Public Instruction, had come within his reach. But he preferred to remain at the Presidency College as a Professor of Science. Here too seniority entitled him to the highest grade, with corresponding rise of pay. Bose, with customary indifference, had never consulted the Civil List. Had he done so, he would have found that his promotion to the top of the Service had been long overdue. For their own reasons the Department had not informed the Government about this promotion: only on the eve of his retirement the claim of a junior officer was brought to the notice of the Government, which then inquired why the question of the prior claims of Bose had not been reported. As no satisfactory explanation was forthcoming, the Government gazetted Bose to the highest grade, with retrospective effect. The large amount thus received was fully credited to the account of the Research Institute, which was to be materialised in a few years' time. A legacy towards this also came from an old and valued friend.

Regarding Bose's claim on Government for facilities of research, it must be said to its credit that the idea was not dropped altogether. Lord Curzon indeed, when Viceroy, desired to revive it. But, as he was not a scientific man himself, he sent a cable to four English men of science for their opinion. The two physicist referees cabled their highest appreciation of Bose's work; but the other two happened to belong to the physiological camp (and as will be seen later) hostile to Bose, and they opposed the idea. In this dilemma, where scientific opinion seemed so evenly divided, the Viceroy, by way of compromise, conferred on Bose at the Delhi Durbar in 1902 the decoration of the Companionship of the Indian Empire.

CHAPTER VI

PHYSICAL RESEARCHES CONTINUED

The Theory of Molecular Strain and its Interpretations

RECALL now from Chapter IV the receiver of the electric waves, the 'radio-conductor' of Branly (called 'Coherer' by Lodge, in terms of his simple and attractive thesis of the fusing together of its metallic particles at their points of contact by the inductive action of the electric waves). Next recall the difficulties and irregularities of its action, more or less felt by all observers, and notably abated by Bose's form of receiver. Bose, as we have seen, succeeded in making his electric wave receiver, at first made of steel springs (afterwards electroplated with cobalt to avoid oxidation), highly reliable. He was also able to devise other receivers which, in addition to their extreme sensitiveness, exhibited automatic recovery. He could exalt the sensitiveness of his receivers to any degree desired by slight increase of pressure of contact, and by increase of electromotive force in the receiving circuit. But after these improvements a new anomaly appeared. When experiments had been carried on continuously for a couple of hours or so, the receiver became less sensitive, and after more prolonged work, still more so, reminding one of fatigue. What could be the meaning of this fatigue? When the fatigued receiver was allowed to rest for several hours, it became sensitive once more. Thinking, naturally enough, that longer rest would render it still more sensitive, Bose left the receiver aside for several days, with the quite unexpected and perplexing result that it had become insensitive once more. This particular insensitiveness could not, as in the case of fatigue, be restored by further rest; but he excited the 'idle' receiver by an electric shock, with the surprising result that its sensitiveness was restored. Two altogether different treatments were thus found necessary in the two cases: rest for the 'fatigued' receiver, and active stimulation foı the 'idle' one.

The theory of the 'Coherer' was therefore inadequate; for if the diminution of resistance by external stimulus were brought about simply by soldering of particles, such diminution would be independent of the previous history of the receiver, i.e. of its moderate rest, restoring sensitiveness as if from fatigue, or of its prolonged rest, reducing this as it were to idleness.

To explain these anomalies, Bose was led into new and wide fields of investigation. Hence two papers.[1] The terms 'Electric *Touch*,' or 'Contact-sensitiveness,' were introduced to avoid the theory involved in the term 'Coherer,' and also because the nature of response depended on the surface of contact, and not on the substratum. An insensitive metal such as copper, when coated with a thin film of a sensitive metal like cobalt, acquired extreme sensitiveness: whereas a highly sensitive material like iron, when given a coating of an insensitive metal like copper, gave little or no response. Bose next embarked on a systematic investigation of the contact-sensitiveness of all the metals, non-metals and metalloids obtainable. Many of the rare metals were at the time not available, but in some cases he isolated the elements from their compounds in an electric furnace; and experimentally overcame many other difficulties encountered at every step.

The investigations on metals were carried out in the

[1] 'On a Self-Recovering Coherer,' *Proc. Roy. Soc.*, 1899. 'On Electric *Touch*, and the Molecular Changes produced in Matter by Electric Waves,' *Proc. Roy. Soc.*, 1900.

sequence of their atomic weights—from Lithium, with its lowest atomic weight 7, to Lead, with high atomic weight 205. He was surprised to find that the 'electric touch' exhibited a periodic change. When a substance exhibits under electric radiation an increase of conducting power, its sign of 'touch' he distinguished as positive. This is the strong characteristic of the 'Coherer' made of iron. This diminution of resistance was by no means general; his investigations revealed the astonishing fact that potassium exhibited an effect which was diametrically opposite, namely an increase of resistance. The receiver made of potassium exhibited, moreover, a rapid and spontaneous recovery, requiring no tapping. It is quite evident that an increase of resistance and automatic self-recovery could on no account be due to the supposed fusion and coherence of neighbouring particles by the induction-spark. The response, positive or negative, is determined by the chemical nature of the substance; and the phenomonen must therefore be one of molecular change.

In arranging the elements in order of their increasing atomic weights, the 'Electric *Touch*' was found, as stated before, to exhibit a remarkable periodicity, approximately represented in the accompanying curve (Fig. 1).

Those above the horizontal line are positive, those below negative, and others which cross the line more or less neutral. Of the neutral substances, copper and silver may be taken as typical.

There are other interesting differences in the behaviours of different metals. In some cases the induced change of resistance under electric stress was not permanent, but the substance completely recovered its original condition. It was as if the molecules were put under strain by the impressed stress. Electrically some were highly elastic, their recovery being quick; in other cases less elastic, and the strained molecules remained in that condition, the recovery being extremely slow. In such cases, however, anything which caused molecular disturbance—e.g. the action of warmth—helped the automatic recovery. Even substances like iron, which remained conducting as an after-effect of electric stimulus, recovered automatically when maintained at a higher temperature.

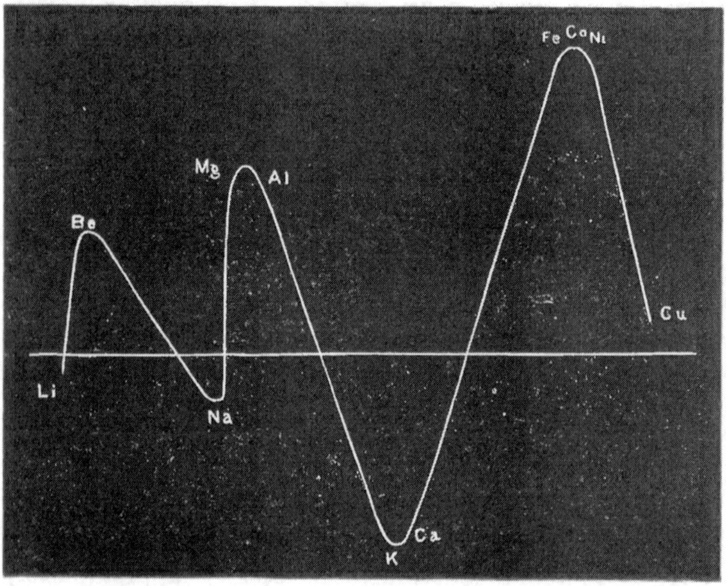

FIG. 1.—Periodicity of Electric *Touch*. Abscissa represents the atomic weight; ordinate the electric *touch* positive or negative.

From the observations of these various characteristics, Bose was led to suppose that electric radiation produced a molecular change of an 'allotropic' nature, similar to the allotropic change induced in sulphur or phosphorus by visible light.

The action of light on various kinds of matter is familiarly known, though little understood. Everyone has noticed how colours are often faded by exposure; while chemists have long known that common yellow phosphorus is transmuted into the red variety, less dangerous because no longer liable to that rapid oxidation in the atmosphere which may readily set the familiar variety on fire. Sulphur exposed to light is not changed to the eye, but treatment with bisulphide of carbon, so convenient a solvent of common sulphur, proves that light has somehow rendered it insoluble. To this phenomenon of 'allotropism' we shall return later: it is enough at first to note that the action of light on bodies, though sometimes within our direct observation, need not necessarily be so, yet may none the less be real and profound.

But how shall we proceed to the investigation of these changes?—how detect changes if they take place?—and how discriminate between the exposed substances and the unexposed? The photographic plate is the familiar instance in point; but though chemists have endeavoured to explain what happens (as by reduction of silver chloride, and the reduction of this to metallic silver), the amount of material altered is too small to admit of analysis and verification. Bose showed how it can be detected electrically, for which the galvanometer is sensitive to a degree incomparably beyond that of chemical estimation.

Now the allotropic variation or change in molecular aggregation in a substance must, according to Bose, change more or less all its properties physical and chemical—e.g. its solubility, its density, its chemical activity, and its position in the voltaic series in consequence of which a current flows from electro-positive to the relatively electro-negative; it would also change its power of electric conduction. Note in this connection the familiar difference of conducting power in the three allotropic modifications of carbon. As charcoal, its conducting power is high; as graphite, its conducting power is only moderate; while diamond is practically a non-conductor. Let us call these A, B, and C. If we could produce any transformation of graphite (B) towards charcoal (A), it would be detected by increase of conducting power, and if towards diamond (C) by decrease

The invisible molecular change may thus be detectible by this subtle electric test, with its great advantage over chemical estimation, which requires large quantities, and long hours of analysis, during which the substance may have automatically returned to its primitive state.

That allotropic transformation may electrically be detected, is also seen in other ways. In a selenium cell the incidence of light causes an increase of conducting power; and removal of light is attended by self-recovery. If the stress has been moderate the recovery is quick; if very great, as by strong light, the recovery is very much protracted. Nor is light the only agent of such allotropic change; heat-rays may also produce it. Thus ordinary iodide of mercury spread out in a thin film is practically a red pigment, but when exposed to heat radiation it becomes transformed into a yellow allotropic variety. On removal of the radiation the substance recovers, the recovery being hastened by a mechanical scratch, and the thin film becomes red once more. Bose found that this visible change had as a concomitant, a change of electric resistance.

In summary, then, we find that in iron-like substances with the positive 'touch' the transformation is towards an increase of conducting power; and in potassium-like substances, it is towards diminution. Just as all substances as regards their magnetic properties fall into two classes, para-magnetic or dia-magnetic, so all substances are divisible into two classes, one exhibiting a positive and the other a negative 'touch.'

Bose had here discovered new classes of electric phenomena; and these two classes of conducting bodies (for only with conductors was experimentation found possible) we may characterise as 'contact-positive' and 'contact-negative.' In at least one almost neutral yet slightly positive substance—silver—Bose succeeded in producing by chemical means a negative variety, which gave the negative response of diminished conductivity. This variety was found less stable, since heating restored the new variety to the familiar one ; and on stimulation he also found repeated reversals from + to –, and back again, thus giving an alternating curve. The change induced in various substances by electric radiation seemed to Bose plainly one of molecular strain in response to external stress. So, he asked himself, do not such variations, sufficiently marked and permanent, give the physicist a peep into the chemist's (hitherto empirical) collection of 'allotropic substances,' and even a method towards their further investigation ? For if the transient allotropism thus discovered be thought of as molecular strain, with the possibility of recovery, then ordinary allotropism, so relatively stable, becomes also comprehensible—i.e. in terms of over-strain, from which spontaneous return is difficult or impossible under ordinary conditions.

This delicate mode of inquiry was rightly claimed as 'full of promise in many lines of inquiry in molecular physics. . . . The varieties of phenomena are unlimited ; for we have in each substance to take account of the peculiarity of its chemical constitution, the nature of its response to ether waves, the lag and molecular viscosity. All these combined give to each substance its peculiar characteristic curve : it is not unlikely that the curves may give us much information as to the chemical nature and physical condition of the different substances.' Bose's new investigations had been to disclose a new class of phenomenon of which electro-optics had given no suggestion, those of the different touch of metals, when employed as materials of so many 'Coherers,' or rather receivers. Here, returning to the chemical suggestions above noted, was an interesting correlation of electric properties with atomic weights, and the disclosure of a new arrangement of these accordingly—one not without suggestive analogies to Mendeléeff's famous classification, and inviting therefore fresh research.

Return now to the nature of the electric radiation discussed in Chapter IV : first, as an extended spectrum of longer and longer waves beyond those of heat, and yet, as Maxwell had foreseen and Hertz had shown, analogous to those of light; and then with their correspondence, increasingly determined by Bose's work, as regards their reflection, refraction, polarisation and other phenomena—in short, an advance of electro-optics.

But now, leaving the direct study of the varied yet profoundly similar rays of this long spectrum of radiation, which we call ultra-violet, luminous, thermal and electric, we come to a third class of problems—touching the effects of diverse radiation on different kinds of matter. As to the effect of electric radiation, Bose was able to show that it induces a state of temporary or permanent molecular strain in matter attended by physical or chemical change in the substance. Since electric waves have turned out to be so similar in their nature and behaviour to those of light, may they not also have molecular reactions more or less similar to the photographic effect? In the concluding part of his Electric *Touch* paper, Bose says:

> The effect of electric radiation (like visible radiation of light) is to produce rearrangement of the atoms or molecules of a substance; so does light produce new atomic or molecular groupings in a photographic plate. The contact-points of the coherer may therefore be regarded as corresponding to the particles of a photographic plate. Investigation on this aspect of the subject has given me some extraordinary results. They seem to connect together many phenomena which at first sight do not seem to have anything in common. I am at present trying to arrange an apparatus which will, by means of the pulsating galvanometer spot of light, automatically record the various molecular transformations caused by external forces.

While the speculative hypotheses with which so many fruitful investigations begin have to be experimentally tested and verified before they can be published as contributions to positive science, it is their inception and development which are the main interest in any biographic treatment. Moreover, is not this view of any investigator, as struggling to criticise his dream, interesting and suggestive to other workers, and so to the teacher of science also? The workers in every laboratory are taught patient accuracy, and so far so good; but must we not encourage their free and varied speculation as well? Have not the great discoveries been great dreams? Are not Kepler's four laws the survivors of innumerable speculations—some say hundreds, if not thousands, of trials and guesses? And did not Darwin defend and recommend even 'fool-experiments,' as he called them? Many a new investigation has begun in this speculative and tentative way.

A further perspective is here of interest. At first it seemed as if the discovery of 'touch,' or contact-sensitiveness, in the field of electric radiation had no parallel in that of optics; but now we see it leading back from newly observed phenomena of electricity to the interpretation of those produced by light, and ultra-visible rays. The fundamental unity of the long spectrum is thus further manifested —and from one of its known extremes to the other, from electric to photographic.

By some instinct or foresight, Bose had already, in 1896, when describing his receiving contact of the electric wave, likened it to a 'photographic particle,' and that premonition he was now able increasingly to substantiate. In a paper which we have here no space to review—'The Continuity of the Effect of Light and Electric Radiation'[1]—it was investigated in many forms of matter, and further generalised as well. Next, 'The Similarities between Radiation and Mechanical Strains,' at first hypothetical, were demonstrated experimentally, as by the construction of a 'Strain-cell,' in which a sudden twist, through measured angles, of one of two similar standard wires of any metal immersed in water, was shown to produce a definite and measurable amount of electro-motive force. The acted wire usually behaves like the zinc plate of the ordinary cell, but not always: some become copper-like. There are thus two classes of bodies, much as we have seen for electric

[1] *Proc. Roy. Soc.*, 1901.

radiation. The effects of recovery from moderate strain, and of overstrain beyond speedy recovery, were also noted.

Hence at length the interesting paper 'On the Strain Theory of Photographic Action,'[1] which, despite its technical detail, is in principle intelligible enough even to the non-photographer. The photographic effect in a sensitive plate is demonstrated by its 'development' after exposure. This effect of light on sensitive substances may be fugitive or persistent, with gradations between. Bose's idea is that the image, with its lights and shadows, produced differential strains on the sensitive matter of the plate; and that these differently light-strained particles are consequently unequally attacked and fixed by the developer. But if this image be correctly interpreted in terms of molecular strain, gradual recovery is to be expected, with a subsequent fading of the image. The early photographers, with their daguerreotypes, were much troubled by this: hence subsequent photographic progress has largely been through making plates of more enduring quality. So that nowadays one goes on taking a series of plates and films to be developed at leisure. Such improved plates, on Bose's theory, simply delay or impede the molecular elastic recovery of the variously strained particles which constitute the image, and hence give ample time for its development. The term 'Sensitiser' may in many cases be a misnomer, since it may actually cause a retardation of recovery.

But the time of recovery should have its limit, and it is here interesting to note that experience confirms this. After Bose's exposition of his theory at the Royal Photographic Society, one of the audience told how after a photographic tour in India the development of a batch of plates had been delayed by circumstances for two years. On then proceeding to develop, he found no image at all: and this he had till then thought of as a

[1] *Proc. Roy. Soc.*, 1901.

mere spoiling by climate. But, as Bose's theory explains, he now saw it as a recovery of the plates from their image-strained condition. For some time later, wishing urgently to take a photograph, at a moment when he had not a single fresh plate available, it occurred to him, as a mere chance, to try one of those spoiled Indian plates, of which the development had been abandoned. To his agreeable surprise the new photograph was successful—in fact, as if the plate had been a fresh one. He now for the first time understood, and brought his experience forward as a vivid confirmation of Bose's theory of strain and recovery.

Substances may be sensitive, yet give no photographic image. For on the same general view, since almost all substances are molecularly affected by radiation, though in different degrees, and with very different rates of recovery, it is theoretically possible that we may alike vary the sensitive material for our photographic images, and find a widening range of developers for them. And in the world of nature our conception of activities of radiant energies through the whole spectrum, and of their effects upon recipient matter, similarly expand thereby. And if this is true throughout the range of inorganic matter, why should it not hold good in the living world as well, sensitive to radiation as we know it to be? Here, however, we are somewhat outrunning the paper before us, though not its author's active mind.

As examples of sensitive substances other than photographic plates with their salts of silver, why not plates of other materials? Moser had already obtained invisible images by prolonged exposure of clean silver and copper plates, which he developed with mercury vapour; and Waterhouse had made similar experiments, even with lead and gold, using the common developers. Since Bose had found all metals sensitive to electric radiation, the sensitiveness to light also was what he expected, while the prolonged exposure found necessary was to provide the necessary strain in materials less sensitive to light than are silver salts.

Mechanical pressures may also produce images capable of development, the so-called 'pressure-marks'; and, by electric strain, the 'inducto-scripts.'

At this time (1901) Bose was interested in the question of obtaining photographs without the action of light. Various radio-active substances were being found whose emanations affected the photographic plate. But Bose worked with substances which ordinarily were not radio-active. A section of a dried stem of a tree exhibits concentric markings, due to unequal growth in different seasons; these different rings, according to Bose, should emit radio-active particles at different rates *under the action of stimulus*. He enclosed a section of a stem in a dark box, with a photographic plate in front of it, but not in contact. Outside the box were two metallic plates, which were in connection with a machine which caused rapid electric oscillation in the intervening space. Under the action of this stimulus the radio-activity of the wood was evidenced by an extraordinarily clear impression of its structure given on the photographic plate—this, be it remembered, without the intervention of light. The accompanying reproduction (Fig. 2) is the photograph of a leaf of Bo-tree taken by the above method. By taking similar photographs, he obtained remarkable results with various stones and crystals, which revealed characteristic differences in their composition. A new field of investigation was opened out for immediate exploration; but all this had to be indefinitely postponed on account of another line inquiry which, as we shall see later, demanded his of undivided attention.

His theory of molecular strain, however, has been fruitful in physical and chemical researches; and subsequently found corroboration from Hartley in his work on the absorption spectra of solutions of metallic nitrates. In summarising his results he refers to 'three remarkable communications by J. Chunder Bose published in the "Proceedings of the Royal Society," 1902. It is supposed on good grounds that "the effect of radiation is to produce a state of molecular strain." Experimental evidence is adduced which shows that the molecular strain caused

FIG. 2.—Photography without light.

by the action of light, changes the physico-chemical properties of substances, so that it becomes possible to develop a latent image through differences in chemical stability as, for instance, by reducing agents.' Dr. Hartley's own experiments lent strong support to this, for the spectra obtained by him showed 'that the solutions of metallic nitrates are in a state of molecular strain.'[1]

[1] *Journal of the Chemical Society*, 1903.

Enough now of this theory of photography: we may pass to Bose's 'Artificial Retina.' His various forms of electric receiver were sensitive to the waves longer than those of heat; whereas the photographic plate is normally sensitive only to the short waves towards the opposite ends of the immensely long and varied spectrum. But, he asked, may it not be possible to find substances of wider and wider range of receptiveness? The ideal substance would be one sensitive through this enormous range, and responding not only to our visible light, but to all the many octaves of the invisible light, which stretch out on each side of the single octave of our colour-sensation. Hence a new and systematic series of tests of the range of responsiveness of natural and artificial substances without number, which is indicated, as begun, in the paper on 'Electric *Touch*,' but has never yet been completed and published. Still, the desired substance was at length found—one so exquisitely sensitive to the long electric waves as to supersede previous materials in the electric receiver of wireless telegraphy, already mentioned; yet giving also the same unquestionable galvanometric answer to thermal, luminous and ultra-violet rays.

To reduce this all-perceiving super-retina to the level of our human perception was next easy; for on placing in front of it a flask of water, to represent the aqueous humour, the electric and thermal rays are now absorbed, and thus can no longer be responded to; and similarly as to some of the ultra-violet rays as well. Thus this 'retina' could now practically only 'see' the rays which are visible to ourselves and signal their impulse to its galvanometric 'brain' behind, while on removing the absorbent water its innumerable octaves of wider perception were restored. As Bose remarked, 'Perhaps we do not sufficiently appreciate, especially in these days of space-signalling by Hertzian waves, the importance of that protective contrivance which veils our sense against insufferable radiance.' Here, then, is a first-class example of 'the wonders of science';

in fact of its 'Natural Magic,' as the old physicist Porta called his book, still memorable for his description of the 'Camera Obscura,' which is now reduced in size into the photographic camera. The camera is indeed a sort of giant eye; and its sensitive plates are a kind of simple and inorganic retina. Correspondingly, the eye is a camera, and its retina an organically elaborated sensitive plate, subtly layered for the perception of different shades of light.

This further invention of Bose's—incredible or uncanny though to some it seemed at first—comes into line with our general and elementary understanding of eye and camera alike: the wonder is in its immense range of sensitiveness. Yet instead of finding any super-retinal elaboration, well-nigh beyond microscopic inquiry, still more beyond mere dissection, when we open the little globe of the electric eye, and take away its lens, this amazing super-retina turns out to be made but of two tiny crystals of galena, adjusted to contact-sensitiveness. That this common lead ore, this heavy sulphide, should of all known things have fullest sensitiveness to all ether-waves, of nature or of laboratory art, is worth reflecting on. Lead—'dull lead'—is less dull than we think! And the characteristic response of the artificial retina next led Bose to discover, as we shall see later, certain unsuspected phenomena in human vision.

CHAPTER VII

RESPONSE IN THE LIVING AND NON-LIVING

INCREASINGLY throughout the preceding chapters there have incidentally appeared various parallelisms between the response of inorganic matter and phenomena we are accustomed to consider as characteristic of life. Indeed, but for the sake of brevity, these resemblances might have been multiplied. Still, to our physicist they were at first but incidental to his main inquiries. But as they multiplied they also grew more impressive, more and more close in their correspondence, and always under investigation of the same experimental and precise character which marked the whole of the preceding physical work. Such precision was in fact unavoidable, since these increasingly physiological studies were carried on by exactly the same methods as he had so often verified, and which had become familiar and well defined. It is important to note this: because so complex are the phenomena of life, and so long have they been regarded as mysterious, that biological speculation and even experiment is open to suspicion of unsoundness, and not least among physiologists in regard to each other; and hence, at their wisest, they are critical of themselves. It was with this caution and self-criticism that Bose began; and not simply with a good deal of that fear and trembling which every respectable specialist feels when he ventures even to look over his neighbour's wall, still more to pluck a handful of the roses which are overhanging into his garden.

For he had become fully aware of the commonly held belief in the West that while the East excelled in metaphysical speculations even to subtlety, it had no special aptitude for methods of exact science. In fact the capacity for concrete investigation was at that time commonly reckoned as due to some phrenological 'bump' absent from the Indian make-up, and towering dome-like upon the Western skull alone. Hence Bose had, from his earliest days of physical work and teaching, the ambition at once of justifying and reviving the scientific aptitude of his countrymen, who moreover, as their old art and commerce show, are not without practical and skilful hands, and cannot have heads so exclusively religious and metaphysical as the concentrated study of Sanskrit literature had induced others to think. The experimental rigour of Bose's work, and the exquisite refinement, yet simplicity, of his apparatus, from this first wave-transmitter and receiver to the unprecedentedly delicate and exactly recording apparatus which his workshop keeps increasingly turning out to this day, are thus explained. And, as a matter of fact, the one criticism of the apparatus and research in the Institute which the writer has ventured to make from time to time is, that one might sometimes be fruitfully enough working with this or that instrument without the delay of demolishing and reconstructing it for the sake of some, after all, minute percentage of extra-exactitude. Yet he cannot but respect this also, and bear his testimony to the physicist's precision, which can endure no trace of inaccuracy.

Let us return, however, to the new investigation, into what we may now begin to call 'the Response of the Living and Non-Living,' since that became the title of the volume of two years later, in which all these studies are summarised. It yielded such abundant and surprising results that Bose, for whom there was still no scientific public in India, nor even a single colleague with whom he could discuss his problems, was feeling the need of a new journey to Europe.

A very cordial invitation fortunately came from the International Congress of Physics, which was one of the many world-gatherings arranged at the Paris Exhibition of 1900.

The surprising results which Bose obtained had roused the interest of the new Lieutenant-Governor of Bengal, and he decided to send Bose on a scientific deputation to Europe, as his predecessor had done four years before. He believed that 'the visit of Professor Bose to Paris will be of great advantage to the singularly original researches in which he is engaged.' Accordingly, Bose reached Paris in August 1900, as a delegate from the Governments of Bengal and of India.

Bose read his paper on the Response of Inorganic and Living Matter before the Paris International Congress of Physicists (1900).[1] Reference has already been made to Bose's observation of the curious phenomenon of fatigue exhibited by the receivers of his electric waves ; and of how fatigue was removed after a period of rest. The receiver, however, became insensitive when left idle for too long a period ; and in this latter case the inertness was removed by the stimulus of an electric shock. In this paper, however, Bose for the first time in science compares and parallelises the responses to the excitation of living tissues with those of inorganic matter.

A muscle-curve registers the history of the molecular change produced by excitation in a living tissue, exactly as the curve of molecular reaction registers an analogous change in an inorganic substance. The two represent the same thing ; in the latter the molecular deformation is evidenced by the change of conductivity ; in the other the same deformation is manifested by the change of form. We have thus means of study of the molecular reaction produced by stimulus, of varying frequency, intensity and duration. An abyss separates the phenomena of living matter from those of inanimate matter. But if we are ever to understand the hidden mechanism of

[1] 'De la Généralité des Phénomènes Moléculaires produits par l'Électricité sur la Matière Inorganique et sur la Matière Vivante,' Congrès International de Physique, 1900.

the animal machine it is necessary to face numerous difficulties which at present seem formidable.

Then follows 'a comparative study of the curve of molecular reaction of inorganic and living substances.' First a curve from magnetic oxide of iron (Fe_3O_4), slightly warmed, and then following it, one of the usual muscle curves, showing a striking general resemblance to the former.

This leads to further study of the behaviour of the iron oxide in comparison with that of muscle : (1) of the effect of a superposition of maximum excitations ; (2) that of summation of moderate excitations slowly succeeding each other ; and (3) that of rapidly succeeding stimuli. Alike for mineral and muscle, these effects are extraordinarily similar, and their curves correspond—so closely in fact that either may be taken for the other. And in detail : (1) when the first excitation is at maximum, no effect is in either case observable from a second stimulus ; (2) moderate excitations are summated ; and when in slow succession, the effect of each shock can be distinguished as steps in the ascending curve ; (3) when the stimuli are very rapid, the effects are combined, and the phenomenon known as tetanus appears in both alike.

He also found that in many inorganic substances, when ordinary stimulus produces the normal 'negative' effect, a feeble stimulus elicits the very opposite, i.e. positive. He was long puzzled by the dual result, not simply as being new to physics, but as yet without parallel in the observed response of living tissues. But, he asked himself, is this a real contrast between non-living and living ?—or may not farther experiment disclose an analogous dual reaction in living things ? The inquiry led him to the discovery of certain living reactions of high significance. These will be treated later in greater detail.

Iron oxide, when warmed, gives an enhanced response under stimulus ; and recovery is also much quickened ; but only up to a certain level, when both are again diminished. The same phenomenon is already well known for muscle, which of course similarly has its optimum, beyond which the response is diminished. Again, just as the fatigue of muscle is removed by rest, or by the gentle mechanical vibration of massage, or by variation of temperature, as by a warm bath, so is it essentially with the iron oxide. For this 'fatigue,' i.e. the diminution of response, can be removed by treatments exactly parallel.

Next as to the effect of the injection of foreign substances. Potassium, as we have seen, has great electric elasticity, and recovers from stimuli almost at once. But when it is treated with certain foreign substances, its first response appears unaltered, but in subsequent responses the power of recovery is almost lost. Similarly with the effect of certain poisons (e.g. veratine) upon muscle.

In all the phenomena above described continuity is not broken. It is difficult to draw a line and say, 'here the physical phenomenon ends and the physiological begins,' or 'that is a phenomenon of dead matter, and this is a vital phenomenon peculiar to the living.' These lines of demarcation would be quite arbitrary.

We may explain each of the above categories of phenomena by making a great number of independent hypotheses, or else discovering a constant property of matter common to all its forms, living and organised, dead and inorganic; we may attempt on the basis of this common property, an explanation of the different phenomena, which at first seem so very different. And in favour of this latter view we may invoke the general tendency of science to seek, wherever facts permit, a fundamental unity amidst the apparent diversity.

Bose's paper came as a great surprise; and the Secretary of the Congress declared that he 'at first felt stunned.' The meeting soon realised the full importance of the subject, and many of its members expressed themselves enthusiastically over the new results. The paper was regarded as one of the most important received by the Congress, and it was published in its volume.

So much for the reception of these ideas among Western men of science. Far deeper was the effect produced on the thoughtful among his own countrymen. Europe was still unconscious of a renaissance in India—the uprising of an intellectual activity which was gathering strength; but Indians rejoiced to find in Bose an exponent of the new in science, whom the West could understand and appreciate. Independent expressions of the feeling came; Swami Vivekananda, who had impressed America by his eloquent enunciation of the philosophical and religious spirit of Vedanta, was then in Paris, and went to hear Bose at the Congress. In one of his letters (collected later as 'The Wanderer') he writes:

> Here in Paris have assembled the great of every land, each to proclaim the glory of his country. Savants will be acclaimed here; and its reverberation will glorify their countries. Among these peerless men gathered from all parts of the world, where is thy representative, O thou the country of my birth? Out of this vast assembly a young man stood for thee, one of thy heroic sons, whose words have electrified the audience, and will thrill all his countrymen. Blessed be this heroic son; and blessed be his devoted and peerless helpmate who stands by him always.

In the field of literature Bose's lifelong friend, Rabindranath Tagore, not yet known in the West, but who had already given a deep impress to Bengali literature, sent him as his letter from India, a poem, of which the following extract is a close translation:

> Whence hast thou that peace
> In which thou in an instant stoodst
> Alone at the deep centre of all things;
> Where dwells the One alone in Sun, Moon, flowers,
> In leaves, and beasts and birds, and dust and stones;
> Where still one sleepless Life, on its own lap
> Rocks all things with a wordless melody,
> All things that move or that seem motionless.

Call thou thy scholar-band come forth
Out on the face of nature, this broad earth.
Let them all gather. So may our India,
Our ancient land, unto herself return;
O once again return to steadfast work,
To duty and devotion, to her trance
Of earnest meditation.

So far, then, goes the story of this Paris paper, told at greater length than usual, alike on personal grounds and because of its importance as including new departures. An essentially similar paper was next read before the Physical Section of the British Association at its Bradford meeting in September in 1900, and was cordially received by the physicists. At this meeting also several of the most prominent of them suggested to Bose to offer himself as candidate for an important chair of physics then vacant, and with warm assurance of their support; but Bose was too loyal to his own country and University seriously to feel the temptation, though he naturally appreciated the compliment. A faint shadow was however felt by Bose at this meeting; for he noticed that while the physicists were warm in their appreciation of his work, and readily took up his interpretations, the members of the Physiological Section, who had been invited to hear the paper—as is the custom when 'boundary questions' are raised—looked perplexed and kept silent; the method of experimentation, by this time familiar to the physicists from Bose's previous papers, being strange and unfamiliar to them. It may here be mentioned that this method of 'conductivity-variation' has since been used with great success in Bose's subsequent physiological work, and has now found acceptance among vegetable physiologists; presumably by this time among animal ones as well.

Before leaving India, Bose had begun to suffer from an illness which subsequently became serious, brought on by too continuous fatigue and constant standing at experiments. After being unsuccessfully treated in

Calcutta, it was neglected by the sufferer until he broke down in London after the Bradford meeting, with the result that two months were lost between operation and recovery. But in this enforced idleness some further thinking was done, with devising of experiment in ways more familiar to physiologists. On recovery, he got to work by December 1900, at the Davy-Faraday Laboratory of the Royal Institution, to which he had been cordially invited by his old friends and teachers, Lord Rayleigh and Sir James Dewar. An assistant was found, Mr. Bull—to whose punctual, intelligent, and skilful carrying out of experimental work Bose still looks back with peculiar satisfaction. For thus so admirably seconded, the lost time was rapidly made up, and new experiments were quickly carried out in many new directions. On leaving London, Bose was able to interest his friends in finding continued outlet for Mr. Bull's abilities. He has since become head of the Photographic Department of the London Polytechnic, where Indian students find from him a ready welcome.

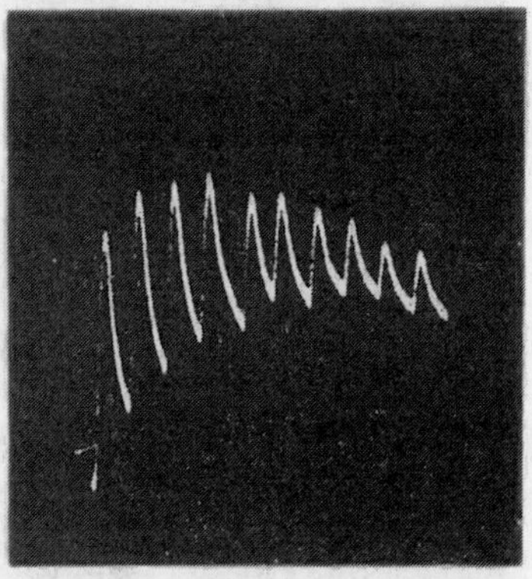

FIG. 3.—Electric response of metal showing fatigue (tin).

This winter's work became more and more physiological; yet, looking at his problems from both sides, he was now occupied not only with the physics of Physiology, but with what we may call the physiology of Physics. The comparison of the responses of the living and non-living, outlined in the above Paris paper, was now attacked afresh, by the electro-motive variation method, to which physiologists were accustomed; and the curves given by metals and muscles were worked out afresh, and with a fuller experimentation, including the effects of fatigue and of stimulating, depressing and poisoning drugs. The non-living and living alike gave responses which were essentially similar.

Revolving these results in his mind, it occurred to Bose in his constant alternation of self-criticism and cosmic outlook, that if the striking continuity between such extremes as metal and animal be real, then a test should be afforded by ordinary plants, hitherto reckoned as unresponsive. Full of this idea, Bose rushed out into the garden plot of his London lodging and gathered the first leaves of its horse-chestnut tree just opening; and on testing one of them, he found it respond vigorously. He next hastened off to the greengrocer, and found his carrots and turnips—despite the stolid and prosaic aspect by which we have too long misjudged them—turning out to be highly sensitive, even in their very roots. Some sea-kale, however, gave little or no response. On inquiry the greengrocer explained that it had suffered on the journey to London from a fall of snow; and fresh specimens on a later day gave full response.

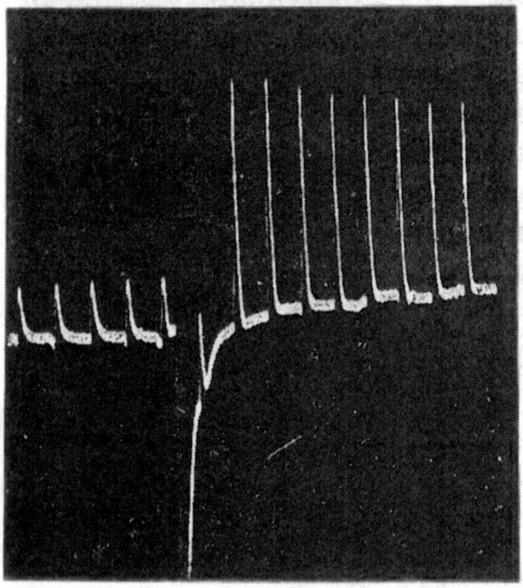

FIG. 4.—Action of stimulant in enhancing response of metal (platinum). In this and in following records the first series exhibit the normal response; the subsequent series show the effect of chemical agent.

The normal similarity in the response of metal, plant, and animal was thus established, by many tracings of their curves; and the next experiments were on the effects of narcotics and poisons. On application of chloroform, plant response disappeared, just as it does for the animal; and with timely blowing off of the narcotic vapour by fresh air, the plant too revived, and recovered to respond anew. Poison was applied to a fresh specimen, and as it absorbed the poison it exhibited a modification of the curve of response extraordinarily similar to that of the dying muscle; and for the plant as for the animal, response came to an end altogether—an apparently clear indication of death. Various drugs, poisonous in quantity, were found to act as stimulants when given in minute doses.

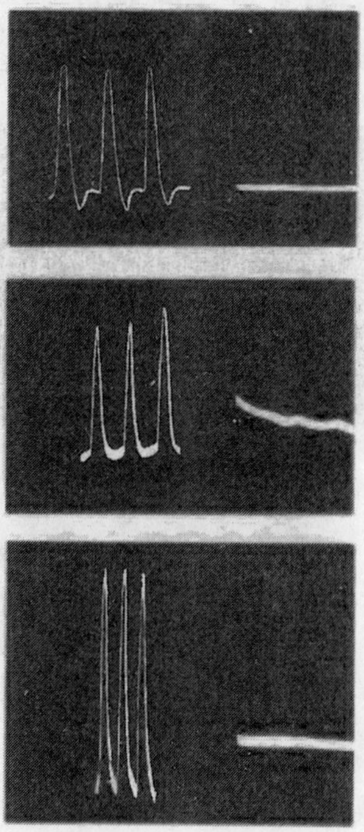

FIG. 5.—Action of poison in abolishing response of muscle (uppermost record), plant (middle record), and metal (lowest record).

Now here comes in the value of a fresh mind, untrammelled by the customary prepossessions of the biologist. Neither botanist, zoologist, nor physiologist had ever thought—or from his outlook would be likely to think—of attempting to poison a metal: he would have considered the very idea of such an experiment absurd. But here the physicist, unburdened by biological tradition, and ruthless in his logic from previous experiences of unexpected correspondence, made all these experiments, and on a whole series of metals. Tin, zinc, brass, and even platinum, were alike dosed in succession with various poisons; with the startling results of curves of response similar to those of the poisoned plants and animals, and like them coming to an end. Oxalic acid was found specially effective, to which tin, the most sensitive of metals, immediately gave way: even platinum, chemically the most inert of the noble metals, soon succumbed. Recalling Darwin's observation of the stimulating action of ammonium carbonate on the sundew, Bose tried this on his metals, and with the surprising result of its augmenting their normal response, even three- or fourfold. Again, toxic

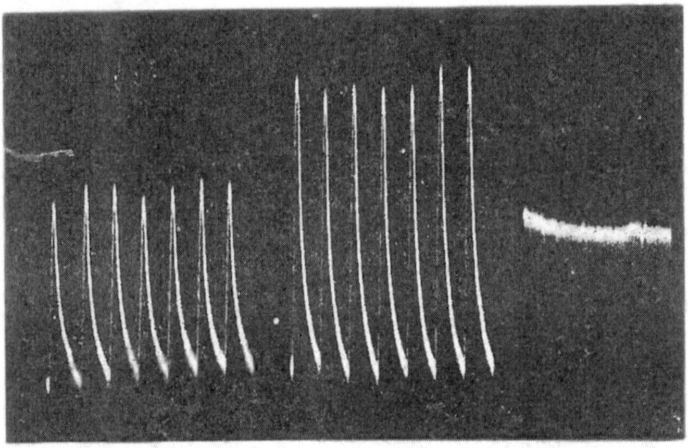

FIG. 6.—Stimulating action of minute quantity of 'poison' which in large doses abolishes the response of metal.

agents, which in large doses poison the plant, but in minute doses stimulate it, were found to have precisely similar effects upon the metals; and similarly with certain other drugs.

So striking was this correspondence, that one day when Bose was beginning to show his records to Sir Michael Foster, the veteran physiologist of Cambridge, the latter picked up one and said, 'Come now, Bose, what is the novelty in this curve? We have known it for at least the last half-century.' 'What do you think it is?' said Bose. 'Why, a curve of muscle response, of course.' 'Pardon me; it is the response of metallic tin.' 'What!' said Foster, jumping up—'Tin! Did you say tin?' On explanation, his wonder knew no bounds; and he hurried Bose to make a communication to the Royal Society, which he (then Secretary) offered to communicate. Finding that Bose was already invited to give an account of these discoveries as a Friday Evening Discourse at the Royal Institution, he said, 'Well, make us a preliminary communication immediately, and thus secure your priority, and that of the Society, and then you can give us a demonstration later on at the meeting next month.' This was done.

In this Royal Institution discourse (May 10, 1901) Bose marshalled the results he had been obtaining for the last four years and demonstrated each of these by a comprehensive series of experiments. But as these are outlined above, it is enough to quote the peroration:

I have shown you this evening autographic records of the history of stress and strain in the living and non-living. How similar are the writings! So similar indeed that you cannot tell one apart from the other. We have watched the responsive pulse wax and wane in the one as in the other. We have seen response sinking under fatigue, becoming exalted under stimulants, and being killed by poisons, in the non-living as in the living.

Amongst such phenomena, how can we draw a line of demarcation, and say, here the physical ends, and there the physiological begins? Such absolute barriers do not exist.

Do not these records tell us of some property of matter common and persistent? Do they not show us that the responsive processes, seen in life, have been fore-shadowed in non-life?—that the physiological is related to the physico-chemical?—that there is no abrupt break, but a uniform and continuous march of law?

If it be so, we shall but turn with renewed courage to the investigation of mysteries, which have too long eluded us. For every step of science has been made by the inclusion of what seemed contradictory or capricious in a new and harmonious simplicity. Her advances have been always towards a clearer perception of underlying unity in apparent diversity.

It was when I came upon the mute witness of these self-made records, and perceived in them one phase of a pervading unity that bears within it all things—the mote that quivers in ripples of light, the teeming life upon our earth, and the radiant suns that shine above us—it was then that I understood for the first time a little of that message proclaimed by my ancestors on the banks of the Ganges thirty centuries ago—

'They who see but one, in all the changing manifoldness of this universe, unto them belongs Eternal Truth—unto none else, unto none else!'

The Royal Institution lecture was highly appreciated; and its totally unexpected revelations naturally created wide interest throughout scientific circles, and even in the press generally. So far Bose's earlier success, both scientific and popular, which had been earned by his previous work and on his visit four years before, had been fully repeated, and even surpassed. But now his troubles began.

Here may be recalled an old and proverbial summary of the progress of ideas—scientific and other—that people first say: 'It is not true'; and next: 'It is not new'; and then often later: 'We knew it all before.' The last is indeed the commonest of these sayings in India; but in Europe we generally begin with the other two.

After his preliminary communication Bose read his paper at the Royal Society on June 6, 1901, with full and detailed experimental demonstration. The paper seemed as well received as usual, but the blow was now to come; and this from no less than Sir John Burdon Sanderson, who was then, and for many years had been, 'the grand old man' of physiological science in England. His work, moreover, had largely lain not only in the study of the behaviour of muscle and nerve under stimulation, but very specially upon the movements of the Venus' fly-trap (Dionæa), to which Darwin had first called his attention, and to the electrical physiology of which he had devoted unsparing labours during many years. He thus stood out as a peculiar authority on the electro-physiology both of animals and plants so far as was then known; and his interest was still so keen that he had come up from Oxford for this paper. He was naturally the person to whom all looked to open the usual discussion after the paper. He began with a compliment on Bose's previous physical work; but then said it was a great pity that he should leave his own sphere of study, in which he had attained such acknowledged distinction, for other fields which properly belonged to the physiologists. Professor Bose's paper was still under consideration for publication; but he might give him the advice that the title should be changed from 'The Electric Response' to 'Certain Physical Reactions,' so leaving to physiologists the use of their term 'Response,' with which physicists are not concerned; and further, as to the electric response of ordinary plants described at the end of the paper, he would say that it was absolutely impossible, since he had tried to detect it for many years past, and never could obtain any. It simply could not be!

Another well-known professor of physiology, also an investigator of the reactions of muscle and nerve, followed Sanderson, and substantially supported him. Two physicists each asked one or two questions, and expressed themselves satisfied with all the experiments just demonstrated. Bose was then called on to reply. He understood that the facts experimentally demonstrated were not questioned by either of his critics. Instead of these being in any way impugned on their experimental evidence, he was asked on mere authority to make modifications, which altered the purpose and meaning of the paper, and to withdraw experimental facts among those which he had just been demonstrating. It seemed to him inexplicable that the doctrine could be advocated—and in the Royal Society of all places—that knowledge should advance so far and no further; so he could on no account alter a word of the paper, even at the risk of a refusal of publication, unless he were shown, on scientific grounds, wherein the experiments he had just shown were faulty or defective.

He expected experimental criticism, and was prepared for it, but not one word of that had been brought forward by either of his physiological critics.

After this no one spoke, and the meeting separated, with formal thanks to the author of the paper; but further trouble was in store. Sanderson from this time felt deeply offended; for his was an intricate and Gladstonian mind, one of authority and influence, accustomed to be unquestioned. He was given, alike in science and in life, to balancing different view-points and interests, and evolving compromises accordingly; and that a young and direct mind would challenge such a courteously-worded compromise, and in such outspoken fashion, must have utterly surprised and wounded him. Moreover, this direct contradiction of his negative results from plants, by Bose's positive ones, could not but be felt very keenly. Yet Bose on his part could not be expected to accept the situation. His physical papers had been judged on their scientific merits, and his papers had hitherto found ready acceptance, his reputation for accurate work being well known. But here was an opposition based on no scientific grounds. He felt that as a physicist he was regarded as an intruder in the domain of physiology. As an unsophisticated man from the East, he had seriously taken the lessons preached by the West about the evils of the caste system; but here he felt he had come against a yet worse system of caste whose etiquette he had unwittingly offended. Lord Rayleigh told him later that he himself had been subjected to ceaseless attacks from the chemists, because he, a physicist, had ventured to predict that the air would be found to contain a new element hitherto unsuspected; yet, in spite of the protests of the chemists, his prediction, as is well known, was verified by the discovery of Argon.

The paper, of which, according to custom, the proof had been circulated among the members before the meeting, was thus not published in the Royal Society's 'Proceedings,' but placed in the Society's 'Archives'—a fate which has befallen other notable papers before: e.g. that anticipation of the kinetic theory of gases which was unearthed and published by Lord Rayleigh a few years ago—decades after its writer's death. Here it may be explained that the practice of the Royal Society with regard to the papers it publishes in its 'Proceedings' and 'Transactions' differs notably from that of the French Academy of Sciences, with its 'Comptes Rendus.' In the latter every paper read is printed, and issued forthwith on its writer's responsibility alone, without thereby suggesting the formal acceptance of the Academy, or even the approval of any of its members, beyond the one who has thought enough of it to present it to the meeting. The Royal Society, on the other hand, has its Publication Committees, so that the issue of any paper indicates that it has passed the scrutiny of one of these, and with at least a preponderance of acceptance. There is something to be said for each method: that of the French is democratic, since strictly in the worker's interest, of getting his idea known, without any delay; that of the English is in the corporate interest, and so far necessarily hierarchic. Bad papers can thus more easily appear in the 'Comptes Rendus' than in the 'Proceedings.' For the latter, novel ones may sometimes be rejected or, as in this instance, shelved. This editorial process in any case is apt to be slow; for while papers read in Paris appear regularly, at least in abstract, the week following, those at London may take months, sometimes even a year or two, especially when publication in the more dignified quarto form of the 'Philosophical Transactions' is concerned. Papers by workers whose habitual soundness and accuracy have become known to the relevant committee, of course get printed with little or no delay, and this had been the case with all Bose's physical papers. For the present one there was also no delay; he had indeed settled its fate himself, and the paper was relegated to the Archives.

Here now was the sharpest of interruptions to a career hitherto so successful; and the contrast was a deeply painful one—indeed as yet the severest shock of Bose's life. The blow was not simply for himself, as for any ordinary man of science in Britain; but, as he clearly saw it, full of threatening omen for his future scientific career in India, imperilling his as yet limited facilities for new work, and his newly risen hopes of scientific support towards their increase. The news in fact at once went out to India, and in crude and exaggerated form—'Bose's work and paper are rejected by the Royal Society'—and thus of course with suspicion thrown upon his previous work as well.

In a fortnight, too, his time in England would be up: his passage was already taken. But he saw that he must fight the matter out and justify himself; so, without delay, he explained the situation and applied to the India Office for an extension of his period of deputation. He was told that this was without precedent, and could not be granted. A year's ordinary leave was due to him, as he had done the necessary service; but it was next pointed out that this could only be arranged for in India, through his own College, as a matter with which the India Office does not interfere. However, it would take advice. Unluckily for Bose, the physiologist to whose advice they referred the matter was one belonging to the hostile group; and the request was naturally declined. But nothing daunted, and determined to burn his boats if necessary, he wrote again, repeating the urgent and overpowering necessity he felt of justifying his result, and saying that he had resolved to remain in England to fight the matter out, and was prepared to take the consequences. The Secretary of State now personally looked into the matter, and—as Bose through life had already, and has since so often, found—his decision was made in the best English way. He was so favourably impressed by this uncompromising courage that he took the responsibility of granting an extension of deputation, and intimated the fact to Bose's College.

Heartened by this, he went to work anew at the Royal Institution Laboratory. He at first feared a cold reception, but was consoled by a brother physicist: 'You can't poach on other people's preserves without some resentment; and you've done worse—you've upset their apple-cart.' He settled down to work for the vacation at his London home, and then returned to the Royal Institution when it reopened in October. Work abated depression, but did not remove it. About this time he was cheered by a letter from Professor Vines, the well-known botanist and vegetable physiologist of Oxford, who expressed interest, asked to see his experiments, and came accordingly to the Royal Institution Laboratory, bringing with him Horace Brown, another effective investigator of the process of plant-life, and Howes, who was Huxley's successor at South Kensington.

With the first application of stimulus to the plant, a wide swing of the galvanometer-mirror's light-beam along the scale demonstrated its sensitiveness. Never before had Bose seen three sober Englishmen so joyously excited: 'they were just as mad as boys.' Said Howes: 'Huxley would have given years of his life to see that experiment.' Said another: 'What did you do to let off steam when you discovered this? You should shout, or you will kill yourself by repressing it.' Then in business mood: 'The Royal Society has not published your paper, so you can give it to the Linnean. We are its President and Secretary this year, so we invite you to read us a full paper. Show us your experiments; and we will invite all the physiologists, and particularly your opponents.'

We have seen how the account of Bose's discovery of Electric Response of Metals and of Ordinary Plants was relegated to the Archives of the Royal Society; his paper before the Linnean Society, where his opponents were specially invited to attend, remained thus the only opportunity to meet all hostile criticism. On the eve of this paper he writes to a friend in India: 'If I ever give up this new line of inquiry it shall be through no compulsion, but through choice. I do not yet see my way clearly, but I shall take it up time after time, if only to show that one man's strength and resoluteness of purpose can face any combination. It is not for me to sit with folded hands in resignation. I do not believe in miracles: but the miracle shall happen this time; for I know that I am fighting for the establishment of truth.'

On the day after his paper (February 21, 1902) he writes again: 'Victory! I stood there alone, ready for hosts of opponents, but in fifteen minutes the hall was resounding with applause. After the paper, Prof. Howes told me that as he saw each experiment, he tried to get out of it by thinking of a loophole of explanation: but my next experiment closed that hole.' All had gone well; the speakers afterwards were glowing in their congratulations, in fact almost to ovation. The President wrote to him:

> It seems to me that your experiments make it clear beyond doubt that all parts of plants—not merely those which are known to be motile—are irritable, and manifest their irritability by an electrical response to stimulation. This is an important step in advance, and will, I hope, be the starting point for further researches to elucidate what is the nature of the molecular condition which constitutes irritability, and the nature of the molecular change induced by a stimulus. This would doubtless lead to some important generalisation as to the properties of matter; not only living matter, but non-living matter as well.

The disaster of the previous year thus seemed completely retrieved; and the paper, with full illustrations of apparatus, went for publication. But now came a new surprise—not less sudden than had been the previous one, and even more painful. For any active scientific mind, confident of its new results, may brace itself up to maintain them, like the theologian of old, against the world. To be told that one's results are not credible, and then to prove them, is thus a triumph for scientific discovery; and Bose accomplished this, within less than a year—an exceptionally speedy success, as too often the sad history of science goes. But now the new blow fell—alleged evidence that these results were not new—that they were known before!—already discovered by some one else! Results substantially similar to those obtained by Bose had been communicated to a London scientific society in November 1901 by the physiologist who had seen Bose's experiments before the Royal Society (June 1901) and had also taken part in the subsequent discussion. Bose learned of the new turn of affairs from a letter from Professor Howes, as the Secretary of the Linnean Society. A new period of depression followed, far deeper than the preceding one, but he rallied himself to reply, formally asking for an inquiry into the matter. This was at once granted. Vines and Howes, both also Fellows of the Royal Society, had fortunately seen proofs of Bose's paper there ten months before that at the Linnean, and five months before the other claimant's communication. Bose's lecture at the Royal Institution, a few days earlier than the Royal Society function, was also in print and in evidence. With all the facts before them, the committee of inquiry had no hesitation. Bose's right to absolute priority was completely established, and the paper was published accordingly.

After Professor Howes, as Secretary of the Linnean Society, had fully inquired into the claim to priority which had threatened to prevent the publication of Bose's paper, he wrote to him unofficially: 'I am fully sympathetic and the facts you cite but confirm my original conviction. You have been mercilessly done by. But my advice to you would be that you should head your paper with a plain statement of facts, and beyond this you should leave fools alone.'

Bose, however, now that he was vindicated, being satisfied with the result, mindful of the chivalrous traditions of his boyhood's tales, not to pursue a defeated antagonist, and desiring the matter to pass, attenuated this statement to the utmost brevity and politeness. But this only renewed Howes's wrath, and turned it fully on Bose: 'I have no patience with you: Eastern courtesy is misplaced here! You are trying to save his face. Mark my words!—People will forget this, and he will soon be your enemy again.'

The prediction indeed proved only too true, as Bose has repeatedly found to his cost; isolated in distant India he could not directly meet the vague insinuations that were industriously spread by his antagonist about the accuracy of his work, thereby prejudicing him in the estimation of English physiologists. This sort of tactics was successful only in so far as it added difficulties to his work for the next nineteen years, but it failed ultimately, especially after Bose's two visits to Europe in 1914 and in the present year, when he had full opportunity of giving public and private demonstrations of his remarkable results. The physiologists who had previously been antagonised by deliberate misrepresentations now fully recognised the value of his discoveries and his new methods of experimentation. Bose has now no stauncher friends than the general body of physiologists who had been at first led to regard him as an intruder.

After the two painful experiences related above, Bose was no longer satisfied with the traditional method of writing papers for scientific societies, with their delays and risks of publication. 'I should have been too lazy to write books, but this forced me.' Hence a new period of concentrated energy began, and some hundreds of experiments were carried out in the next few months. The mass of these are included in his volume 'Response in the Living and Non-Living,'[1] which thus not only embodies the result of all his previous London lectures and papers, but notably extends them in various directions. Of these advances some indications are given in a fresh paper to the Royal Society

[1] Longmans, Green & Co., London, 1902.

in May, 1902.[1] This one was printed promptly, and without any criticism or objection, although the writer made it the occasion of re-stating the very matters previously objected to. For though the paper is essentially physical, and in the physicist's form of technical expression, his curves of response of metals are more convincing than ever; and no summary of what was coming to be his main thesis could be more unmistakable than what appeared in the paper now accepted by the Royal Society. 'The various phenomena connected with the response in inorganic substances—the negative variation—the relation between stimulus and response—the increased response after continuous stimulation—the abnormal response converted into normal after long-continued stimulation—the diphasic variation—the increase of response by stimulants, decrease by depressors and abolition by "poisons" so-called—all these are curiously like the various response-phenomena in living tissues. A complete account of the mutual relation between the two classes of phenomena will be found in a work to be shortly published, "On the Response in the Living and Non-Living."'

Here, then, was at any rate a reversal of that decision which had consigned his results to the Archives of the Society.

Herbert Spencer too, who was alive to scientific advances, acknowledged 'Response in the Living and Non-Living' in cordial terms and with regrets that it was too late to avail himself of the new results in his 'Principles of Biology.'

Enough, however, for the present of scientific researches and their controversies. For reader, as for writer, it may be a welcome change to turn to another side of experience and character, as developed in widely different environments from those of laboratory science.

[1] 'On Electromotive Wave accompanying Mechanical Disturbance in Metals,' *Proc. Roy. Soc.*, 1902.

CHAPTER VIII

HOLIDAYS AND PILGRIMAGES

It is one of the many conventional beliefs of the industrial age, with its railways, steamers and telegraphs of yesterday, its aeroplane routes for to-morrow, that abundant and extended travel, still more world-commerce, are essentially modern affairs, and that our forefathers, in any and every land, were practically all quiet stay-at-home people, knowing little beyond their self-sustaining village or their country town. But, as we look into the past, this too simple idea becomes shaken. Even in the early stone age we find flints unmistakably brought from afar; and in this or that museum of Western Europe one may see a well-wrought neolithic jade, dug up in its own neighbourhood, which cannot have had a nearer origin than the Kuen Lun mountains in Central Asia. So the shell ornaments, frequently found in early inland burials, have been brought from shores often far distant. Later, again, the amber of the East Prussian shores is found in the excavations of Babylon. That ships of Solomon brought gold from its old workings in South Africa is a familiar suggestion, and likely enough; and so on over the world. And though to our modern age of commerce and war, it has been the ancient weapon and the buried treasure which have most attracted attention, the religious past has also been steadily advancing its claims to what we now call internationalism. Of the wide and rapid extension of Buddhism throughout India and far beyond, and with return pilgrimages accordingly, we have the clearest evidence, from Hiuen Tsaing and earlier, to this day. Again, even this great religion was but one of a whole series of spiritual movements broadly contemporaneous and surely interesting: witness the Zoroastrians in Persia, 'the discovery of the Law' in Jerusalem, the Pythagoreans of Greece and beyond, and so on, from the early founders of Rome to the Druids of the Celtlands from Gaul to the Hebrides.

To understand Modern India we need better guidance than any of our modern writers, so often too strident, even to harshness, when not more or less narrowly specialised. For this we should need some truly European-spirited historian like Comte, or like Lord Acton; and when he comes—since we must first realise ourselves before understanding others—he will set before us those prehistoric and semi-historic traditions above touched on. He would next revive the unity of Roman days, from Clyde to Euphrates, and its interaction, not always hostile, with the northern barbarian world as well. He will not only renew for us Arthur, Alfred, Charlemagne, and more, as heroes of Europe, but behind all such champions of Christendom, show us Christendom itself, at its gentlest and best. He will make us feel anew the significance of the wanderings of St. Paul as a source of enduring impulse to the missions of Rome, of Ireland, of Iona and Holy Isle; as of Austin, Benedict, and others, throughout European lands; and of later teachers farther still. He will trace the effect of such universally diffused re-idealising of life in these medieval lay pilgrimages of all our peoples, with their faces set henceforward not only towards Rome or Santa Sophia, but to Jerusalem itself, of which even the Crusades were but the exasperated intensification. Within each land too, and even between them all, he will trace the pilgrims. Chaucer's genial company, riding towards Canterbury, is but a swan-song of this old spirit. To realise it more fully we must join all the great pilgrimages, as to Compostella, to Chartres, to Cologne and farther, for the West; and similarly with East Europeans to Holy

Novgorod and Kieff, to Mount Athos, and again to Jerusalem. And even in our Western cities, though the modern noises of machinery and cannon may have deafened us to the varying and ever-returning cadences of this pilgrims' chorus, we may feel its old spirit. Even in Ulster itself, that world-central survival of fanatic bitterness, we may still stand near St. Patrick's tomb and see the peasant, before he takes ship for America, scraping from above it a few grains of its soil into an old envelope to carry in his bosom till he dies, so that in that far-away alien land he may lie amid dust thus hallowed for his folk and faith. And if we have human feeling enough to respect a scene like this, however strange to our modern ways, why not also, on our way to India, respect the Haj, which unifies another great faith, after all a kindred one, albeit unitarian and abstaining? Without some such sympathy how shall we understand our own most modern as well as most ancient fellow-citizens, the Jews, who beat us at our own games of business and politics, because they bear so deep in their hearts the memories and aspirations of their Holy City, and are even now carrying these into its renewal?

It is with such preparation then—and not simply with the help of Baedeker and Murray, though brightened by all the picturesquely-coloured reporting of Kipling, of Steevens, and the rest, or dulled by the school and college examination-routine of our administrators, our professional and business men, or by the conventionalities of politically-minded writers of whatever school or race—that we may best approach and understand the greater aspects of India. For it is as a spiritual unity, underlying all the innumerable but more superficial differences, that India has primarily to be realised.

We thus come to the Boses and their Indian travels. The physical sciences are based on observation; the natural sciences yet more so; but the social sciences need it most of all. In and through travel the social interests of men are peculiarly educated; so that, though the traditionally religious motive of pilgrimage has faded in Europe and is fading in India, there is still no fear but that it will return upon our modern spiral. Neither Cook's tourists nor American ones may strike us as models of reverence; but none the less it is their element of reverence which has sent the bulk of them—so far therefore on true pilgrimage—to the historic places of their world. Much more is this reverence persistent in India. So for both East and West; as real and living education vitalises or replaces the traditional official and commercial sorts, the socio-religious education of travel will grow up into a very real revival of the pilgrimages of old, however largely we may as yet prefer to describe it in more secular-looking terms, as of the wander-years of higher education.

Now though here perhaps more consciously and definitely stated, yet none the less in essential spirit, we have been preparing to appreciate that side of Bose's life and larger education which may at first sight seem apart from his scientific studies, yet which none the less has nerved him for his best work, and above all for his Indian ambitions beyond his personal interests and achievements. Immediately after marriage he began, with his young wife, to devote the two annual vacations to seeing and knowing India and to realising what India has stood for; and their experiences, especially if illustrated by a selection of the multitude of photographs which were thus made, might in themselves assuredly have made one of the best of individual records of Indian travel. But alas! a few years ago a new and well-meaning servant, instructed to dust the collection of negatives, had thoroughly cleaned off every plate before his well-meant exertions were discovered; while the pressure of scientific work through college term-times has kept the journal from being written. Yet vivid recollections survive, and the educative experience has been gained; so that this Western-educated modern physicist also peculiarly and widely knows his country; knows it as an Indian of Indians.

Beginning broadly in historic order, with old centres and shrines before later ones, one of the young couple's first journeys was to the Sanchi Tope built by Asoka's queen over a relic of Buddha ; and with the life of the time carved upon its gigantic gateways. It was from Sanchi that Asoka's son and daughter went on the mission which established Buddhism in Ceylon to this day. Our present pilgrim-pair, having some adventure with dacoits by the way, went next to Mandhata with its huge old megalithic-based and iron-clamped gates of the temple, built at the junction of two sacred rivers—which so readily and fitly becomes a sacred spot in India—of the thrice sacred Nerbudda with the Tapti. They visited the adjacent temple ruins, whose legends link them with the heroes of the 'Mahabharata'—Bhima, Arjuna, and others. Another inspiring visit was to the noble old hill-city of Chitor, once and again the heroic centre of Rajput chivalry and woman's sacrifice—tales of defeat surpassing those of its famous Towers of Victory. Ajmere too, with its pilgrimage-centre of Pushkar on the lake, was duly visited. Next came the striking contrast of modern Jaipur, laid out with formal magnificence by its astronomer-prince, and of Amber, his ancestral hill-city—one to the Western eye recalling, perhaps surpassing, that of Edinburgh, new and old. Agra and Delhi were, of course, also included. Another year, for health reasons, Naini Tal was taken as centre, with a visit to Lucknow by the way. From Naini Tal Bose went alone to the Pindari Glacier. A hairbreadth escape for guide and self proved only stimulating ; so the next year, starting by way of Almora, he piloted his wife and several friends to the glacier again. Another year, starting from Rawal Pindi, then the railway terminus, they made their way up to Baramulla, hired a house-boat for Srinagar, and saw much of the landscape beauty, the gardens and monuments of Kashmir. In two later years Kashmir was revisited, the last time as guests of the Maharaja, and so with fuller acquaintance, and a standing invitation to return.

Another journey was through Orissa, with its famous temple of Bhubaneswar, its caves of Udaigiri and the great rock-inscription of Asoka, Puri with its Jagannath temple, the neighbouring ruins of Kanarak, the Chilka lake, and so on. The famous caves of Ajanta and Ellora were visited together; and then again on a later journey with Mrs. (now Lady) Herringham and her group of Indian and other artist-collaborators on their task of copying the Ajanta paintings —Sister Nivedita (Margaret Noble) being also of the party. At Bankipur the excavations of Pataliputra, and the famous Persian and Moghul library, were duly visited; and also the birthplace of Govinda Singh, one of that notable succession of saints and heroes who founded the Sikh religion. Another year the Sikh interest was followed up at its main centre—Amritsar, with the golden temple. One journey to Lahore was to lecture in the University; but again there were extended visits. Similarly the Bombay district was wandered through, largely for its cave-temples of Elephanta, Karli and Kenhari, and next the Mahratta country, with its associations of the struggles of the warlike Shivaji.

Again on their last return journey from Europe and America, in 1915, these ardent travel-comrades, landing at Colombo, travelled through Ceylon, visiting the ancient Buddhist temples, and thence came northwards through the great temple-cities of the south, from Rameswaram by Madura and Tanjore, to Trichinopoly and Srirangam—places of which the writer has lately written an interpretative eulogy, even venturing to correct the estimate of Ferguson.[1] At the last named Bose was not only shown all that ordinary Indian visitors may see, but invited to enter the inmost precincts—the Holy of Holies. He explained that he was not an orthodox Hindu, and no longer believed in caste, and had lost it in any case by his journeys to foreign countries across the sea; and so he had no right to enter the

[1] 'The Temple Cities,' *Modern Review*, March 1919.

sanctuary. 'No, no,' said the priest. 'Come in. You are a Sadhu.'[1]

Several visits too were made to the Kumaon district, one with a stay with the monks at Mayavati; and each time with visits to the villages—an element indeed running through all these journeys, and an interest no less real than that in the monuments and associations of the past. And in India, though definite historic record be too often lacking, in the present village and the past legends, the traditional spirit none the less survives; and the simplest-seeming villagers are thus often deeply imbued with Hindu culture and mythology. With all these journeys such interests could not but strengthen.

At Budh-Gaya—under whose pipal tree, still represented by its descendant, Buddha attained his illumination—a vacation was largely spent as guests of the Mahanta (the Abbot), whose conversations increased their insight into the spirit of Buddhism. Then too they saw the old city of Rajgir, where Buddha pleaded for the lives of the goats from its king, and which was the scene of the first assembly of his faith after his death.

Such interest in the ancient centres of Indian learning had an old and natural nucleus in youthful memories of Vikrampur and its traditions. Hence our pilgrims went at one time to Taxila, with its excavations now guided by Hiuen Tsaing's travel-journal of thirteen centuries ago; and at another time to the ruins of Nalanda, to which Hindus look back as a great University, which had in the days of Athens thousands of students, including some from other lands beyond India. But of all journeys the best remembered seems that which was most of the traditional pilgrimage character—to Badrinath and Kedarnath, the goal of the last journey of Judhisthira, one of the heroes who there sought his end. For this long journey the start begins with what is the terminus for

[1] A Sadhu is a man who has devoted himself to the contemplative and religious life, whether as hermit or wanderer.

most pilgrims—Hardwar, where the Ganges emerges from the mountains and enters on the plain. Three weeks' journey uphill from the railway was needed, with mules carrying all necessities of life, Bose riding or walking, Mrs. Bose sometimes walking, sometimes carried on light stretchers. On this journey, more fully than ever before, they felt themselves as in and of the pilgrim throng from all parts—from Ceylon and Comorin, Bengal and Orissa, in fact every part of India. Never had they seen such intensive influence of religion at once traditional and natural; for all the pilgrims were attuned and in accord, and greeting each other as friends without thought of caste. Every face was glowing with fervour as the great snows appeared; and the cry of 'Jai Kedarnath!' (Glory to the God of Snows!) passed from lip to lip. Men and women alike were transfigured in trances of prayer and its reward of ecstasy. A blind man groping his way up a narrow and dangerous path, a mere cliff edge, when told, 'Friend, take care!' answers, 'Why need I be afraid when He is leading me by the hand?'

No wonder then that Bose, after recalling these memories, should say, 'With all these experiences, India has made me and kept me as her son. I feel her life and unity deep below all.'

This essential unity of India, which lives most deeply in the spirit of religion and in the soul of woman, is also clear in old-world statesmanship; a vivid illustration of this was given as recently as the late eighteenth century by Queen Ahilyabai, the gentlest, but not the least effective, ruler of the notable and warlike dynasty of the Holkars. From her beautiful little capital of Maheswar on the Nerbudda—itself a place of pilgrimage, some forty miles or so south of the present State capital of Indore, and hence a representative spot for Central India—she sent the funds and chose the builders to erect four new temples at the extreme points of India—north, south, east and west; and thus encouraged further pilgrimage.

The notion is often expressed by English journalists, and even by officials who ought to know better, that Indian unity is a recent ideal of lawyers and politicians taken from Mazzini and absorbed by unrestful youth; and it is true enough that there are minds which thus too simply view it, through that education in European nationalism and liberalism which an orator can so logically adapt and so eloquently re-voice. But India's real unity is something incomparably older and deeper: it rests on sacred and epic literature and legend for the people, and on great and ancient philosophies, which are not merely cultivated by the classically educated, but deeply diffused, for good and evil, throughout the people as well. All this variety of cultural influences, in essential harmony and (to us strangely) free from intolerance, has from unnumbered ages been steeping into the Indian villages with their old economic self-sufficiency and moral solidarity: hence the apparent heterogeneity, of languages and castes, and of mingled and changing Hindu, Mohammedan and European rule, has mattered far less than we are wont to suppose.

India then, though not a nation in a European sense, is something not merely less, but more. It is rather the analogue of Europe: and though even vaster in population, and more varied in climates and peoples, has a more diffused and an often deeper community of spirit. Not simply then through any mere political changes can this unity be more adequately realised—though on the modern spiral some may think so—but also, and more deeply and surely, through her cultural spirit. That spirit not even the conquests of Islam have broken, nor yet the modern rule and other influences of the West. This it is which is stirring towards its renaissance,. as the religious groups of the past generation, or the political groups of the present, alike show: and this it is which will more fully revive its old values, and adjust them anew with those of the Western world. This indeed is what many of its pioneers, like Bose among others. have throughout their lives, and each in his own way, been doing, and yet more fully preparing for.

Instead then of always looking at India as a country with everything to learn from the West, and nothing to teach it, as the superior Western fashion has too long been, we are finding that we also have something to learn—though as yet we may think only from Indians in the first rank, like Bose, Tagore, and perhaps a few others. But we have to learn something from the Indian culture itself; and perhaps especially now—in the present situation of Europe, torn into embittered halves, and these again subdividing without end along every old division of languages and nationalities, intensified by the recent Germanic, Anglo-Saxon, and other mythologies of race. And with even all those divisions more or less splintering across and estranged anew by the spreading rift of labour towards revolution.

Suppose now we students, men of science, of letters, or of art, though hitherto so non-political, begin to consider how we may help forward something of that true peace and good will to which our best statesmanship indeed aspires, but can never by mere treaties realise, nor by political leagues obtain. Must we not again look to all that is best in each country's history and civilisation?—which should be found in its rural villages, its cities' past? How else, for instance, has that old and bitter feud and mutual hate, so long second to none in duration and intensity in Europe—that between Scots and English—come to an end? By growth of mutual knowledge and understanding, even more than by common advantage. How else abate the old bitterness, and the renewed alienation of Ireland?—how inspire a saner feeling in England where for so long it has been so far from that desirable? Without some respect and good will for France as for Belgium, would the English people have risen to support them as they have done, even despite their admitted and manifest material interest? And without that increasing sympathy with European culture which American travellers have been taking home these two generations, would their present virtual reincorporation with Western and Mediterranean Europe have been possible ?

The reunion of Europe, then, can most strongly, even if slowly, be made through the education of travel. Not merely in the recent tourist spirit, at least in the cruder forms ; but in that combining of the best of modern cultural travel with something of the old spirit of pilgrimage which that helps effectively to renew. The Brownings and Ruskin in Italy were examples of this union in their day : why not renew it more widely ? As Europeans grow more tolerant and more sympathetic, like the Indian travellers we have been following, our scheme of educational travel will grow and spread into fuller pilgrimages, which should be on the Indian scale —throughout Baltic and Mediterranean lands alike, from Scandinavia to Spain, and thence to Greece and beyond. Why not east and west, from Russia to Ireland, indeed to America as well ?—with ever increasing appreciation of all their regional and civic interests, the natural, the spiritual and the temporal together, and in aspects historic, actual and incipient. Does this seem 'Utopian' ? It is after all but what the tourist and the wandering nature-lover, the art-student, and the historian have long been doing, and what the regional agriculturist and town planner are now in their turn doing. To-day it lies with re-education, with reconstruction, and with re-religion as well, to organise all these contacts more fully. In view of the real and profound unity and all but universal tolerance, in spite of many imperfections and drawbacks, the recovery of some such measures of spiritual unity as her children feel cannot be unattainable in the West, the more since this once was a living force in the old days of Christendom—a force which, so far from having lost its old appeals, is indeed for ever reviving.

Not only is the cultural and spiritual value of a large

LADY BOSE.

PROFESSOR J. C. BOSE (1907).

experience of travel manifest in Bose's general outlook, at once ranging over India and the West; but it was also of more than frequent scientific suggestiveness. One cannot, of course, explain mental incidents like the unexpected flash of this or that new physical or biological insight, or fresh plan of investigation, amid some scene of natural beauty or venerable antiquity, beyond the emotional and mental stirring such scenes so readily give. But Bose's ardent temperament could not but feel Asoka's inscription of old as a vivid call and command to his own life: 'Go forth and intermingle; and bring them to the righteousness which passeth knowledge. Go forth among the terrible and powerful, both here and in foreign countries—in kindred ties even of brotherhood and sisterhood . . . everywhere.'

Nor is it to be wondered at that among the excavations of Taxila, and again among the ruins of Nalanda, he should feel that it was not only their old University spirit thrilling within him, but the common spirit of all Universities. These visitings peculiarly awoke and strengthened in him the perception that his life-work was to be more than one of personal purpose and scientific character—more even than the organisation of a physical laboratory, even of the best; and that what he must henceforth aim at, and think out, and work for should be nothing less than recreation of some yet fuller centre of intellectual quest and diffusion, like those of old. First of all for India: yet also, like those, with contacts and impulses to all the world beyond. In this old pride of India as she was, and hopes of her as she may be, on one hand, no less than in his peculiarly full and wide participation in Western science on the other, we see at once the two uniting forces which found expression in the foundation of the Bose Research Institute.

And with this better understanding of the man, upon his Indian side, and his ever-widening cultural sympathies and outlooks, we may return to his scientific work.

CHAPTER IX

PLANT RESPONSE

AT the outset of this intricate subject a brief and personal outline may be given. In his investigations on response in general Bose had found that even ordinary plants and their different organs were sensitive—exhibiting, under mechanical or other stimuli, an electric response, indicative of excitation. If this were so, it puzzled him greatly that so-called ordinary plants should not give any indication of excitation by visible movement. In the best known of sensitive plants, Mimosa, the leaves, on being irritated, strikingly respond by a sudden fall of the leaf, due to contraction of the lower half of the cushion-shaped and joint-like leaf-base, the 'pulvinus.' Bose noted that the contraction of the pulvinus was small; it was the long leaf-stalk which here acted as a magnifying index. He therefore thought that the contraction due to excitation may be present in ordinary plants, and may only have escaped the attention of other workers. To test this anticipation, he attached a similar magnifying device to ordinary plants, and was rewarded by finding that they too answered to stimulus by a distinct contraction. He therefore entered into a long series of investigations in which the mechanical response of the plant indicated its state of excitation.

For recording the responsive movement Bose employed his device of the 'Optical Lever,' by which the movement was greatly magnified. He was thus able to demonstrate that '*all the characteristics of the responses exhibited by the animal tissues, were also found in those of the plant.*' The results of these extended investigations, embodied in a series of seven papers, were communicated to the Royal Society in December 1903. They were regarded as of such importance that the Royal Society accepted them for publication in their 'Philosophical Transactions.' But the same hostile influence which had attempted the suppression of his Linnean Society paper was again in full activity. Bose was now away from England, and his opponents had their way. The Royal Society then informed Bose that their appreciation of the value of his work was shown by their willingness to accept his papers for the 'Transactions.' His results were, however, so unexpected and so opposed to current theories that nothing short of the plant's automatic record would carry conviction; his papers would therefore be placed, for the present, in the Archives of the Society.

This postponement, and virtual refusal, of publication —for the condition laid down seemed at that time an impossible one—was of course widely taken, and in India especially, as a strong, if vague, confirmation of the dubiousness of Bose's alleged discoveries. But happily Bose's response to this combination of environmental stimuli, by turns so depressing and so exasperating, was of the intensity and duration required for the large and sustained experimental productivity summarised in the two books which Bose wrote for publication.[1] They include an amount of work and fresh result during the three years of their production to which there can be few parallels in science; so that, despite the painfulness of these experiences, we can now hardly regret them. We must, in fact, rather congratulate their sufferer upon stimuli which have proved to be of such effective increase to his own movements and growth.

[1] *Plant Response*, 1906, and *Comparative Electro-Physiology*, 1907. Longmans, Green & Co.

In taking up his researches on the response of plants Bose asked himself:

> How are we to know what unseen changes take place within the plant? If it be excited or depressed under some special circumstances how are we to be made aware of it? The only conceivable way would be, if that were possible, to detect and measure the actual response of the organism to a definite testing blow. In an excitable condition, the feeblest stimulus should evoke a large response. In a depressed state, even a strong stimulus should evoke only feeble response; and lastly when death overcomes life, there would be an abrupt end of the power to answer at all. In short, under successive uniform stimuli, the change in the magnitude of the response should reveal to us the physiological changes induced by the environment.
>
> We might therefore have detected the internal condition of the plant if we could have made it write down its response. In order to succeed in this, we have to discover some compulsive force which will make the plant give an answering signal; secondly we have to supply the means for an automatic conversion of these signals into an intelligent script. And last of all we have ourselves to learn the nature of these hieroglyphics.

Hence, then, is the essential transition in Bose's work from physics to physiology. Now for a fuller outline of the series which opened with the Response of Inorganic Matter. They comprise a succession of six volumes, representing many years of work, and each not only summarising separate investigations and papers communicated to the Royal or other Societies, but with large accession of new material. The first of the series, 'Response in the Living and Non-living' (Longmans, Green & Co., 1902), with 199 pages, has been already summarised above; the second, 'Plant Response' (Longmans, 1906), amounts to 781 pages, detailing 315 experiments; the third, 'Comparative Electro-Physiology' (Longmans, 1907), goes to 760 pages, with 321 experiments described, and as usual largely figured also. The next six or seven years' work was largely devoted to the perfecting of recording instruments; but substantial results of work with them are also embodied in the fourth volume of this weighty series, as 'Researches on Irritability of Plants' (Longmans, 1913), with 376 pages and 180 experiments. The work of the years following appeared in the 'Philosophical Transactions' of the Royal Society for 1913. That of 1917 and 1918 has been mainly published as 'Life Movements in Plants,' this being Vol. I of the 'Transactions of the Bose Research Institute' (Calcutta, 1918), with its 251 pages, including 21 papers. Vol. II of the 'Transactions' for 1919 is just published, with its 344 pages and 30 papers. After the publication of one more volume their fertile author hopes to conclude his researches on Plant Movements, and thus to turn to other classes of problems old and new, each long meditated, but practically delayed.

Given this long series of six vclumes, with well over 2500 pages describing a full thousand and more of experiments, with summaries of their results, the writer has found it no easy problem to attempt any reasonably intelligible account of their main results, such as has been already offered above in Chapter IV, for Bose's initial work with electrical waves. To do this at all adequately, for such a multiplicity of problems in the plant world explored by our author, within the limits of present space is impossible; since fuller explanation, rather than further concentration, would often be desirable. For adequate summary, even of main results, an entire volume is needed, and such a volume only Bose himself can write.

Moreover, a biography is like a portrait: it seeks essentially to depict the man, and it can at best only indicate the scope, the principle and process of his life-work; its volume of accomplishment must in general be left to the specialists to whom they are addressed, while even their principal results in the present case are still only beginning to be adequately summarised for students of bio-physics and of vegetable and animal physiology (indeed of experimental psychology too) in the various text-books and treatises of these subjects which are from time to time prepared for them, in various countries and their languages.

Still the reader may reasonably expect some broad indications; and towards such the writer has laboured. Instead of attempting fully to summarise any of the volumes either singly or in succession, a fresh method has presented itself which, despite its diagrammatic (and therefore at first sight unfamiliar) aspect, may be found helpful towards expressing the main stages of the active life-work here before us. If we can outline such a graphic presentment, it should be applicable to kindred interpretations, of scientific work and individual development together. At any rate, as our physiologist has so long been striving to trace the curves of life in plants (and also in animals), let us try to mark down some essentials of his own life-curves of interests and growing achievements, and of his aims beyond.

As the pool or lake reflects the starry sky, so we may think of the mind of science in general as the would-be complete mirror of the cosmos. But the action of each individual scientific mind, with its own rhythm of growth and development, is like a widening wave-circle, which we watch as it starts from its excited centre and extends upon the surface of the pool. It reflects fresh images to us as it advances; yet it is none the less the same wave-circle all the time, continuous with its own past, as it presses on towards its widening future. Its photographs then, at different phases of this development —conveniently those of notably vivid reflections to our eyes—preserve for us its characteristic record, its essential biography.

The succession of books just named are, as it were, so many records of what has been fundamentally one and the same thought-advance, in its extension; and also of course in its deepening. Each book is thus a record up to its date of this extending curve, or at least of a large arc of the curve, while this or that intervening paper is a minor arc of this again, or on the way to it. In the present series this process is peculiarly clear, in fact as typical as may be.

Of course, no mind's survey is all-comprehensive ; hence a semicircle is ample for our diagram. This again we may divide into parts, for the elements of an extending survey, and these are four : the response of metal, of plant, of animal muscle and nerve, and finally the corresponding physico-psychological interpretation as far as may be. A reconsideration of the facts already known to physiologists of the responsive behaviour to the stimuli of the physical environment of animal tissues, muscle and nerve, when taken in conjunction with our physicist's discoveries as regards the behaviour of inorganic matter under stimulus, led him to that remarkable discovery of the curve of response of metals so strictly similar to the response of animal tissues already noted ; and this correspondence next naturally led to that inquiry as to the possibility of corresponding responses from the plant, hitherto reckoned so passive and inert, which we have also seen as successful. Here, then, was a new and substantial unification of phenomena previously supposed to be strictly confined to animal physiology, and an extension of them first to the field of vegetable physiology and then to that of physics, in which no such close comparison had ever been suspected. Furthermore, since in all sciences it is man who is observing and interpreting nature, and thereby learning something towards the better understanding of himself, the field of human physiology is also successfully entered; especially perhaps with the chapter on 'Visual Analogues,' and the discovery of the binocular alternation of vision, and so on. Moreover in this way it generally happens, and specifically with such observations as those on 'unconscious visual impression,' that the field of psychology is entered, and found so far harmonious with preceding ones ; while further inquiry in this field is also indicated, as will be seen in a subsequent chapter. Leaving experimental psychology aside, however, for the present—or rather, let us say, leaving it as implicated within the human and comparative fields—we may conveniently divide the range of inquiries of this first volume of the series—'Response of the Living and Non-Living'—into its four main factors: of Non-Living, Vegetable, Animal, and Human; and thus we see all comprehended in the generalising sweep of a semicircle.

The Response of the Non-Living has not been inquired into further; for henceforth our investigator has been devoted to the Organic field. The next volume, as its name implies—'Plant Response'—is essentially confined to its chosen department of Vegetable Physiology, as closely as may be; but in the immediately succeeding, and indeed complemental, volume—'Comparative Electro-Physiology'—we find not only an intensive application of all then known of that department of animal physiology to the further elucidation of plant-behaviour, but also vigorous incursions into the animal physiologist's own fields of labour; with the ensuing development of many of his classic experiments to more refined observation and record, and larger comparative treatment of them, and often accompanied by fresh inquiries.

Thus from a study of the response of leaves (in course of which Burdon Sanderson's and other previous work on Dionæa—Venus' Fly-trap—is reviewed and interpreted) we are led on by his consideration of the ordinary leaf as an electrical organ to that of the curious electric organs long known in certain fishes; and thence to 'the theory of electrical organs.'

This line of work is further extended into a whole chapter of comparisons of the 'response of animal and vegetable skins'—in which grape and tomato on one side, and frog, tortoise and lizard on the other, are all shown to behave substantially alike. So again Bose compares the behaviour of the epidermic and the secreting tissues of plants to those of animals; and similarly with regard to the response of digestive organs, from the tentacle of the sun-dew, or the pitcher of Nepenthes, which Darwin's 'Insectivorous Plants' had brought into great prominence a good few years before, to the stomachs of frog, tortoise and other animals: and in all this comparative study unexpected agreements are found even of detail. So from a chapter on 'the response to the stimulus of light given by leaves,' our writer passes boldly to the response of the retina to the same stimulus. Again, from the determination of the velocity of transmission of excitation in plant-tissues and the comparison of the conducting powers of two parts of an identical nerve by the original device of a 'Conductivity Balance,' we come to a new method for the quantitative stimulation of nerve; and thence again to the electrical response of isolated 'vegetable nerve' (isolated, that is, by the withdrawal of the fibro-vascular bundle, with its conducting elements included within its sheath, from the leaf-stalk of the fern), in which the analogous behaviour to animal nerve is demonstrated, in normal condition, under tetanisation, under influence of heat and cold, and under anæsthetics, like ether and chloroform.

In such ways of investigation, at once broader in scope and bolder in comparison than heretofore, while more experimentally elaborated—generally with improved methods and newly invented and finer apparatus—this incursion into animal physiology proceeds, often with fresh results. The further investigations into the electro-physiology of nerve are too elaborate and technical for outline here; but the animal physiologist has had since to reckon with them increasingly.

It is now time to return to the earlier of these two correlated volumes, the one on 'Plant Response,' and to note something of its advance upon its predecessor, which indeed now appears to be the introduction to Bose's wide and varied inquiry in vegetable physiology which has become increasingly predominant. The essential problem is thus stated:—Is the plant a mysterious entity, with regard to whose working no law can be definitely predicated? Or can it be interpreted as a machine — i.e. as transforming the energy supplied to it in ways more or less capable of explanation? So diverse are its movements that the first hypothesis has often seemed the only one. For light may induce sometimes positive curvature, sometimes negative; gravitation induces one movement in the root and the opposite in the shoot, and so on: whence it appeared to many, even to evolutionists, as if the organism had become endowed with various specific sensibilities for its own advantage, but that a consistent physico-chemical explanation of its movements was out of the question, However, the thesis is here clearly affirmed, and justified in detail, that 'the plant may nevertheless be regarded as a machine; and that its movements of response to external stimuli, though apparently so various, are ultimately reducible to a fundamental unity of reaction. This demonstration has been the object of the present work, and not that treatment of known aspects of plant-movements which is to be found detailed, together with the history of the subject, in standard books of reference on Vegetable Physiology.'

Of this large thesis the first chapter is a model of explicit statement. 'The plant, like a machine, responds either to the impact of external forces, or to energy latent within. As the working efficiency of an engine is exhibited by indicator-diagrams, so the physiological efficiency of a living machine may be inferred from the character of its pulse-records.' The making of the records, and the mode of exhibiting them during their progress (even to the largest audiences), are explained and clearly figured; this 'Optical Pulse-Recorder' may therefore here be figured (Fig. 7), as at once simple and convincing. The apparatus consists of a twin drum, over which is wrapped a band of paper to serve as the recording surface. The drums are kept revolving by clock-work. The excursion of the spot of light caused by the responsive movement of the plant-organ, is followed

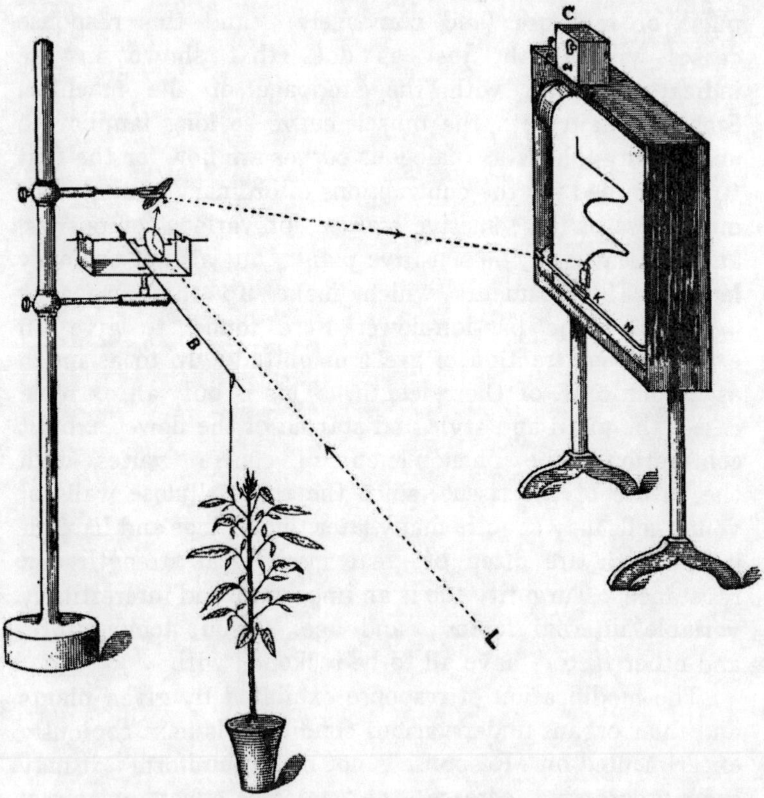

FIG. 7.—The Optical Pulse-Recorder. B, arm of optical lever attached to moving leaflet; L, ray of light, which after two reflections from the two mirrors falls on the recorder; C, clock-work, which keeps twin-drum—on which is wrapped the recording paper—revolving; H, horizontal guide bar; K, inkwell with projecting sponge.

by means of a sliding inkwell, from which projects the ink-sponge. By this means, the tracing of the response-curve and its various modifications under the action of different influences can be demonstrated. In the figure here reproduced the short arm of the optical lever is attached to the pulsating leaflet of the Telegraph-plant.

Again it is shown that agencies which depress the physiological condition of a tissue also depress its pulse of response (and conversely); and this response ceases with death, just as does that shown in the indicator-diagram with the stoppage of the machine. Starting again with the muscle-curve so long familiar to animal physiologists, analogous curves are now for the first time obtained for the contractions of ordinary plants: not only those of the sensitive stamens of various composites, and the leaves of the sensitive plants, but also of ordinary leaves. The filaments which make up the corona or 'glory' of the passion-flower were found to give an excitatory contraction of great magnitude, up to as much as 20 per cent. of their length. This is only an extreme case: the pistil and style and stamen of the flower exhibit contraction. The phenomenon, of course, varies with the nature of the tissue, since the thin cellulose walls of young cells may acquire many later thickenings and hardenings, which are often of great mechanical strength and resistance. Turgidity too is an important and interestingly variable internal factor; and age, season, temperature, and other factors have all to be reckoned with.

The modification of response exhibited by given plants and their organs under various conditions is next copiously experimented on. Response is not merely uniform: it may show progressive increase—the 'staircase effect' of animal muscle. Nor is fatigue merely a muscular phenomenon. Plant-records also amply exhibit it; for these readily become 'tired out' by long-continued previous stimulation. The accompanying tracings (Figs. 8 and 9), taken by his automatic recorders, show how the successive responses under different conditions of experiment, undergo a 'staircase' enhancement or a 'fatigue' depression. Indeed some of the more intricate phenomena of fatigue, nowadays being so actively studied, alike for educational, athletic and industrial purposes, are seen not to be without their parallels in the plant; not merely in the sensitive Mimosa, but even in the undemonstrative radish.

The discussion of the various theories of response must be left to the professed physiologist: it is sufficient here to emphasise the more general conception underlying the whole work and increasingly verified as it proceeds. Not simply is the mechanical response to stimulus expressed in obvious

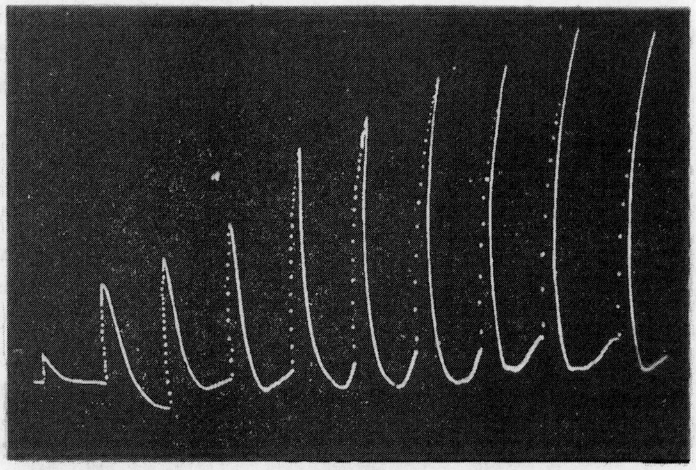

FIG. 8.—The 'staircase' enhancement of response in plant.

movements like the fall of the Mimosa leaf, but by mechanical response of organs of ordinary plants when their record is magnified, as by the optical lever. Such excitatory reaction caused by external stimulus expresses itself not only in mechanical movements, but also by generation of electric current, and by change of electric conductivity; and doubtless also in other ways, both physical and chemical. Just as the passage of one and the same electric current may be manifested not only by the swing of the galvanometer needle, but also in chemical change—or in terms of light and heat, or by sound, as from an electric bell, according to the nature of the detecting apparatus upon its circuit—so essentially it is with the organism, which may exhibit a variety of different responses to the same stimulus, in accordance with its differing functional and structural means of expression. Its mechanical response, its responsive electric current, its variation of conductivity are but different expressions of an identical reaction which underlies excitation.

This conception of the concomitance of these different

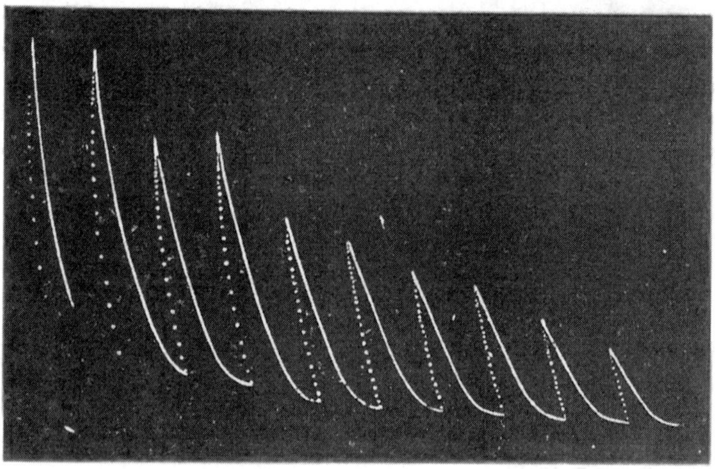

FIG. 9.—' Fatigue ' depression of response in plant.

manifestations, when taken along with the further investigation of their optimum, and also of their maximum and minimum—especially those of temperature, at which inaction appears, and even death supervenes—next led to the unexpected discovery of a ' death-spasm ' in all plants. Furthermore, this death-spasm, when experimentally scrutinised and recorded by each of these independent methods—mechanical, electro-motive, and conductivity variation—was found to show the same simultaneity of all the three changes.

For determining the critical temperature at which the

death-spasm occurs, a perfected form of apparatus—a 'Death Recorder'—was devised. The death-point—at any rate for all the dicotyledonous plants observed and their different organs—was found to be almost as definite as a physical constant; for, using very diverse specimens and methods, the critical temperature is always at or very near 60° C. The death-contraction in the plant is in every respect similar to the same phenomenon in the animal, and is an instance of true excitatory effect. Yet different plants have their characteristic death-curves, and the same species may exhibit variations under changed conditions of age and previous history. Thus when the plant's power of resistance is artificially depressed, whether by poisons or by fatigue, its death-spasm occurs at a temperature often considerably lower—even as much as 23°. This phenomenon, of course, also shows that the death-spasm is no mere phenomenon of coagulation; for even if it takes place at 60° or thereabouts, it cannot also happen at 37° C.

As stated before, there is an electrical spasm corresponding to the mechanical spasm at death. The electromotive force generated at death-temperature is sometimes considerable: Bose shows that in each half of a green pea it may be as high as half a volt. If five hundred peas are suitably arranged in series, the electric pressure will be five hundred volts, which may cause even electrocution of unsuspecting victims. And so Bose drily remarks: 'It is well that the cook does not know the danger she runs in preparing the particular dish; it is fortunate for her that the peas are not arranged in series!'

All this complex investigation necessarily depended on contriving and adjusting three different systems of apparatus for recording different modes of response, mechanical and electrical. Though the instruments employed were so widely different, yet the responses obtained were found to agree in every important detail.

Much investigation has been devoted in these books, and also, more recently, to the nature and causes of 'automatic' movements, of which those of the Telegraph-plant (Desmodium) are the extreme examples in the vegetable world. Briefly stated, the automatism turns out to be but apparent, in so far as these activities are proved to be dependent on external stimulus previously absorbed. The half-way house between this 'automatic' activity and the simple response of a Mimosa leaf was discovered in Biophytum, a common weed of Bengal (akin to Oxalis) and also in the somewhat allied Averrhoa Carambola, an acid fruit-tree of Indian gardens. For while in these a single moderate stimulus gives rise to a single response, as in Mimosa, a strong stimulus produces a whole succession of responses, recalling the automatism of Desmodium. This observation suggested the idea that Desmodium might be depressed in its automatism, and even reduced to the single response of Mimosa; and this condition was experimentally realised: the leaflets ceased to pulsate accordingly, and came to a standstill. Conversely, why should not Mimosa have its simple response exalted towards a multiple response, which is the transition stage on the way to automatism? This was not at first demonstrable mechanically, but was proved by the electrical mode of response-record; while now more lately, with the finer recorders since invented, it has been successfully recorded in Mimosa. That is, its natural single response is developed into a slow rhythm of multiple response; and this is practically equivalent to the automatism induced in Biophytum. The ascent of the whole series of sensitive plants from ordinary (but as we now know, only apparently) insensitive ones, first to simple response as in Mimosa, and thence through transitional forms like Biophytum to the habitually automatic Desmodium, has thus been made intelligible—surely no small gain to our conception of the evolutionary process.

Another remarkable comparison is here also made—that between the automatic pulsation of the telegraph-plant and that of animal heart-muscle. The comparison is worked out in considerable detail, and the result is wholly confirmatory, in variously modified as well as in normal conditions, such as temperature, drugs or poisons. So exact is the correspondence that a poison which stops the heart in its phase of contraction also stops Desmodium in its contracted phase, while the poison which stops the heart in relaxation does the same for the plant. And while for the heart it has been known that one poison may be used as the antidote to the other, so it turns out with the poisoning of Desmodium.

Yet another point of interest appears. The actively rhythmic muscle of the heart is more resistant to external stimulus than is ordinary muscle: e.g. it resists tetanisation by external electric shock. Similarly for the active Desmodium leaflet. Thus that passive yielding of the organism or organ to external stimuli, of which we have so often seen cases above, has here its limit: and we see the internal energy of the organism now, as it were, vindicating itself against interferences from the outside environment. We may thus still speak of 'automatic movements,' and concede a certain independence to the organism, and individuality to the organ.

The general thesis that plant and animal physiology—despite all differences of aspect and habit of life, and of organisms in detail—are yet profoundly analogous is again strikingly confirmed.

Turning next to the section on Growth, our knowledge is greatly advanced, as will be found in greater detail in a subsequent chapter. It is, however, enough here to note that for the vegetable physiologist the most interesting of all these new conceptions may lie in the reinterpretation of the growth-process, as itself a phenomenon of automatism, comparable to that of Desmodium pulsation. For here we have the rhythmic activity controlled by inner stimuli, which present a certain autonomy of their own, and yet are also dependent for their continuance upon energies ultimately derived from the environment and sensitive to its changes. In both cases depletion of energy by isolation stops activity. Yet from this state of standstill, growth can be renewed by fresh stimulus from outside. Even an organ in which growth has normally ended may be started anew, as demonstrated by Bose, by electrical or other appropriate stimuli. So here is, at any rate, some support for the ever-recurring dream of rejuvenescence. And even if this be no more, at least for the higher species, than a mirage of life, we may at least suggest the possible fruitfulness of discussion, perhaps even collaboration, between—say—one of Bose's experimental assistants and one of the young neurologists before whom the war has so strongly brought problems of this nature.

CHAPTER X

IRRITABILITY OF PLANTS

As in the world of matter, so also in the world of thought, there is an inertia which retards movement and change; and this is especially the case in the adoption of new methods of scientific inquiry. Bose's 'Plant Response' and 'Comparative Electro-Physiology' (1906–7) gave detailed descriptions of his methods, but want of opportunity of following the practical demonstration stood in the way of their wider adoption. In spite of this drawback, various workers in different parts of the world followed closely Bose's work, and employed his method with success. The Optical Lever has been used in certain physiological investigations in the Cambridge Laboratory; van der Wolk of Utrecht has followed with success Bose's lines of investigation; while his electro-physiological investigations have been incorporated in a course of advanced work under Professor Harper at Columbia University, New York.

In response to a widely expressed desire that workers in the West should become acquainted first-hand with the practical working of his methods, the Government sent Bose in 1907, on his third scientific deputation, to England and America. After a short stay in England he visited the United States, and lectured before highly appreciative audiences in the different American Universities.

On his return to India Bose concentrated his attention on the invention of a complete set of apparatus by which the experimental plant would be automatically excited at definite intervals of time by successive uniform stimuli. In answer to this the plant should make its own responsive records, and embark on the same cycle over again without any assistance at any point from the observer. After several years of trials and efforts, the problem was at last solved to the utmost particular, both in refinement and with high magnification. His instruments, embodying a new principle, will no doubt react towards the improvement of the relatively crude myograph of the physiologist. The most important of the series of these instruments—the Resonant Recorder—is based on the principle of sympathetic vibration. The difficulty of friction of contact, which made the direct record of the feeble plant-movement impossible, is here completely eliminated. The sensibility of the apparatus may be gauged from the fact that the automatic records obtained by this instrument give measurements of time as short as a thousandth part of a second; the results obtained with the instrument show that the sensitiveness of the plant is not so feeble, and its power of perception so sluggish, as have been supposed

Inventions and discoveries are by some regarded as the fortunate products of flashes of insight, and such minds are reckoned as 'gifted' accordingly, even up to 'genius'—a quality not further explained. For others genius seems but the highest development of patience, and its results as rewards of continuous attention and reflection. As a matter of fact, both processes intermingle. Hence for Newton the suggestive fall of the apple is insufficient without his own answer, when asked how he came to his discoveries: 'I know not, save it be by constantly intending my mind thereunto.' Indeed the man of science, despite his apparent gravity of aspect and of subject, is peculiarly continuous with his own childhood. Hence, when we watch a child striving to solve a puzzle, to make a mechanical toy, or to build his bricks into a tower, we see that very alternation of patient endeavours amid failures, with moments of new constructive insight, which make up the essential progress of science. In our day everywhere, and not least in India, one who can do any such things on the adult scale is reckoned an 'expert' —a term which again precludes further inquiry; but the inventor and the discoverer alike know themselves better, and but advance in their childlike way by alternate steps, not unmingled with falls, but guided by flashes of freshened insight and hope.

On such general grounds, as well as for coming to a further understanding of plant-movements, it is here worth the reader's while to look into this problem, of how to enable the plant to make its own record of its movements—whether in nature or under stimulus of altered conditions. For one thing, the time-relations of every phase of movement must be found, and determined with the physicist's exactitude. Though for everyday use the second hand of our watches marks our ordinary limit, the starter and judge of a race, or the physician feeling a pulse, have to take note of fractions of a second; hence the stop-watch, with its finer graduation, down to tenths of a second. But for physical measurements far smaller fractions are often necessary; hence the interest of the tuning-fork, with its hundreds of vibrations per second. Better still than the tuning-fork is the vibrating reed; for of this we may adjust the length to any required quickness of vibration, within a wide and sufficient range, say from ten to a thousand times per second. It may easily be made to write its tracings on a recording surface—conveniently a smoked plate. The vibrating reed soon gives off its initial energy, but continuous vibration may be maintained by electric means. The steel reed, with its required frequency of vibration once adjusted, is made to dip its bent point into a small cup of mercury; so that the metallic contact should start a current which passes through a small coil wire fixed above the reed, and containing a soft iron of core, which the current converts into a temporary magnet. The attraction of the magnet upon the reed pulls it up out of the mercury. But this stops the current. The small electro-magnet thus becomes inert; the magnetic attraction ceases, and the reed is set free to swing and fall anew towards and into the mercury thus renewing the current and with

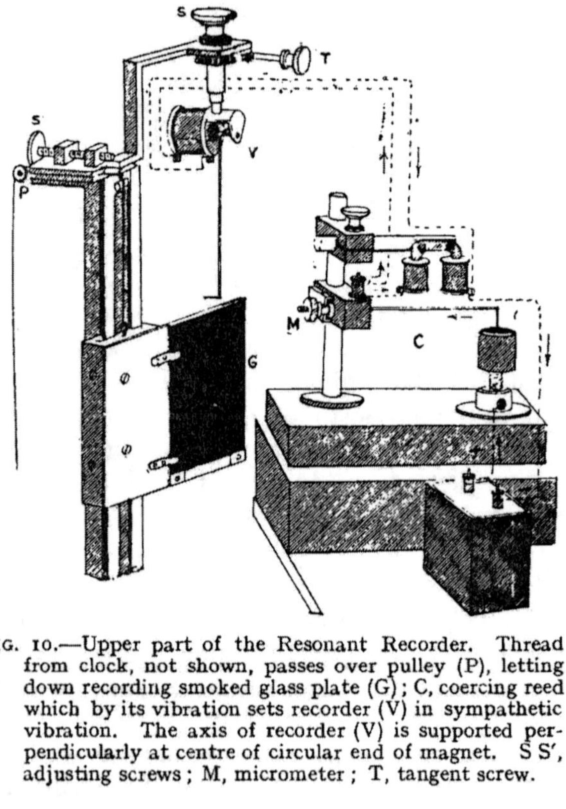

FIG. 10.—Upper part of the Resonant Recorder. Thread from clock, not shown, passes over pulley (P), letting down recording smoked glass plate (G); C, coercing reed which by its vibration sets recorder (V) in sympathetic vibration. The axis of recorder (V) is supported perpendicularly at centre of circular end of magnet. S S', adjusting screws; M, micrometer; T, tangent screw.

it the magnet, pulling up the reed and so on. Thus the desired rhythm, appropriate to the reed's length, can be maintained steadily, and for any required length of time. So much for the Coercer of Bose's apparatus, which has to set the resonating writer in sympathetic vibration.

This resonating writer—a fine steel wire, with a bent tip, and of length suitable to the required rate of vibration —is suspended vertically by means of pivots supported on jewel bearings. One of the bearings is fixed at the centre of a soft iron core, and the other bearing is carried by a flat metallic plate. The soft iron core is surrounded by a wire spiral through which flows the same current which activates the reed; so this second iron core becomes an electro-magnet, and for exactly the same periods; the reed and the writer are kept in perfect unison. The bent tip of the writer taps regularly upon a smoked plate, placed at right angles to it. These taps must always be on the same point so long as the recording surface is stationary; but if it be made to travel we shall get a row of dots, made at the time-intervals predetermined. It was next found most conducive to good records to let the plate descend by its own weight, thus giving a vertical series of dots; for though successive distances between them are slightly increasing in course of the acceleration of the falling plate, this matters little for time-measurements, since their numbers per second are identical. An ingenious compensatory device has, however, been provided for use when required.

The tapping method has now secured a double advantage: (1) the precisely comparable time-records, and (2) the practical elimination of friction; since the bent tip of the writer gives a series of taps, and is therefore not in continuous contact with the recording surface. A fine cocoon thread is securely tied to the leaf to be observed, and its other end is attached to the short arm of a very light wire lever which has been already fixed to the writer. The movement of the leaf pulls the writer to one side or other, giving dots no longer in mere vertical row, but now recording every movement of the plant. The conspicuous fall of the Mimosa leaf, or the minutest quiver in pulsating leaflet or of contraction under a stimulus, will thus cause a pull on the attached thread; and this will be transmitted and magnified by the writing lever. The dots are seen to lie in definite and characteristic order; and the dotted curve gives the whole history of the plant-movement from start to finish.

The Resonant Recorder is shown complete and in use upon the accompanying illustration (Fig. 11). An actual record is

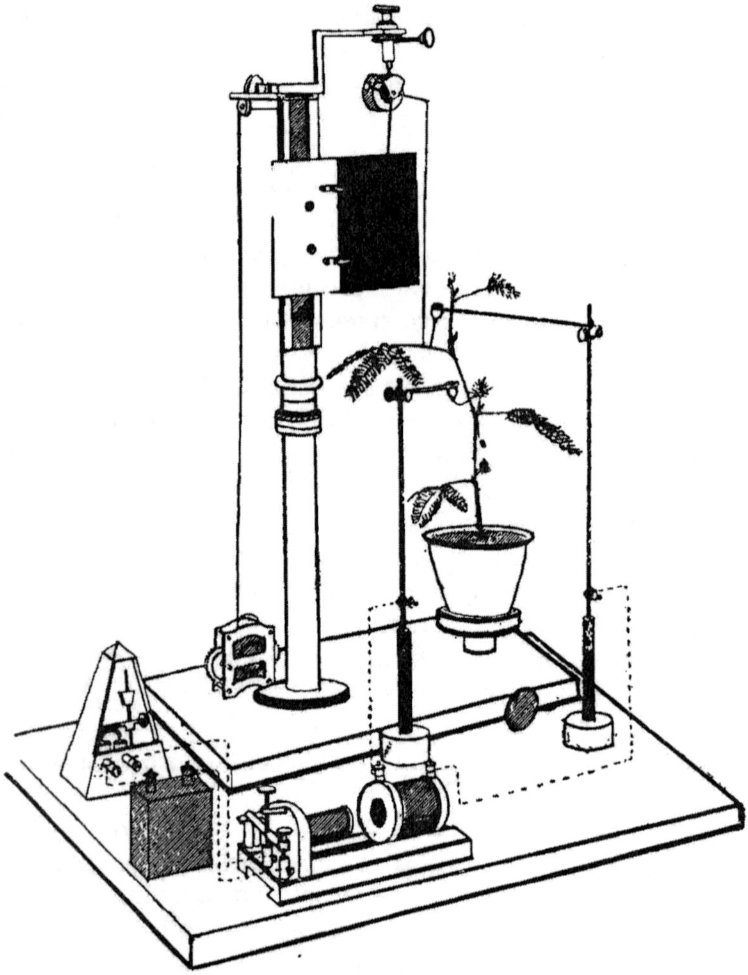

FIG. 11.—General view of the Resonant Recorder and the electrical connections by which excitatory shock of a definite duration is given to the plant; duration of shock determined by metronome, which completes electric circuit.

given in the next figure which measures the time taken by the plant to perceive and answer to the shock given at the vertical line in the record. The successive dots are at intervals of two hundredth part of a second, and the leaf-movement began at the fifteenth dot after the shock (Fig. 12). The perception-time of the plant is thus 0·75 of a second. When the plant is fatigued, its perception-time becomes very sluggish : when excessively tired, it temporarily loses its power of perception. In that condition the plant requires at least half an hour's absolute rest to regain its equanimity.

For some purposes, however, the Resonant Recorder

FIG. 12.—Record for determination of the latent period of leaf of Mimosa. Shock given at vertical line ; successive dots at intervals of 0·005 second.

has its limitation. It measures movements which are exceedingly quick ; there are, however, other movements which are relatively slow, and Bose still needed an instrument which could take slower records, lasting for hours and days. Moreover, some movements may be so slight and weak that even the recording system just described —being necessarily of magnetisable metal though at its finest—may be too heavy for the excessively limited mechanical power of certain plant-movements.

Hence, instead of the writer oscillating so many times per second, he now set the smoked glass plate oscillating, to come up periodically against the point of the writer. The oscillation can now be as slow as we please, since by various ingenious adaptations of clockwork we can obtain any required period of oscillation—in practice usually from once in a second to once in a quarter of an hour, as may be required—while the oscillations and their dotted records can go on as long as the winding of the clock is attended to. Further, the mechanical mode of oscillation dispenses with the necessity for the steel writer, and a light grass awn, or a hair-drawn glass fibre, can take its place. In the Resonant Recorder the magnification is limited by the proportions of the writing lever, usually to 25 times or thereabouts; but now in the Oscillating Recorder with a single lever this may easily be raised to 100 times, and with compound lever to 10,000 times. The Oscillating Recorder, moreover, admits of lateral extension, so as to carry four plates, and it may have as many plants recording themselves side by side at the same time under identical conditions.

It is now time to see what results they have yielded. First of all they afforded complete verifications of the essential accuracy of the curves of plant-movements given in the 'Plant Response' taken by the simpler method of the Optical Lever. The phenomena of nervous impulse were demonstrated by the 'Resonant Recorder'—against the generally accepted view that there was nothing in the plant comparable to the nervous system in animals. Bose's results were thus so convincing that the Royal Society accepted them for publication in their 'Philosophical Transactions' (1913). Following this and the publication of his 'Researches on Irritability of Plants,' Bose received several invitations to lecture before different Universities and scientific societies of Europe and America, and was accordingly sent by the Government on his fourth scientific deputation in 1914.

Bose determined not only to carry his delicate instruments but also the plant-specimens—Mimosa and Telegraph-plant (Fig. 13)—from India, so that they should give their autographic records before the audience. In Europe most of the plants go through their periods of hibernation in the season when the scientific societies are in full session. In a world-tour the carrying of his delicate instruments was difficult enough; but to take tropical plants in hope of their retaining vigour and sensitiveness in the freezing climates of Europe, and particularly of America, seemed an impossible venture. But Bose, with his characteristic determination and resourcefulness, faced

FIG. 13.—The two plants Mimosa pudica and Desmodium gyrans that accompanied Professor Bose round the world. The small leaflets of the Desmodium (to the right) pulsate up and down.

the problem. A special glass case was provided for their journey and every possible care taken of them by his admirably devoted and skilled experimental assistant. Only half the number of the plants survived the voyage, but once in London they were safely housed in the Regent's Park tropical greenhouse. This done, Bose fitted up his temporary laboratory at Maida Vale, where the difficulties connected with experiments on tropical plants transferred to a cold climate were observed, and means devised to overcome them.

He was now asked to lecture before various Universities, and first at Oxford, where his demonstrations were received with high appreciation. Next at Cambridge, Sir Francis Darwin presiding. Here also his audience was most enthusiastic. In London he lectured before the Royal College of Science. His Friday Evening Discourse before the Royal Institution was given in May 1914, and proved a great success. His Resonant Recorder registered the speed of transmission of excitatory impulse, the Oscillating Recorder traced the throbbing pulsations of the Telegraph-plant, and demonstrated their striking similarity with the pulse-beat of the animal heart. Finally, the Death Recorder indicated by its tracing the death-throe of the plant.

His private laboratory at Maida Vale was visited by various scientific and literary men. Among these were Sir William Crookes, then President of the Royal Society, and other leading men of science. A very distinguished animal physiologist was so strongly impressed by the unexpected revelations made by the plants that he frankly blurted out: 'Do you know whose casting vote prevented the publication of your papers on Plant Response by the Royal Society? I am that person. I could not believe that such things were possible, and thought your Oriental imagination had led you astray. Now I fully confess that you have all along been right.'

Among the men of letters came Mr. Balfour, who at once saw the psychological importance of the discoveries. Mr. Bernard Shaw, being a vegetarian, was unhappy to find that a piece of cabbage was thrown into violent convulsion when scalded to death. Editors of leading journals also came, and the following departure from the usual gravity of *The Nation* will indicate the popular impression made by the new revelations of plant life:

In a room near Maida Vale there is an unfortunate carrot strapped to the table of an unlicensed vivisector. Wires pass through two glass tubes full of a white substance; they are like two legs, whose feet are buried in the flesh of the carrot. When the vegetable is pinched with a pair of forceps, it winces. It is so strapped that its electric shudder of pain pulls the long arm of a very delicate lever which actuates a tiny mirror. This casts a beam of light on the frieze at the other end of the room, and thus enormously exaggerates the tremor of the carrot. A pinch near the right-hand tube sends the beam seven or eight feet to the right, and a stab near the other wire sends it as far to the left. Thus can science reveal the feelings of even so stolid a vegetable as the carrot.

The Royal Society of Medicine also became keenly interested in Bose's work on the effect of drugs on vegetable tissues, and asked him to deliver a discourse before the Society. Sir Lauder Brunton wrote to him:

> Ever since I began the study of Botany in 1863, and still more since I made some experiments on the action of poison on plants in 1865, the movements of plants had a great attraction for me. For Mr. Darwin I made some experiments on digestion in insectivorous plants in 1875. All the experiments I have yet seen are crude in comparison with yours, in which you show what a marvellous resemblance there is between the reactions of plants and animals.

The lecture before the Royal Society of Medicine was highly appreciated by the leading members of the medical profession, and the Secretary of the Society officially addressed the Government of India, expressing their high appreciation of the work which was 'so entirely new in biological science.'

He was next invited to lecture before leading Universities of the Continent. He first visited Vienna, where amongst his audience were many leading physiologists of Austria and Germany, who paid the generous tribute that 'Calcutta was far ahead of them in these new lines of investigation.' In Paris he met with similar success. He received cordial invitations from different German Universities for a series of lectures. He was to have begun these lectures from the 3rd of August, 1914, and was actually on his way to Bonn, but fortunately was just in time to retrace his steps and escape internment. Two nephews, then also in Germany, were less fortunate.

He next visited America and lectured before a number of the principal Universities there. He also addressed the American Association for the Advancement of Science at Philadelphia, and the New York and Washington Academies of Science. At Washington he was invited to address the State Department and also the Bureau of Agriculture, where the great importance of his work in practical agriculture was fully realised. He lectured at Harvard before the Departments of Philosophy and Psychology, and also before Clark University, whose President, the well-known psychologist, Dr. Stanley Hall, had been keenly interested in Bose's work from his earliest publications. Everywhere Bose's work received the warmest appreciation.

We may now return to the phenomena of Irritability, so successfully explored by the invention of Bose's new instruments. It is, however, impossible to give in such short space all the interesting results ; and it must suffice to give a few extracts from Bose's popular lectures.

One of his inquiries related to the physiological effect of different gases on plants :

According to popular science, what is death to the animal is supposed to be life for the plant ; for does it not flourish in the deadly atmosphere of carbonic acid gas ? But instead of flourishing, the plant gets suffocated just like a human being ; note the relief on readmission of fresh air (Fig. 14). Only in the presence of sunlight is the effect modified, by photo-synthesis. In contrast to the effect of carbonic acid, ozone renders the plant highly excitable.

The plant is intensely susceptible to the impurities present in the air. The vitiated air of the town has a very depressing effect. Sulphuretted hydrogen, even in small quantities, is fatal to the plant. Chloroform acts as a strong narcotic, inducing a rapid abolition of excitability. The ludicrously unsteady gait of the response of the plant under alcohol could be effectively exploited in a temperance lecture. But the next result is in the nature of an anticlimax, where the plant has drunk—pure water—not wisely, but too well. The gorged plant loses all power of movement. The plant was restored to normal condition by extracting the excess of liquid by application of glycerine.

Does the plant feel the depressing effect of darkness? Fig. 15 records the effect of a passing cloud; the slight variation of light was detected by the plant much earlier than by the observer. Any sudden change of light is found to exert a marked depressing effect. The plant partially regains its

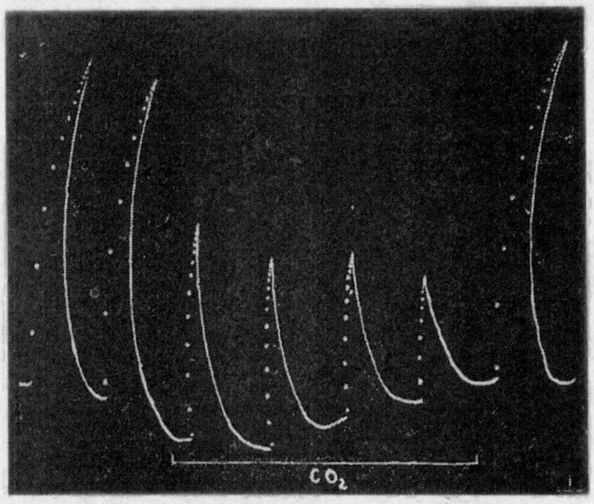

FIG. 14.—Depression of excitability under carbonic acid and revival on readmission of fresh air.

sensibility when accustomed to darkness. When brought suddenly from darkness to light, there is also a transient depression followed by enhanced excitability.

Again as to the effect of wounds:

I undertook three investigations, on the effect of wounds on plants. The first enquiry is as to the effect of injury on growth; the second is the change manifested in the pulse-beat of rhythmic tissues in plants. The third investigation had for its object the study of the paralysing effect of wounds.

In the first of these the normal rate of growth and change of that rate by injury were found from the automatic records given by the Crescograph. When the growing plant was pricked with a pin, the normal rate was at once depressed to a fourth, and it took about two hours for the plant to recover from the effect of the pin-prick. A slash made with a knife was found to arrest the growth, the inhibition persisting for a very long period. Severe shock caused by a wound thus retards the growth in normal healthy specimens.

The reactions in exceptional cases are highly interesting. Certain plants, for reasons at present obscure, remain stunted

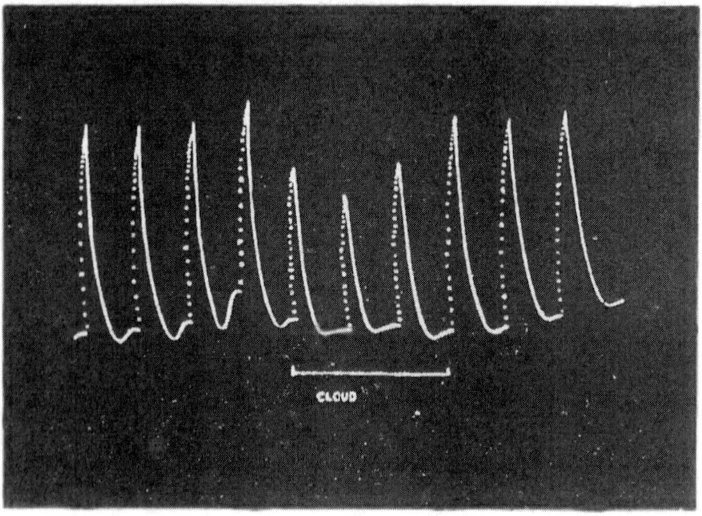

FIG. 15.—Depressing effect of a passing cloud on the response of Mimosa.

in growth, the branches and leaves presenting an unhealthy look. Lopping off the offending limb, curiously enough, is found good for the plant. The stimulus of severe shock renews the growth that had remained arrested.

Another series of investigations was carried out with the leaflet of the Telegraph plant, which pulsates up and down, like the movement of a semaphore. When the leaflet is cut from the parent plant, and the cut end placed in water, the pulsation is found to be arrested by the shock of operation. After a time the pulse-throb is slowly renewed, and maintained for nearly 24 hours. But death had found an unguarded spot at the wound; and its march, though slow, is sure. The death-change thus reaches the throbbing tissue, which becomes permanently stilled with the cessation of life (Fig. 16). But the rate of the death-march has been successfully retarded by means of nourishing solutions; the throbbing life of the cut leaflet has thus been prolonged from one to seven days.

In cutting off the leaf of Mimosa the sensibility of the plant is paralysed for several hours. The paralysing effect of the wound was determined by means of testing shocks, the response being at the same time taken down by the automatic recorder. The parent plant gradually recovered, and showed signs of returning sensitiveness. The detached leaf also recovered its sensibility in a few hours, and exhibited its normal responses. But this vehemence lasted only for a day, after which a curious change crept in; the vigour of its responses began rapidly to

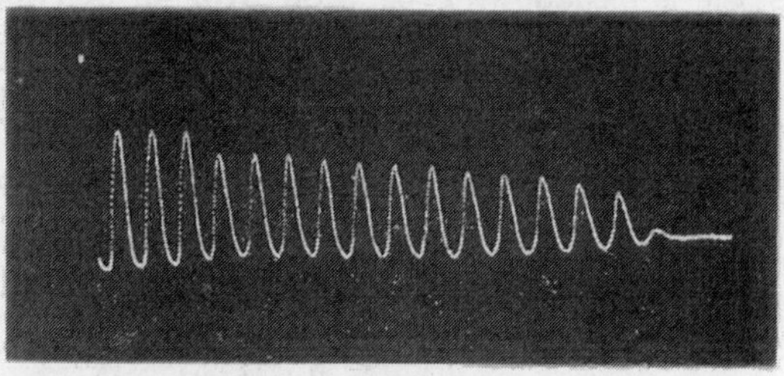

FIG. 16.—Abolition of pulsation at the death of the plant.

decline. The leaf, hitherto erect, fell over death had at last asserted its mastery.

As regards the comparison of the general phenomenon of Irritability in plants and animals, Bose says:

We find that the plant is not a mere mass of vegetative growth, but that its every fibre is instinct with sensibility. We find it answering to outside stimuli, the responsive twitches increasing with the strength of the blow that impinges on it. We are able to record the throbs of its pulsating life, and find these wax and wane according to the life conditions of the plant, and cease with the death of the organism. We find the different parts of the plant are connected together by conducting threads, so that the tremor of excitation initiated at one place courses through the whole, this nervous impulse, as in man, being accelerated or arrested under the several actions of drugs and poisons. In these and in many other ways the life reactions of plant and man are alike; thus through the experience of the plant it may be possible to alleviate the sufferings of man.

Bose thus concluded his Royal Institution Discourse:

These our mute companions, silently growing beside our door, have now told us the tale of their life-tremulousness and their death-spasm in script that is as inarticulate as they. May it not be said that their story has a pathos of its own beyond any that we have conceived?

In realising this unity of life, is our final sense of mystery deepened or lessened? Is our sense of wonder diminished when we realise in the infinite expanse of life that is silent and voiceless the foreshadowing of more wonderful complexities? Is it not rather that science evokes in us a deeper sense of awe? Does not each of her new advances gain for us a step in that stairway of rock which all must climb who desire to look from the mountain-tops of the spirit upon the promised land of truth?

CHAPTER XI

THE AUTOMATIC RECORD OF GROWTH

THE movement of the leaf of Mimosa is very sudden and conspicuous, while the movement of growth is almost imperceptible. But the large movements of stems, leaves and roots under the action of various forces such as light, warmth and gravity are ultimately due to excessively minute variations in the rate of growth. The discovery of laws relating to the movement of growing organs thus depends on accurate measurement of normal growth and its changes. Apart from theory, the subject is a matter of great practical importance since the world's food supply is so intimately dependent upon vegetative growth.

The extreme difficulty of the investigation arises from the extraordinary slowness of growth; of this we may form some idea from the following examples. Taking the annual growth in height of a tree to be five feet, which is a liberal estimate, it would take a thousand years for growth to cover a mile. The slowness of the snail is proverbial, but its pace is 2000 times faster than the average movement of growth. Yet one more instance. We take a single step, covering two feet in about half a second; during this period the plant grows through a length of $\frac{1}{100000}$ part of an inch, or half the length of a single wave of light. It is evident that some very strongly magnifying arrangement must be employed to observe growth and its changes. The instrument hitherto used in the botanical laboratory—the 'auxanometer'—magnifies about twenty times or so. Even here several hours must elapse before growth becomes perceptible; but during this long period the external conditions such as light and warmth can hardly but change, thus confusing, if not even vitiating, the results.

The external conditions can be kept constant only for a few minutes; and it is therefore necessary to obtain growth-magnification to something like ten thousand times. The difficulty of obtaining such magnification is so great that it took Bose about eight years to overcome it, and his 'High Magnification Crescograph' (Fig. 17) may be regarded as a veritable triumph in invention. The apparatus not only produces this enormous magnification, but also automatically records the rate of growth and its changes, in a period as short as a minute.

Bose employs for the purpose a compound system of two levers; the first magnifies a hundred times, and the second enlarges the first a hundredfold, the total magnification being thus 10,000 times. But the double system of levers introduces difficulty on account of their weight; this was surmounted by the employment of an alloy of aluminium, which combines great rigidity with exceptional lightness. The friction at the bearings increased by the deposit of invisible dust particles introduced a further difficulty; bearings even made of ruby did not obviate the trouble. Bose was finally able to devise a new form of suspension by which all difficulties were fully overcome.

These high magnification records show that growth is often not steady and continuous, but proceeds in rhythmic pulses. In normal Calcutta conditions these average about three per minute. Each pulse exhibits a rapid uplift, and then a slower and partial recoil, amounting to a recession of about a fourth of the distance at first gained; and from the resultant progress it starts for its next rise. Our mental image of the growth-process is thus transformed by these tracings from a steady mechanical progress to that of the wavelets of a rising tide. Still, there are also tracings in which growth appears as practically uniform; but such may be due to the resultant of the growth-pulses at different levels and in different layers of tissue. Another example of the extreme sensitiveness of the apparatus is

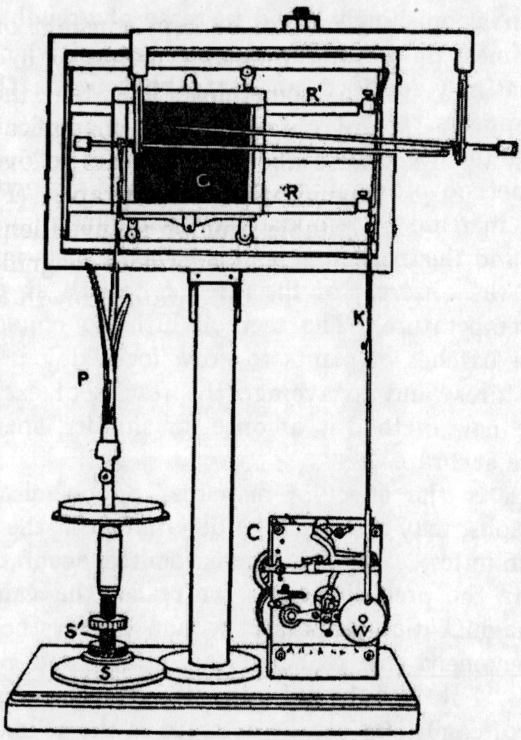

FIG. 17.—The High Magnification Crescograph. P, plant; C, clockwork for periodic oscillation of recording smoked glass plate (G); S S′, micrometer screws; K, crank; R, eccentric; W, rotating wheel.

seen from the fact that it even detects the retardation of growth caused by a mere touch, while a more violent irritation arrests growth altogether. Though rough handling is harmful to a vigorous plant, Bose found that its effect was, however, beneficial to a plant which had remained backward in its growth. Corporal punishment has therefore its uses!

Peculiarly obvious is the result of any temperature change upon the rate of growth. The application of cooled water of course depresses, until at the critical minimum all growth is arrested. Conversely, warmed water may effect an astonishingly rapid increase of growth, even by many times, up to the optimum; beyond which growth is increasingly retarded, until at about 60° C. the death-spasm appears.

By a further refinement of experimentation, an automatic method provides records of a plant's growth during gradual increase of temperature from minimum to maximum; and the inspection of this 'Thermo-crescent Curve' informs the observer of the rate of growth at each and every temperature. The method hitherto employed was to place batches of plants to grow for a day in different temperatures, and to average the results of each batch; but the new method is at once far simpler, speedier and far more accurate.

Similarly the effect of manures and chemicals, drugs and poisons, may now each be determined in the course of a few minutes, and with unprecedented accuracy. Here too, as in the preceding cases, we realise the value of this high magnification apparatus: not merely because all the phenomena are rendered far clearer and more conspicuous, but also because the result of any particular change of conditions can be detected in the course of a few minutes, during which the other conditions may remain constant, or be artificially kept so.

It will be understood that it is only by the discovery of laws of growth that any marked advance in scientific agriculture is possible. We have been using only a few stimulating agents, whereas there are thousands of whose actions we have no conception. The rule of thumb method hitherto employed in the application of a few chemical stimulants and of electricity has, moreover, not been uniformly successful. The cause of the anomaly is found from the discovery of an important factor—namely, the dose of application, which had hitherto not been taken into account. Thus Bose found that while a particular intensity of electrical current accelerated growth, any excess above a critical point retarded it. The same was true of chemical stimulants. A striking practical result was obtained with certain poisons which in normal doses killed the plant, but in quantities sufficiently minute acted as an extraordinarily efficient stimulant, the treated plants growing far more vigorous and flowering much earlier. The treated plants, moreover, successfully resisted the insect blights. Such facts lead to the inquiry into the critical point at which depressant passes into a stimulant, or conversely. At this point we see how a fresh line of research has here been opened for Pharmacology and Medicine. And similarly another for speedily testing the action of manurial agents, and other means of accelerating growth for Agriculture. The immediate test needs only a few minutes instead of a season, while the changing conditions of the latter are avoided.

Very striking also is the personal equation of the given plant, i.e. its permanent 'constitution' and its changing 'tonus.' The latter is found to be experimentally modifiable. Thus a given batch of similar seedlings was divided into three groups: one was kept normal for reference, another depressed by less favourable temperature to a sub-normal condition, and the third put in an optimum condition. The small dose of poisons which the normal plants could just survive after a period of struggle was found to produce immediate death in the sub-tonic specimens; but the same dose actively stimulated and exalted the growth of the super-tonic ones. Here, again, suggestiveness for medicine and for agriculture will be manifest.

The most perplexing phenomena in the life of plants are the 'tropic movements,' which will be described in a subsequent chapter. They are generally brought about by the action of the environment inducing slight modifications in the rate of growth. No satisfactory explanation of these movements has been forthcoming, since the apparatus in use was too crude to detect the *variation* of growth-rate, which was itself very minute. But with the High Magnification Crescograph, Bose succeeded in obtaining tracings which measured the rate of growth as small as $\frac{1}{100000}$ inch per second. He was thereby able to record changes induced in normal growth by the action of various agents, by contact, by variation of temperature, by radiant heat and light, by the stimulus of gravity, by electrical currents, and by various chemical agents. From these fundamental reactions he was able, as we shall see later, to offer a complete explanation of the diverse movements in plants.

After observing in the laboratory the extraordinary sensitiveness of this Crescograph with its magnification of ten thousand times, the writer offered the opinion that surely the utmost perfection had at last been reached; but to this Bose made the naïve and cryptic rejoinder that 'man is never satisfied'; and forthwith began to push on his investigations towards obtaining still higher magnification. He at first tried increasing his system of levers from two to three. But he soon found that, though theoretically possible, a limit to magnification is imposed on account of additional weight, and friction at the linking of one lever to another. He therefore thought of a weightless lever, and of linking without material contact. This he succeeded in effecting by the invention of his Magnetic Crescograph (Fig. 18); here the movement of the lever of his ordinary Crescograph upsets a very delicately balanced magnetic system. The indicator is a reflected spot of light from a mirror carried by the deflected magnet. In this way Bose obtained a range of magnification from one to a hundred million times.

Our mind cannot grasp magnification so stupendous. We can, however, obtain some concrete idea of it by finding what the

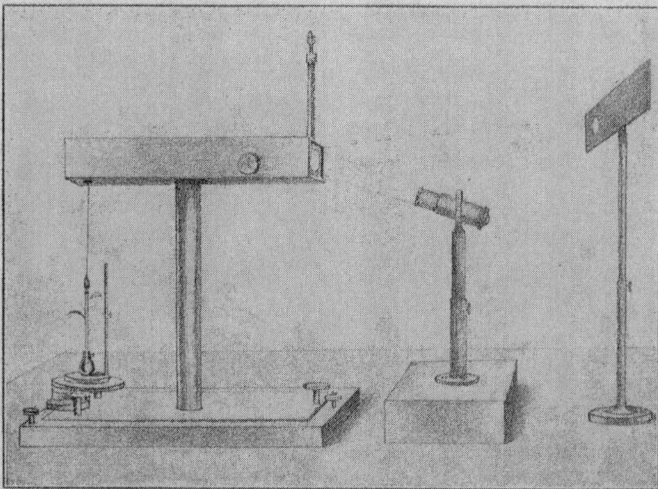

FIG. 18.—The Magnetic Crescograph for magnifying imperceptible growth of plants ten million times.

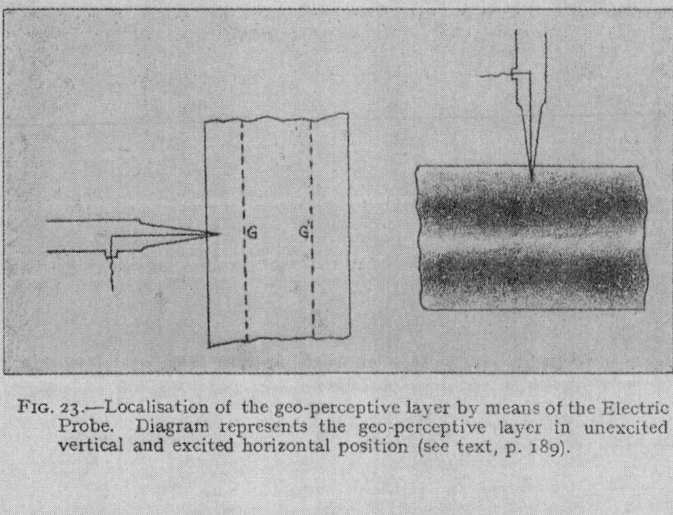

FIG. 23.—Localisation of the geo-perceptive layer by means of the Electric Probe. Diagram represents the geo-perceptive layer in unexcited vertical and excited horizontal position (see text, p. 189).

speed of the proverbial snail becomes when magnified ten million times by the Magnetic Crescograph. For this enhanced speed there is no parallel even in modern gunnery. The fifteen-inch cannon of the *Queen Elizabeth* throws out a shell with a muzzle velocity of 2360 feet per second or about 8 million feet per hour; but the Crescographic snail would move at a speed of 200 million feet per hour or 24 times faster than the cannon shot. Let us turn to cosmic movements for a closer parallel. A point on the equator whirls round at the rate of 1037 miles per hour. But the Crescographic snail may well look down on the sluggish earth; for, by the time the earth makes one revolution, the snail would have gone round nearly forty times!

Bose has been using his Magnetic Crescograph for demonstration purpose before large audiences. The movement of the spot of light indicating magnified growth is seen to rush across the screen. A stop-cock is turned on, admitting cooled water into the vessel containing the plant. The movement of the spot slows down and ultimately comes to a stop: the growth activity is now held in a state of arrest, a thermometer indicating the exact temperature-minimum. The plant-chamber becomes gradually warmed, and with the removal of lethargy the growth-movement is renewed, gathering increasing speed. Another stop-cock turns on a depressing agent, and the growth becomes paralysed; but a dose of a stimulant instantly removes the depression. The life of the plant becomes subservient to the will of the experimenter; he can exalt or depress its activity; he may thus bring it near the point of death by application of poison, and when the plant is hovering in an unstable poise between life and death resuscitate it by the timely application of an antidote. It all looks like magic! But are not the achievements of science more wonderful than magic?

'It is by the extension of man's power beyond his sense-limitations that he is enabled to probe into the deeper mysteries of nature.'

The enthusiasm aroused during Bose's recent scientific visit to England (1919–20) is not a little due to the extraordinary advance in investigation rendered possible by his Crescograph. No experimental conditions for exhibition of growth could have been more difficult than in the depth of an English winter, when the plants were in a state of hibernation. In spite of this they were made to shake off their stupor, and the rate of growth was exhibited by the indicating spot of light rushing across a 10-foot scale in the course of some twelve seconds, the actual rate being less than a hundred thousandth part of an inch per second.

Bose's magnifying methods, which far surpass the powers of the ultra-microscope, are now calling him back to employ them for the continuation of his physical researches, which have been interrupted for nearly twenty years. He foresees the possibility of making a new Micro-Radiometer, also a galvanometer of surpassing sensitiveness, and other finer detectors for the exploration of the effect of forces on inorganic matter. Though he is opposed to the classifying barriers used to divide the branches of knowledge, yet he is true to his old love. He is still a physicist without its implied limitations, trying to include in its imperial domain the realm of the living, and to use the subtler skill he has learned from its exploration to reveal activities which seem only to be veiled by the apparent inertness of matter.

CHAPTER XII

VARIOUS MOVEMENTS IN PLANTS

As a teacher of botany for nearly forty spring and summer seasons, and from the first interested in certain plant-movements, and also in trying to teach the elements of vegetable physiology in practical classes, the writer has had some experience of the intricacies and obscurities of the subject. From Sachs, the great teacher of vegetable physiology in our young days, he received inadequate light; and though Darwin's 'Movements of Plants' (1889) seemed helpful, and his discovery of 'circumnutation' —for him a common property of shoots and leaves, and even of roots, from which more specific movements might be viewed as evolutionary specialisations under definite influences—was highly attractive, yet this theory did not fully carry conviction. For such records of circumnutation might be but complex resultants of the plant's responses to many changing conditions. But how to analyse these? Experiments and observations have of course increased, and also attempts to co-ordinate and interpret them; witness the portly third volume of Pfeffer's great 'Vegetable Physiology,' which is very largely thus occupied, but still without bringing to the subject the needful simplicity and generalisation. We now see a twofold reason for this failure of vegetable physiology hitherto. First because the vegetable physiologists, despite many and praiseworthy endeavours, but with their imperfect instrumentation and correspondingly slow and little magnified records, could not fully succeed in the needful analysis of the different environmental factors and their resultant responses. But, as we have seen above, the experimental resources of instrumentation and record have now been raised to an entirely new level through Bose's labour. And secondly, because of the inadequate recognition of organic control in the plant, fully analogous to that presented by animal life—in fact what we have always recognised in the animal as essentially associated with nerve action.

The reader may here fairly ask, What clearer interpretation of plant-movements—not only of the motile organs of Mimosa and its like, but of other movements associated with growth—is now being obtained through these advances? A fully adequate answer to the question will be found in Bose's recent volumes on 'Life Movements in Plants'; here we must endeavour to give such an outline of main results as may be possible within the present narrow limits, alike of space and of avoidance of technicalities. So instead of following the order of existing treatises, or even of Bose's own discoveries, which have been partly determined by circumstances, let us start with such movements of plant responses as seem simplest and most undifferentiated, and thence proceed to the subtler and more evolved.

To realise concretely something of the problem of vegetable physiology in general and of plant-movement in particular, let the reader imagine himself accompanying a botanist among his students in the garden some day when he is pointing out to them many of the phenomena of plant-movement with which they have broadly to acquaint themselves in living nature before proceeding to their experimental studies.

Here, then, are seedlings in abundance, alike in cultivation and as springing weeds. Some are growing erect in ordinary light; others in shaded corners are bending their stems to the light, and exposing their cotyledons and young leaves accordingly. This may lead us to notice the way in which the leaves of many plants expose their upper surfaces as fully as may be to the light, partly, as we may see, in terms of their spiral origin upon the stem, though with definite individual and collective adjustments, and of various kinds. Thus a rosette-plant, like Dandelion, may have its leaves all practically on the ground-level; but where there is some little stem, the lower leaves may have longer stalks, so as not to be shaded by those above. In most herbs and shrubs, when we look at their leafage from the mid-day sun's point of view, we may often admire the co-adjustment by which leaves avoid shading each other, fitting themselves into a pattern, often recalling those of wall-papers, or stuffs adorned with decorative plant-designs. For this there is manifestly some adjustment: some movement has taken place to turn this and that leaf into a better position for light than that of their simple and regular development upon the stem. This further adaptation is effected through the varying growth and movement, not only adjusting the level of the leaf, but also, it may be, twisting it; and we seek to note how this is done. It is often effected by the more or less enlarged and swollen-looking, because turgid, leaf-base, the 'pulvinus,' which is conspicuous in many plants, and highly sensitive in Mimosa.

There are many other adaptations for that quest of light on which the whole green world depends, and to utilise which is the essential photo-synthetic activity of the leaf, on which all animal life also depends, directly or indirectly. Here, for instance, is the great practical value of the stem and copious branches of tall herbs and shrubs, and above all of trees; for by the help of these they more and more increase their available leaf area for light exposure, so that a single tree of moderate magnitude is enabled by the vast collective surface of its leaves to absorb a very large amount of light.

The light-quest of the plant-world appears in yet more striking ways, so that each organ may find its place in the sun. And there are many means besides that of individual strengthening of stem to attain stature. Weak stems, like those of roses on the lower levels, or of lofty climbers, may scramble up by help of hooking prickles upon the solid stem-plants, and so get the better of them. Others again climb in gentler though not less efficient ways, like many tendril-bearers, e.g. peas and vines. Yet others swing their slender growing shoots, and so become twiners, like the convolvulus, the hop, and many more among herbs. Many have shrubby, tough and rope-like stems like clematises, or even attain the fullest loftiness, like the lianas, which often grow to almost tree-like stems, twisted constrictor-fashion round their victims. Some again can climb on rocks and walls, like Ivy with its adhesive stem-roots, or like Ampelopsis with its tendrils cementing their tips to their supports.

Yet even of life-sustaining light, plants may have more than they can bear, especially when water, their other necessity, is scanty. Hence we note plants which turn their edges to the light, like many peas to some extent, and some eucalyptuses much more; and others yet more completely, like the famous Compass-plant of America. And though the palms and bananas bear their immense leaves in full sunshine, even these are not without some moderative adaptations; while many plants have reduced the ordinary size of leafage of their family, sometimes even to the leaf-stalks, or to the stipules, parts which every one may have noticed at the base of the rose-leaf. Thus the acacias of desert regions, as notably in great tracts in inland Australia, may lose the beautiful bipinnate leaves so characteristic of their genus, sometimes indeed only producing one or two in the seedling, and henceforward have but leaf-stalks, flattened out in somewhat leaf-like fashion, yet now vertically instead of horizontally so as to catch less light, and also of tough and leathery character, so as to reduce the transpiration of water. Extreme cases are found in the Cactus and the Euphorbia families; for here the leaves may vanish early, or even be represented by mere prickles or hairs, leaving the swollen stem, which now remains green, to do such slow and limited vegetation as it can in their place—whence sometimes its flattening as in the prickly pears, or its ridging in yet more reduced forms.

Many other forms attract us ; for the plant in its evolution is like Proteus in his changing dance through the world and throughout life, and with the same extreme and dramatic contrasts. Leaving the cactus forms standing immobile like pillars, or lying like stones upon their rocks (sometimes only distinguishable from rocks by the scrutiny needed for mimetic form), we turn to moister situations. Here we may even find a variety of plants increasingly sensitive, up to the Mimosa itself, for which Bose's long years of research serve to express, and to deepen, the age-long wonder of the children of every age since man was intelligent at all. Less conspicuous sensitives there are, which—suggestively to evolutionists—lead back to the common and passive forms (yet these as Bose has shown merely passive-looking) ; while conversely we also find that further marvel of the Telegraph-plant (Desmodium), which to Bengal children seems to move to the clapping of their hands. It moves child-like, but in its own way: with its restless signal-like leaflets rising and falling by day and night alike, while health endures, and throughout the season. From utmost apparent passivity, then, we find activity more tireless than any animal's, and seeming no less determined from within.

So we might go on ; but questions meantime have been arising among the students—assuming them to be students, and not merely those parrots of the cram-book cage, into which evil enchanters, of Eastern traditions and Western convention alike, have so largely transformed them. The botanist guide is asked at every turn—How is this ? And how is that ? How did the seedling shoot grow up, and how does the root go down ? And how of this upset one, trying, and successfully, to right itself anew ? The book answer of the crammed parrot is too much like that one for which Molière's invaluable satire on would-be medical and scientific education two centuries and a half ago is still needed. 'Why does opium make one sleep?' 'Because it has a dormitive virtue,' replies the candidate, and passes with 'honours' accordingly. So the earthward root has 'geotropism,' an earthward property. And why does the shoot ascend in the very opposite direction?—By 'negative geotropism'—surely the very poorest term in science for this loftiest adventure of life upon the globe. And why does the branch of the leaf stand out laterally? —By 'dia-geotropism'!

Again, how do leaves turn to light?—In virtue of their 'heliotropism' or 'phototropism.' Yet why sometimes also turn from the light?—By 'negative phototropism.' And so on. This facile verbalism gives us 'hydrotropism' for the root's water-quest, and 'rheotropism when roots in water are observed to bend against the stream; 'chemotropism' for its utilisation of salts, and so on. The tendril's touch is its 'thigmotropism'; and there are yet more uncouth names.

Intellectual activities have their verbalisms, their confusions and misdirections, as well as emotional ones; and these may also accumulate into what are practically diseases. Every science of course needs its technical terminology—as definite, precise and full as need be; but all have suffered from verbosity of nomenclature, and notoriously botany most of all. Thus—apart from the systematic names for each and every species and order which are of course indispensable—there are some fifteen or twenty thousand technical terms in the botanical dictionaries, of which the majority have lapsed; but too many still survive, even in modern text-books, to the perplexity of the student; too many even of these are given him by his professor in lectures, and still he uses too many himself, though fewest of all. It is of real advantage for the advance of our science, as well as of necessity for its most general understanding, to reduce this nomenclature to its necessary technical and logical minimum, without impairing sufficiency.

There are so many cases and kinds of plant-movements that terms have gone on multiplying far faster than the understanding of them. True, despite all this superficial nomenclature, and by the very authors of it, there have been many experimental endeavours to elucidate and interpret the real causes underlying these phenomena, i.e. to observe and measure the effects of various stimuli, as of light and others. Yet the terminology employed is not only redundant, but often wrong. And though Pfeffer summarises the literature of the subject up to the coming of Bose, and often with research and interpretation of his own, and uses these terms with moderation, since after all they do help to group the obvious phenomena, he so far sees their limitations. For the terms employed give no explanation of the phenomena they are used to connote.

'When we say that an organ curves towards a source of illumination because of its heliotropic irritability, we are simply stating an ascertained fact in a conveniently abbreviated form without explaining why such curvature is possible, or how it is produced.'[1]

The weakness of the situation is recognised by Pfeffer's clear-headed translator, Professor Alfred Ewart, who also protests against this excess of names, and with the needed general criticism: 'Error lies in supposing that a dissimilar response necessarily indicates a totally distinct form of irritability, and hence needs a new term, or that phenomena are made simpler or easier to understand by giving them a classical terminology.'

Great uncertainty thus prevails as regards the explanation of various movements of plants. Hence the need for Bose's thoroughgoing reinvestigation of the phenomena; and these now taken in relation with the sensitiveness to

[1] H. Pfeffer, *Vegetable Physiology* (Clarendon Press), 1903, ii. 74.

all forms of stimuli and the resulting response, which he has demonstrated in the growth and life of ordinary plants. Hence, too, the need of comparative study of all those vegetable responses, not only in relation to each other but in comparison with the response of inorganic matter on the one hand, and of animal muscle and nerve on the other. But the study of such nervous phenomena, in higher animals and in man, have long been under inquiry by the psycho-physiologist or physiological psychologist; and if their organic substratum, their physiological processes, be now demonstrated in the vegetable world, the study of some of their elemental psychological bearings can hardly but be of comparative and evolutionary suggestiveness also. In this way Bose is widening out our range of inquiry far beyond the initial outlooks of our gardens; or rather, let us say, those outlooks are deepening, and beyond all previous anticipation.

After this garden ramble, which might of course have been extended to notice many other examples of plant-movements, we start Bose (as it is happily easy to do, for no man can be fuller of his subject, or more willing to explain it) to give us a fresh outline of his discoveries and their interpretations. He cannot begin better than with his long-loved Mimosa; and in this he first sets us clearly to observe the form and movements. We note the long leaf-stalk or petiole rising from the distinct and swollen leaf-base or 'pulvinus,' which we soon find to be the main sensitive organ, and especially its lower surface; we also see it to be the pivot from which the leaf falls. Next, at the far end of the leaf-stalk, we note the four secondary petioles, which answer to the two basal pairs of pinnæ in a compound Acacia leaf. As in this, they bear on each side a row of small leaflets, the pinnules, of which each has its base distinctly swollen, as a 'pulvinule.' But the leaflets show up-movement, whether independently excited, or when the main leaf falls. The main sensibility of their pulvinules is thus found to be more on their upper surface, the very opposite from that of the main pulvinus. Besides these two movements in opposite planes, down and up respectively, we see that the midway pulvini, those of the four main leaf divisions, behave differently again; for though they may fall a little, their main movements bring all four almost close together from their normal divergent position, so their sensibility must obviously be in each case on their sides, and in right and left pairs. A wonderful leaf-mechanism, with its tri-dimensional contrast; yet after all in analogy with that of our own build.

The leaf thus visualised, and its sensitive working practised on, till we can in various ways not only make a whole leaf fall, and thence all the rest, but also stir a single leaflet, and so compel the fall of the whole leaf, and even thence of other leaves through the plant. We thus prove conductivity of impulse in each direction. We are now ready for finer observation, experiment and interpretation. First the older explanation, still surviving in text-books; Pfeffer had offered a hydro-mechanical theory of transmission of stimulus, and Haberlandt—the very best of microscopic analysts of plant-tissues, since most devoted to applying his observations towards the interpretation of their uses and functionings in detail—had offered, and with fairly general acceptance by physiologists, a too simple explanation of the fall of the Mimosa leaf. He compared its pulvinus to an indiarubber tube filled with water and tied in at both ends—so having a definite hydrostatic pressure of turgescence, and which, when a pinch is given at one end, of course exhibiting an increase of pressure, and even a certain flow, which are transmitted along the tube as an undulatory wave.

It is here worth noting clearly that in this contrast of interpretations of transmission of stimulus—(1) as essentially hydro-mechanical, for most vegetable physiologists hitherto, but (2) as fundamentally 'excitatory' for Bose—that it is our physicist who has here taken up the essential physiological point of view, and the physiologists who had so far lost it. For they were thinking but anatomically that, since their sections had not revealed any striking nervous tissue like that of animals, nothing nervous could be there: whereas, had they held to their own fundamental experience and conception of the physiology of living protoplasm—that it presents respiration, though without gills; digestion, though without stomach; and movement, though without muscles—they would have realised the possibility of conduction of excitation without a highly developed nervous system. Moreover, intercellular continuity between vegetable cells has now long been known to microscopists; and this not only in many cellular tissues, but more distinctly in and throughout certain elements of fibro-vascular bundles, in which there is more or less protoplasmic continuity, which is essential for conduction of excitation, and to these it was not unreasonable to suspect conducting powers. Just as Lavoisier at once grasped the universality of the principle of the respiration process in living beings, and boldly correlated this with the process of oxidation, from slow rusting to active combustion, on the inorganic plane, so Bose, with similar range of comparison, has made and verified the analogous step with regard to irritability in the plant and transmission of excitation to a distance, thus extending our conceptions of the highly evolved muscle and nerve of animals to the simpler, yet fully similar contractile cells and conducting tissues in plants.

Bose's researches on conduction of excitation in plants have now received full acceptance, and his conclusions are published in the 'Philosophical Transactions' of the Royal Society.[1] In this paper Bose was able to show that the transmission is not hydro-mechanical, as has been previously supposed, for the impulse was shown to be initiated in the complete absence of any mechanical disturbance. All the

[1] 'On an Automatic Method for the Investigation of Velocity of Transmission of Excitation in *Mimosa*,' *Philosophical Transactions*, vol. 204.

characteristics of the nervous impulse in the animal were shown to be present in the corresponding impulse in the plant; thus rise of temperature accelerated the velocity in both, lowering of temperature causing a retardation or arrest. Anæsthetics and poisons arrested the impulse in an identical manner.

The crucial test of a new theory is in its power of predicting phenomena hitherto unknown, and Bose's prediction of certain unexpected characteristics of impulse in animal nerve has recently been verified. Bose discovered that the nervous impulse in plant is of a dual character, a positive followed by a negative. The positive gives rise to expansion and erectile movement of the motile leaf; the negative on the other hand gives rise to contraction and down movement of the leaf. Certain investigations now being carried out by Bose seem to indicate that the nervous impulse in the animal may also exhibit a dual character. Of still higher importance is the possibility of control of nervous impulse, for which Bose obtained his clue from investigations carried out with plants. He was thus able to confer on the nerve two opposite 'molecular dispositions' at will. Under one disposition the nervous impulse was greatly enhanced during transit, and under the opposite disposition it was retarded or became arrested. We shall, in a subsequent chapter, dwell on the high significance of these results.

CHAPTER XIII

THE RESPONSE OF PLANTS TO WIRELESS STIMULATION

THE distinction that used to be drawn between plants and animals, that the former did not possess any conducting tissue analogous to the nerve of the animal, has been by Bose's work proved to be groundless. It was nevertheless urged that the sensibility of plants was comparatively of a very low order. Bose undertook to show that this was by no means the case. The most sensitive organ for the perception of electric current is the tip of the human tongue, and a European can detect by his tongue a current as feeble as 6 micro-amperes, a micro-ampere being the millionth part of a unit of electric current. Bose's pupils, however, possessed a higher sensibility, inasmuch as some of them could detect a current which was only 4·5 micro-amperes. This highly sensitive tongue was then matched against the sensitive leaflet of the plant Biophytum. A very feeble current which could be gradually increased was passed through the tongue and the leaflet, and when it reached the intensity of 1·5 micro-ampere the leaflet wagged in response, while the overrated tongue had nothing to tell as regards its perception of the current, which had to be increased threefold before it was perceived. Thus by this test the plant was three times more sensitive than the Hindu and four times more so than the European!

A record has already been given in a previous chapter (Fig. 15), which shows that the plant becomes depressed by a slight diminution of daylight, which is hardly noticed by a human observer.

Bose also found that the growth of plants was affected by changes in the environment which were below the limit of human perception. For this new range of investigation he had to turn his attention to a new type of apparatus, the sensitiveness of which had to surpass those which he had already invented. The High Magnification and the Magnetic Crescograph enabled him to measure the most minute rate of growth. For the detection of the effect of impact of external stimulus, he had first to measure the normal rate, and afterwards the changed rate induced by the stimulus. The effect of stimulus, whether stimulating or depressing, could be found from calculation of the difference in the two cases. He now wished to eliminate the necessity for calculation and the consequent loss of time. The idea that now possessed him was to devise a new method which would *instantly* show by the up or down movement of an indicator- the accelerating or retarding effect of the agent on growth.

The desideratum was to compensate the up-movement of growth by some regulating device; this involved the problem of making the plant descend at the exact rate at which the growing tip of the plant was rising, whatever that rate may be. Some such regulator has to be introduced as in the compensating movement of an astronomical telescope, by which the effect of earth's movement round her axis once in twenty-four hours is neutralised. But the problem that confronted Bose was far more difficult, for instead of compensating a definite rate he had to obtain adjustment for widely varying rates of growth in different plants, and even of the same plant under different conditions.

The difficult problem was successfully solved in his Balanced Crescograph (Fig. 19). A train of revolving clock-wheels, actuated by the fall of a weight, lowers the plant exactly at the same rate at which it is growing. The exact adjustment is obtained by the gradual turning of a screw to the right or to the left, by which the rate of compensating fall is retarded or accelerated. In this way the rate of growth becomes exactly compensated, and the recorder now dots a horizontal line instead of the former curve of ascent. The turning of the adjusting screw of the Balanced

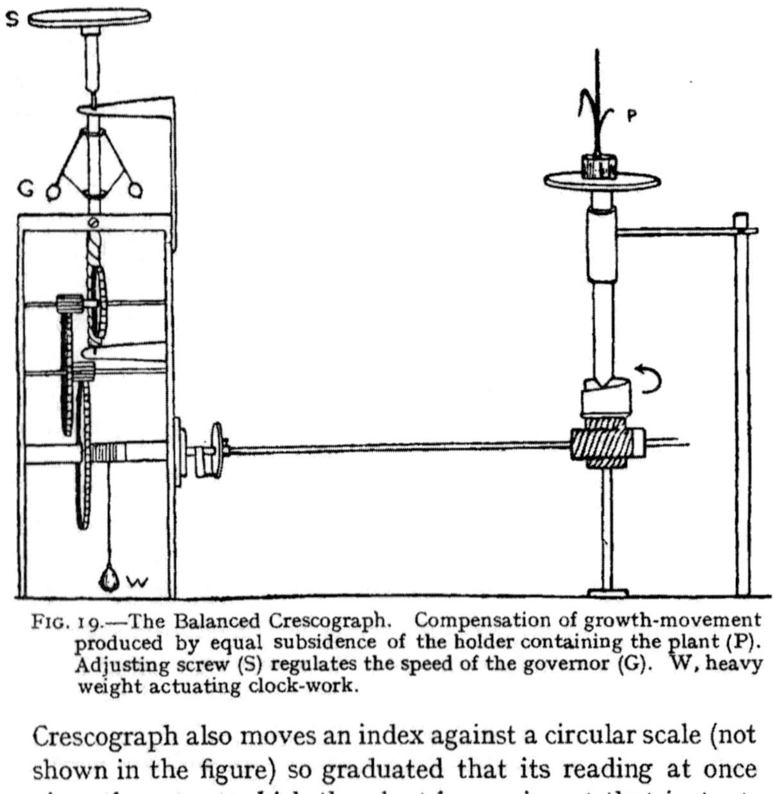

FIG. 19.—The Balanced Crescograph. Compensation of growth-movement produced by equal subsidence of the holder containing the plant (P). Adjusting screw (S) regulates the speed of the governor (G). W, heavy weight actuating clock-work.

Crescograph also moves an index against a circular scale (not shown in the figure) so graduated that its reading at once gives the rate at which the plant is growing at that instant. When balanced, the recording apparatus is extraordinarily sensitive. Any change, however slight, in the environment is at once indicated by the upset of the balance with up or down movement of the curve. This method is so extremely sensitive that Bose has been able to detect variation of rate of growth so excessively minute as $\frac{1}{1500}$ millionth of an inch per second.

As an illustration of the delicacy of this method, a record is given of the effect of carbonic acid gas on growth (Fig. 20). A jar is filled with this gas, and emptied over the plant ; the invisible gas, on account of its heavier weight, falls in a stream and surrounds the plant. The

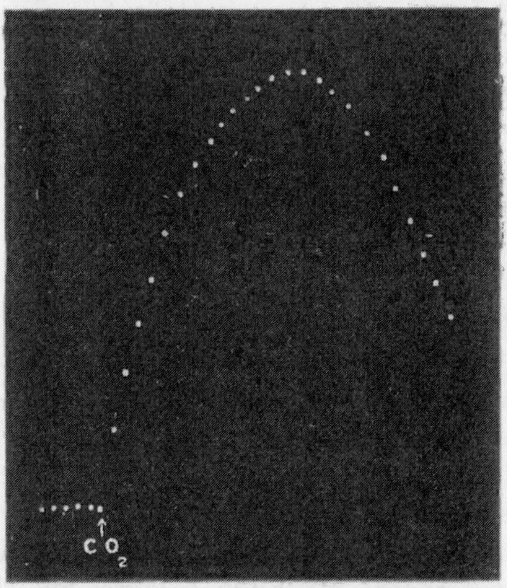

FIG. 20.—Record showing the effect of carbonic acid gas on growth. Horizontal line at the beginning indicates balanced growth. Application of carbonic acid gas induces enhancement of growth, shown here by up-curve, followed by depression, exhibited by down-curve. Successive dots at intervals of ten seconds.

record shows that this gave rise to an immediate acceleration of growth, and this continued for two and a half minutes ; this preliminary acceleration was followed by retardation of growth as shown by the down curve. With diluted carbonic acid, the acceleration may persist for an hour or more. Thus the Balanced Crescograph not only shows us the beneficial effect of an agent, but also tells us the dose which prolongs the beneficial effect.

Plants are regarded as extremely sluggish : and it is

thought that they are unable to perceive a stimulus unless applied for a considerable length of time. Thus for the perception of geotropic stimulus it is supposed that 'even in rapidly reacting organs there is always an interval of about one to one and a half hours, before the horizontally placed organ shows a noticeable curvature, and this latent period may in other cases be extended to several hours (Jost).' Bose finds that the latent period of geotropic perception is often as short as a second.

As regards perception of light, it has been supposed that the period of effective exposure must at least be of seven minutes' duration. With his extraordinarily sensitive apparatus Bose investigated the question of the plant's capability to respond to stimulus of light of excessively short duration. We can hardly conceive of anything so fleeting as a single flash of lightning. Bose now subjected a growing plant, balanced in his Crescograph, to an artificial flash of lightning—that is to say, to the light emitted by a single electric spark between two metallic balls. The plant perceived this light of incredibly short duration, as was manifest from the upset of the balance, and the resulting automatic script made by the plant.

So much as regards the perception of plants to minimum duration of stimulus. The next question is as regards their range of perception, and Bose's astonishing discovery of the response of plants to wireless stimulation has caused something like a sensation among the scientific public. The account of this discovery is best told in Bose's own words taken from the second volume of the 'Transactions' of his Institute, and from his letter in *Nature*:

A growing plant bends towards light; this is true, not only of the main stem, but also of its branches and attached leaves and leaflets. This movement in response is described as the tropic effect of light. Growth itself is modified by the action of light: two different effects depending on the intensity are produced; strong stimulus of light causes a diminution of rate of growth, but very feeble stimulus induces an acceleration of growth. The tropic effect is very strong in the ultra-violet region of the spectrum with its extremely short wave-length of light; but the effect declines practically to zero as we move towards the less refrangible rays, the yellow and the red, with their comparatively long wave-length. As we proceed further in the infra-red region we come across the vast range of electric radiation, the wave-lengths of which vary from the shortest wave I have been able to produce (0·6 cm.) to others which may be miles in length. There thus arises the very interesting question whether plants perceive and respond to the long æther-waves, including those employed in signalling through space.

At first sight this would appear to be very unlikely, for the most effective rays are in the ultra-violet region with wave-length as short as 20×10^{-6} cm.; but with electric waves used in wireless signalling we have to deal with waves 50,000,000 times as long. The perceptive power of our retina is confined within the very narrow range of a single octave, the wave-lengths of which lie between 70×10^{-6} cm. and 35×10^{-6} cm. It is difficult to imagine that plants could perceive radiations so widely separated from each other as the visible light and the invisible electric waves.

But the subject assumes a different aspect when we take into consideration the total effect of radiation on the plant. Light induces two different effects which may broadly be distinguished as external and internal. The former is visible as movement; the latter finds no outward manifestation, but consists of an 'up' or assimilatory chemical change with concomitant increase of potential energy. Of the two reactions, then, one is dynamic, attended by dissimilatory 'down' change; the other is potential, associated with the opposite 'up' change. In reality, the two effects take place simultaneously; but one of them becomes predominant under definite conditions.

The modifying condition is the *quality* of light. With reference to this I quote the following from Pfeffer: 'So far as is at present known, the action of different rays of the spectrum gives similar curves in regard to heliotropic and phototactic movements, to protoplasmic streaming and movements of the chloroplastids, as well as the photonastic movements produced by growth or by changes of turgor. On the other hand, it is the less refrangible rays which are most active in photosynthesis.' The dynamic and potential manifestations are thus seen to be complementary to each other, the rays which induce photosynthesis being relatively ineffective for tropic reaction, and *vice versa*.

Returning to the action of electric waves, since they exert no photosynthetic action they might conceivably induce the complementary tropic effect. These considerations led me to the investigation of the subject fourteen years ago, and my results showed that very short electric waves induce a retardation of rate of growth; they also produce responsive movements of the leaf of Mimosa when the plant is in a highly sensitive condition. The energy of the short electric waves is very feeble, and undergoes great diminution at a distance; hence the necessity for employment of a plant in a highly sensitive condition.

I resumed my investigations on the subject at the beginning of this year. I wished to find out whether plants in general perceived and responded to long æther-waves reaching them from a distance. The perception of the wireless stimulation was to be tested, not merely by the responsive movement of sensitive plants, but also by diverse modes of response given by all kinds of plants.

The Wireless System.—For sending wireless signals I had to improvise the following arrangement, more powerful means not being available. The secondary terminals of a moderate-sized Ruhmkorff's coil were connected with two cylinders of brass, each 20 cm. in length; the sparking took place between two small spheres of steel attached to the cylinders. One of the two cylinders was earthed and the other connected with the aerial 10 metres in height. The receiving aerial was also 10 metres in height, and its lower terminal led to the laboratory, and connected by means of a thin wire with the experimental plant growing in a pot; this latter was put in electric connection with the earth. The distance between the transmitting and receiving aerial was about 200 metres, the maximum length permitted by the grounds of the Institute.

I may state here that with the arrangement described above I obtained very definite mechanical and electric response to wireless impulse. For the former I employed the plant Mimosa; the latter effect was detected in all plants, sensitive and ordinary.

Effect of Wireless Stimulation on Growth.—For the detection of variation of growth it was necessary to devise the extremely sensitive Balanced Crescograph. In this apparatus a compensating movement is given to the plant-holder by which the plant subsides exactly at the same rate as its growth-elongation, so that the tip of the plant remains at the same point. This perfect balance is attained by a variable regulator. The compound magnifying lever attached to the plant records the movement of growth. Under exact balance the record is horizontal. Any induced acceleration of growth upsets the balance and, with the particular arrangement of the apparatus, causes a resulting

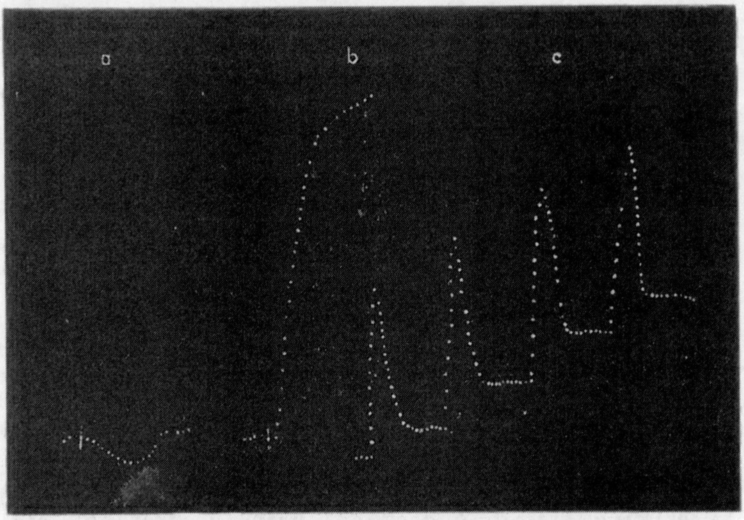

FIG. 21.—Record of responses of plant to wireless stimulation. (*a*) Response to feeble stimulus by acceleration of growth; (*b*) response to strong stimulus by retardation of growth; (*c*) response to medium stimulation—retardation followed by recovery. Down-curve represents acceleration, and up-curve retardation of growth (seedling of wheat).

down record; induced retardation, on the other hand, brings about an upset in the opposite direction and an up curve. The results given above (Fig. 21) show that growing plants not only perceive, but also respond to the stimulus of electric waves. These effects were found in all growing plants. The records were obtained with the seedling of wheat.

Effect of Feeble Stimulus.—I first studied the effect of feeble stimulus. This was secured by decreasing the energy of sparks of the radiator. The response was an acceleration of rate of growth as seen in Fig. 21 (*a*). This is analogous to the accelerating effect of light stimulation of subminimal intensity.

Effect of Strong Stimulus.—The maximum energy radiated by my transmitter, as stated before, was only moderate. In spite of this, its effect on plants was exhibited in a very striking manner. The balance was immediately upset, indicating a retardation of the rate of growth (Fig. 21, *b*). The latent period, i.e. the interval between the incident wave and the response, was only a few seconds. The record given in the figure was obtained with the moderate magnification of 2000 times only; but with my Magnetic Crescograph the magnification can easily be raised ten million times, and the response of plant to the space-signalling can be exalted in the same proportion.

Under an intensity of stimulus slightly above the subminimal, the response exhibits retardation of growth followed by quick recovery, as seen in the series of records given in Fig. 21 (*c*). The perceptive range of the plant is inconceivably greater than ours; it not only perceives, but also responds to the different rays of the vast æthereal spectrum.

These revelations are as unexpected as they are startling. They show that the pretension of man and animals for undisputed superiority over their hitherto despised 'vegetative brethren' does not bear the test of close inspection.

CHAPTER XIV

TROPISMS

We have now to refer to the various tropic movements of plants in response to the multifarious stimuli of their environment; the stimulus may be (1) of touch, in consequence of which tendrils twine round their support; (2) of the action of light, under which the plant-organs move sometimes towards, and at other times away from, light; (3) of the action of gravity, which causes opposite movements in the shoot and the root, the shoot moving upwards and the root downwards. There are also numerous other complicated movements associated with the recurrence of day and night. The intricacies and apparent contradictions of the responsive movements are so baffling that no consistent explanation appeared possible. This led to the supposition that a particular movement was due to some unknown specific sensitiveness; organs possessed of positive sensitiveness moved towards the stimulus, while others characterised by negative sensitiveness moved away from it. Such use of merely descriptive phrases is, however, no real explanation of the phenomena. The idea of specific sensibility is, moreover, quite untenable when we find cases where, under continued stimulation, an organ moves at first towards the stimulus and afterwards away from it. An identical organ cannot evidently be possessed of both the positive and the negative sensibility.

Bose pursued for many years the quest of discovering some fundamental reaction which was at the basis of phenomena so extremely diverse. What, then, is the characteristic reaction in response to stimulus, and what are the agents which cause stimulation? The term 'stimulus' has been used, in vegetable physiology, in a vague and indefinite sense, giving rise to much confusion. Thus light and warmth have both been regarded as stimuli; but Bose was able to show that they bring about physiological effects which are diametrically opposite to each other. He carried out long series of experiments, the results of which enabled him to classify factors which cause stimulation. He showed that, generally speaking, agents which cause a contractile twitch in animal muscle also bring about the contraction of plant-tissue. The following modes of stimulation are thus found effective in causing excitation of vegetable tissues:—(*a*) Mechanical (contact or friction, prick or wound); (*b*) radiation (the entire æthereal spectrum including visible light, radiant heat and electric waves); (*c*) electrical (make or break of a current, induction shock and condenser discharge); certain chemical agents also act as stimuli. The first great generalisation established by Bose is that *the direct application of all forms of stimuli, mechanical, electrical or radiant, cause similar physiological response of contraction.*

He next shows that the excitation caused by stimulus may remain localised or transmitted to a distance according to the conducting power of the particular tissue. In this respect there are numerous gradations of highly conducting, semi-conducting and non-conducting tissues. Taking the sensitive plant Mimosa as the type possessing high power of conduction and a motile pulvinus, he demonstrates the sensitiveness of the plant by all modes of stimulation and the consequent response. He shows how the sensitiveness of the under surface, eighty-fold greater than that of the upper, was measured; as also how he determined the speed of transmission of excitation from petiole onwards, usually at 30 mm. per second. This speed, while inferior to that in higher animal nerve, notably surpasses that of lower animals, like the mussel, so that we are ready to understand how he and his assistants can now dissect out a petiole-pulvinus preparation for investigations as definite and complete as those long familiar to physiologists of the nerve and muscle of a frog, and with his present apparatus carry their inquiries substantially further.[1] He shows in this connection that in Mimosa the conducting power in a transverse direction is only $\frac{1}{400}$ that in the longitudinal direction of the stem.

We may next take the case of tissues in which the power of conduction is exceedingly feeble ; the contraction caused by direct stimulus remains, in this case, localised. A very remarkable reaction is, however, produced at a distance, which is of a diametrically opposite character and distinguished as the 'Indirect' effect of stimulus. The effect of 'Direct Stimulus' applied immediately on the responding surface is a diminution of turgor, a contraction and a negative electrical variation shown by the galvanometer. The effect of 'Indirect Stimulus' is, on the other hand, an increase of turgor, an expansion and a positive electric indication. The discovery of this hitherto unsuspected effect of Indirect Stimulus is one of Bose's most far-reaching results ; for many of the apparent contradictions in the responsive movements in plants are shown to be due to this very important factor having remained so long unknown.

We may next proceed to Bose's special contributions to the understanding of plant-movements. A very important generalisation established by him is the unity of reaction in all plant-organs, growing and non-growing. Most significant of these advances towards the understanding of the movements brought about by growth, is the conception, experimentally worked out, that the growing organ and its responses are like those of Mimosa pulvinus and its responses. He records the effect of all forms of stimulus on growth, and shows that direct

[1] *Transactions of the Bose Institute*, vol. i., 1918.

stimulus checks growth or brings about an 'incipient' contraction; when the intensity of stimulus is increased, the effect culminates in an actual contraction. This is exactly parallel to the contraction in the pulvinus under direct stimulus.

He next demonstrates the effect of Indirect Stimulus (applied at some distance from the responsive region of growth). This produces an expansion and acceleration of the rate of growth. The opposite effects of Direct and Indirect Stimulus are diagrammatically shown in Fig. 22 (*a* and *b*). He thus establishes his Law of Effects of Direct and Indirect Stimulus :—

Direct Stimulus induces contraction; *Indirect Stimulus causes the opposite effect of expansion.*

The same law applies when stimulus acts on one side of the organ. When stimulus of any kind acts on the right side (Fig. 22, *c*), the directly stimulated right side contracts and the indirectly stimulated opposite, or left side expands, with the result of tropic curvature towards the stimulus. And from these fundamental reactions, experimentally demonstrated, Bose explains the diverse movements brought about by the various forces of the environment.

He thus leads us to the explanation of the movements of tendrils. Whether these be branch-like, i.e. at first uniform and radial, or from the first more or less bifacial, like the leaves, leaflets or stipules which also often develop into tendrils—in all these the same reactions to direct and to indirect stimulus appear. Hence it is that the rubbed tendril contracts towards this direct stimulus, and its coiling in this useful direction is thus not a special marvel of natural selection between alternative chances, but is of the nature of all response (though of course the selectionist may then fairly emphasise its special and useful development). From this simple beginning onwards, all tendril-behaviour may be worked out in detail.

The many cases of the lightward movement of plant-growth—of which every one must have noticed some, as of plants grown in a window—may next be understood in the main; since the light acts upon the stem and leaf-stalks

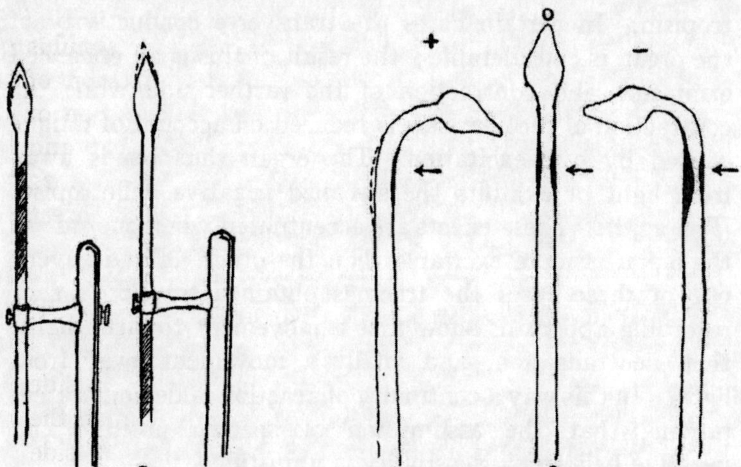

a b c d e

FIG. 22.—Effects of Direct and Indirect Stimulus.

(*a*) Stimulus applied Directly at the growing region inducing retardation of growth or contraction as represented by dotted line. Stimulated area represented in this and in following by shade.
(*b*) Stimulus applied Indirectly (at some distance from growing region) gives rise to acceleration of growth and expansion.
(*c*) Stimulus applied to right side of organ causes contraction of that side and expansion of the opposite side, thus giving rise to positive curvature towards stimulus.
(*d*) Excitation transmitted to the opposite side causes neutralisation.
(*e*) Excitation caused by intense stimulation is transmitted across and thus reverses the normal curvature to negative, i.e. away from stimulus.

just like the touch of the support upon the tendril. For in this case again the directly stimulated side is contracted and the opposite side is expanded, so bending the shoot lightwards.

When the light is very strong and long continued the over-excited plant-organs may begin to turn away: how is this effected? Bose's experiments show that the strong excitation percolates into and traverses the stems and petioles, and provokes their contraction on the further side, thus neutralising their former bending (Fig. 22, *d*). The organ now places itself at right angles to the light, and this particular reaction has been termed dia-heliotropism. In certain cases the transverse conductivity of the organ is considerable; the result of this is an enhanced excitation and contraction of the further side, while the contraction of the near side is reduced on account of fatigue caused by over-excitation. The organ thus bends away from light or exhibits the so-called negative heliotropism (Fig. 22, *e*). These effects are accentuated when one side of the organ is more excitable than the other. But in every one of these cases the tracings obtained by Bose's self-recording apparatus show first a movement towards light, then neutralisation, and finally a movement away from light. In this way a continuity of reaction is demonstrated, proving that the assumption of specific positive and negative heliotropic sensibility is unjustified.

With this comprehension of the dual effects of light-stimulus, the adjustment of leaves to receive light—and also in certain cases, as above noticed in the garden, to escape excess of it—may alike be unravelled: since we now see that the more or less sensitive surface of the pulvinus on which the leaf-adjustment usually depends may be variously affected, even to definite twistings, as when a leaf-organ is placed edgewise to the light.

So far, then, for these common phenomena we have now got a simple and uniform dynamic explanation behind the familiar utilitarian one. But every botanist knows cases of further difficulty. The common Indian cress (*Tropaeolum*) turns towards light in winter, but away from it in summer. Bose shows that the conduction of 'nervous' excitation in the plant is exalted, as in the animal, by the rise, and lowered by the fall, of temperature. The transverse conduction of excitation is thus enhanced by higher temperature in summer; the excitation in this season more easily percolates across the stem, reversing the normal positive curvature seen in winter. It will thus be seen how diurnal, seasonal and climatic factors may bring about modification in the response.

Next we pass to 'Geotropism, Positive and Negative,' the explanation of which offered difficulties almost unsurmountable. From the youngest seedling to the lofty tree, the shoot rises upwards, while the roots descend. When laid flat, or inverted, the plant begins to right itself, shoot and root turning in their respective directions. The righting of the shoot is very manifest, and on the great scale, in corn 'laid' by the rain, of which the nodes soon renew growth-activity and so raise the shoot anew. In itself, the organism is thus as definitely bi-polar in its way as is a magnet in its own. In and for this characteristic behaviour gravity is evidently the external factor, to which the organism has to adjust itself. Yet to understand what may be this functional co-adjustment of organism and environment has long been puzzling botanists. It was at first thought that the descending root might be merely sinking under its weight; but with a basin of mercury set below it, the root forces its way down against this potent resistance, which would, of course, float it were it passive. Again, how can the shoot rise tens, even hundreds, of feet against gravity? And how can the same uniform stimulus of gravity produce dual and contrary effects?

For the solution of these most difficult problems Bose undertook investigation on the following subjects :—

1. What is the mechanism of the movement of response under the stimulus of gravity?

2. Which is the particular layer of cells which perceives the stimulus and acts as the sense-organ?

3. What is the reason of the opposite signs of response in the shoot and in the root?

The research necessitated the invention of new methods of investigation of extreme delicacy and reliability; of these may be specially mentioned the Method of Geo-electric Response, and the Localisation of Geo-perceptive

Layer by means of the Electric Probe. A description of the methods and their applications will be given presently.

As regards the mechanism of the up-curving of a horizontally laid stem, it may be due either to the expansion of the lower or contraction of the upper surface; and no experimental test had been devised to decide between the two alternatives—the prevalent opinion, however, being that the movement was due to expansion. Here then is an apparent exception to Bose's demonstration that all forms of stimulus induce contraction as their direct effect, and expansion as the indirect effect.

In order to subject the question to a crucial test, Bose devised his extremely delicate electric method to find whether the upper side of the horizontally laid stem remains passive or exhibits an active state of excitation. He had in his previous work on 'Comparative Electro-physiology' demonstrated that the state of excitation in a vegetable tissue is exhibited by two simultaneous reactions—of contraction and of an electric change of negative sign. Thus the state of active excitation of any point of the tissue can be detected with the greatest certainty by means of a galvanometer. Bose connected two sides of a stem with the galvanometer, and the displacement of the stem from the vertical to the horizontal position was immediately followed by the clearest indication that the upper was the excited side. The electrical response was found to increase as the angle of inclination to the vertical was increased from zero to 90 degrees. This direct stimulus of the upper surface involves its contraction and results in the geotropic curvature of the stem upwards.

The next puzzling question is in regard to the sense-organ which enables the plant to perceive the vertical direction and move accordingly. We get our idea of direction of force of gravity by means of plumb-lines, and our own orientation in space is so far understood as dependent on the semicircular canals associated with the internal ear; and these are believed to function through the effect of gravity on their contained fluid in our varying positions, and its changing flow and pressure with our movements. In water animals, whose specific gravity is little different from that of the water they inhabit, heavy solid bodies come into service: the large 'otoliths' of the fish's ear, and the sand-grains, mingled with tactile hairs, in the lobster's. So if it be by such stimulus of solid particles, with their always vertical fall, that animals are oriented, must not the solid granules of various composition, albuminoid, starchy and other, which are found free in many vegetable cells, have a similar action on their protoplasm and practically serve as otoliths, giving the needed signal and stimulus for proper orientation? Definite layers of starch grains have been found in microscopic sections of the plant, and from anatomical considerations of their distribution the theory of statoliths has been ably advocated by Noll, Haberlandt, Němec and others.

The direct test needed for the localisation of geo-perceptive layer is, however, the physiological reaction of the *living* plant, giving unmistakable signal of its perception of geotropic stimulus as it is disturbed from its normal vertical position. Bose now worked out the highly original device of his Electric Probe, by means of which he is able to explore the interior of the plant and detect the state of excitation in its different layers. Suppose G and G^1 to be the layers of cells in a stem concerned in the perception of the stimulus of gravity, G G^1 being the longitudinal section of an annular ring (Fig. 23, p. 158). As long as the stem remains vertical, geotropic stimulation will be absent, but inclination to the vertical will cause irritation. Bose's Electric Probe consists of an exceedingly fine platinum wire, enclosed in a capillary glass tube, the probe being electrically insulated except at the extreme tip. When the probe, suitably connected with a galvanometer, is slowly thrust into the stem so that it enters one side and comes out at the other, the galvanometer will by its deflection show the state of irritation of every layer of cell throughout the organ. Holding the stem vertical, Bose sent his exploring probe step by step across the organ and found no sign of local excitation. The passage of the probe itself, it is true, causes a slight irritation, but this is reduced to a minimum by making the probe excessively fine and by making the passage of the probe very slow.

The case will be very different when the stem is displaced from the vertical to a horizontal position. The geotropically sensitive layer now perceives the stimulus and becomes the focus of irritation; the state of excitation is, as explained before, detected by negative electric response exhibited by the galvanometer, and the electric variation would be most intense at the perceptive layer itself; the excitation at the perceptive layer will irradiate into the neighbouring cells in radial directions with intensity diminishing with distance. Hence the intensity of responsive electric change will decline in both directions outwards and inwards.

The distribution of the excitatory change, initiated at this perceptive layer and irradiated in radial directions, is represented in the right hand of Fig. 23 (p. 158) by the depth of shading, the darkest shadow being on the perceptive layer itself. Had excitation been attended with change of light into shade, we should have witnessed the spectacle of a deep shadow, vanishing toward the edges, and spreading over the different layers of cells during displacement of organs from vertical to horizontal; the shadow would have disappeared on the restoration of the organ to the vertical position.

Different shades of excitation in different layers are, however, capable of discrimination by means of the insulated electric probe, as it is pushed into the organ from outside. In actual experiment the probe exhibited increasing excitatory electric change during approach to the perceptive layer, which reached its climax when the probe came in contact with that layer. When it passed beyond this point, the electric indication of excitation underwent rapid decline and abolition. The electric indication at the perceptive layer itself became abolished as soon as geotropic stimulus was removed by the restoration of the organ to the vertical position. Bose is thus able to map out the contour lines of physiological excitation inside a living organ.

After localising by means of his electric explorer the perceptive layer, Bose made section of the organ and found that the particular cells contained large-sized starch-grains, which were instrumental in causing gravi-perception by their weight.

If the fall of the heavy particles on the sensitive ectoplasmic layer of the lower side of the cells be the cause of geotropic excitation, then the geotropic response should take place after an interval necessary for the heavy particles to fall from the base to the side of the cell. This period could not exceed more than a few seconds, but the geotropic reaction, as hitherto observed, seemed to be initiated much later—after periods varying from several minutes to an hour or more. Bose, however, with his magnifying recorder, was able to detect the commencement of geotropic curvature in less than a minute; his electric method also showed the latent period not to exceed a few seconds.

In geotropic response the only anomaly that remained was in regard to the response of the root being opposite to that of the shoot. Bose showed that every cut portion of the growing region of the shoot responds to the stimulus of gravity by bending upwards. The growing region of the shoot is therefore both sensitive to stimulus and responsive to it. *Hence geotropic stimulation of the shoot is direct.* But this is not the case with the root. Here it is the tip of the root which perceives the stimulus, for Darwin showed that when the root-tip is amputated the root loses its orientation. The actual geotropic bending takes place in the growing region at some distance from the tip. The stimulus is received at the tip and transmitted to the distant responding region of growth. *Hence geotropic stimulus acts indirectly in the root.* Bose had shown that the effects of direct and indirect stimulus on growth are antithetic; it therefore follows that the responses of shoot and root to the direct and indirect stimulus must be of opposite signs.

Bose went further and carried out direct experiments on the characteristic responses of the root. He applied various forms of stimuli, first directly on the responding growing region of the root, and found that the induced curvature was towards the stimulus; he next applied the same stimuli on one side of the root-tip, and the response was by movement away from the stimulus. His generalisation that direct stimulus and indirect stimulus induce opposite responsive movements became verified even in the case of roots.

Objections had been raised about Darwin's experiment on the decapitation of roots abolishing geotropic response; it was urged that the shock of operation might of itself abolish all sensibility. In order to meet this objection Bose carried out his electric experiments on the reaction of different zones of intact root under the stimulus of gravity. When he made his electric contact at one side of the root-tip, displacement of the root from vertical to horizontal position at once gave the *negative* electric response, showing that the root-tip had become directly stimulated. Restoration of the root to the vertical position was followed by disappearance of all signs of irritation. He next applied his electric contact at the responding growing region of the root, which on displacement from a vertical to a horizontal position gave rise to *positive* electric response, which is the indication of indirect effect of stimulus. By this crucial experiment carried out on an intact plant Bose was able to establish an underlying unity even in responses which appeared to be so diametrically opposite.

CHAPTER XV

THE SLEEP OF PLANTS

DIFFERENT organs of plants are in a state of constant movement which is not immediately noticeable. But a striking change is observed in their respective positions at day and night. The explanation of this particular phenomenon of Nyctitropism has hitherto proved very baffling, as will be seen from the following summary given by Jost in his 'Physiology of Plants.'

> Many plant organs, especially foliage and floral leaves, take up towards evening positions other than those they occupy by day. Petals and perianth leaves, for example, bend outwards by day so as to open the flower, and inwards at night so as to close it. . . . Many foliage leaves also may be said to exhibit opening and closing movements, not merely when they open and close in the bud, but also when arranged in pairs on an axis they exhibit movements towards and away from each other. In other cases, speaking generally, we may employ the terms night-position and day-position for the closed and open conditions respectively. The night-position may also be described as the sleep-position. . . . A completely satisfactory theory of nyctitropic movements is not yet forthcoming. Such a theory can only be established after new and exhaustive experimental research.

Bose has recently carried out a complete investigation on the subject, the results of which are given in Vol. II of the 'Transactions of the Bose Institute.' Without entering into details, it may be said that the new advance here consists in distinguishing—for a series of simple cases chosen as typical—the various factors which are predominant, as notably the response (1) to variation of temperature, (2) to variation of light, and (3) to the variation geotropic response under daily variation of temperature. This last phenomenon, hitherto unsuspected, is the determining cause of a very large number of day and night movements. In many instances the resulting effect is due to different combinations of various factors. Light and heat may be strong or weak; moreover, radiant heat has quite the opposite effect to that of mere raising of temperature; light may give rise to after-effects, and the plant's responses may also vary from simple to more or less multiple and automatic. Thus the independent variables are many. Calculation shows the possible variety of effects to be enormous, and observation increasingly shows that nature has realised no small number of these. Bose's demonstration of the reaction in typical cases will enable the inquirer to predict the effect of combination of different factors.

His success in these investigations is due to the perfection of his newly invented apparatus by which the movement of the plant becomes automatically recorded throughout the day and night. The periodic variation of environmental conditions is also recorded at the same time by his thermograph and recording photometer. Confirmatory experiments are carried out where light is maintained constant, the plant being subjected to the daily variation of temperature; in others the temperature is maintained constant, and it is the diurnal change of light and darkness that affects the plant. The results of such protracted investigation enabled him to unravel the complexities of the daily movement of different plants. The following extract from Bose's popular lecture given at his Institute will be found interesting as regards the 'sleep' and 'waking' movements of the water-lily Nymphaea, and the investigation which led to the discovery of the cause of this movement.

The Night-Watch of Nymphaea

The poets have forestalled the men of science. Why does the water-lily *Nymphaea* keep awake all night long and close her petals during the day? Because the water-lily is the lover of the Moon, and like the human soul expanding at the touch of the Beloved, the lily opens out her heart at the touch of the moon-beam, and keeps watch all night long; she shrinks affrighted by the rude touch of the Sun, and closes her petals during the day. The outer floral leaves of the lily are green, and in the day-time the closed flowers are hardly distinguishable from the broad green leaves which float on the water. The scene is transformed in the evening as if by magic, and myriads of glistening white flowers cover the dark water. The recurrent daily phenomenon has not only been observed by the poets, but an explanation offered for it. It is the moon-light then that causes the opening of the lily, and the sun-light the movement of closure. Had the poet taken out a lantern in a dark night, he would have noticed that the lily opened its petals at night in total absence of the moon; but a poet is not expected to carry a lantern and peer out in the dark; that inordinate curiosity is characteristic only of the man of science. Again the lily does not close with the appearance of the sun; for the flower often remains awake up to eleven in the forenoon. A French dictionary maker saw Cuvier the zoologist about the definition of the crab as 'a little red fish which walks backwards.' 'Admirable!' said Cuvier. 'But the crab is not necessarily little nor is it red till boiled; it is not a fish, and it cannot walk backwards; but with these exceptions your definition is perfect.' And so also with the poet's description of the movement of the lily, which does not open to moon-light nor yet close to the sun.

Nor has the scientific explanation hitherto offered proved more satisfactory. The eminent plant-physiologist Pfeffer regarded the 'sleep and waking movements' to be due to the recurring action of light and darkness, of sunrise and sunset. The opening and closing of the water-lily has, however, little or no connection with the rising or setting of the sun; the opening could not be due to setting sun for the flower remains open in light up to about 11 o'clock in the morning; neither could it be due to the rising sun, since the flowers are already open at night. Finding that light exerted little or no effect, Bose turned his attention to the action of daily variation of temperature.

We may next enquire whether the daily variation of temperature has any effect in producing the alternate movement of opening and closing of the lily. If the curve of movement of the flower resembled the curve of variation of temperature, we should then have no hesitation in ascribing the floral movement to diurnal change of temperature. In the determination of the influence of temperature on the movement of the flower it is therefore necessary to obtain a diurnal record of the movement of the petal, and also that of the change of temperature throughout the 24 hours.

The automatic recorder should thus fulfil two different requirements. It should, in the first place, record the magnified movement of the petal, and indicate the time when such movement took place ; it should also trace the fluctuation of temperature, both the rise and fall, throughout day and night. For obtaining magnification of movement, one of the petals of the flower is attached by a fine thread to the arm of a light lever made of fine aluminium wire. The lever is supported on jewel bearings which reduce the friction to a minimum. The tip of the longer arm of the lever is bent so as to serve as a writing point. This traces the magnified record of the movement of the petal on a smoked piece of glass, which is moved by clockwork through its entire length in 24 hours. The tip of the writer rubs off the smoke where it touches, and thus leaves a white line on a dark background. The difficulty met here is that there is a considerable friction at the point of contact of the writer with the glass plate. The free movement of the flower is thus greatly hampered and the record thus becomes distorted. This difficulty is overcome by keeping the glass plate, for a greater part of the time, away from contact with the writing point. By a special contrivance of clockwork, the plate is made to approach the writing point intermittently, say once every fifteen minutes. The successive dots thus record the movement of the leaf during successive quarters of an hour during day and night.

There now remains the method of recording the diurnal variation of temperature. For this I use the simple device of a compound strip, made of the more expansible strip of brass, soldered to the less expansible strip of steel.

When temperature rises, the brass expands more than the steel; hence the compound strip undergoes a curvature, the brass surface becoming convex. The free end of the strip is attached to a second magnifying lever which thus records the variation of temperature.

The curves of daily variation of temperature, and the movement of the petals, show an astonishing resemblance to each other. There can therefore be no doubt that the cause of the opening and closing of the flower is the diurnal change of temperature. The flower is in a position of 'sleep' during the day; a rapid fall of temperature occurs from 6 P.M. and the petals begin to open at first slowly, then very rapidly. The flower becomes completely open and fully expanded by 10 P.M. at night. Though the temperature continues to fall, there is no further possibility of expansion beyond the maximum. At about 6 A.M. the temperature begins to rise, and the reverse movement of closure sets in. The flower continues to close very rapidly till the closure or 'sleep' movement becomes complete before 11 A.M.

It is thus seen that the closure of the flower is brought about by a rise of temperature, the opening being due to a fall of temperature. Both sides of the petals are in a state of growth, but the outer side is the more sensitive to changes of temperature. Thus it happens that during rise of temperature the growth of the outer side is relatively fast; during cooling it becomes relatively slow. The two opposite reactions give rise to two different curvatures, namely of closure during rise, and of opening during fall of temperature. Other flowers are known, e.g. the Tulip, where the inner side is relatively the more sensitive. Pfeffer has shown that in this flower, rise of temperature brings about an accelerated growth on the inner side of petal. Hence the flower *opens* during rise and *closes* during fall of temperature.

Thus different flowers through their sensitiveness to heat and cold execute the so-called movements of 'sleep' and of 'waking.' Some of them have the healthy habit of normal humanity to sleep at night and keep awake in the day-time. Others turn night into day and make up for their long night-watch by sleeping it off in the day-time!

The daily movement of the water-lily is thus shown to be due to the predominant effect of variation of temperature on growth. Bose next describes the effect of variation of light and darkness on organs which are sensitive to light.

This type is exemplified by the leaflet of Cassia alata. A rapid movement of closure of leaflets is initiated in this plant at 5 P.M., when the light is undergoing a rapid diminution. The movement of closure is completed by 9 P.M., and the leaflets remain closed till 5 A.M. next morning, after which they begin to open; the opening is completed by 9 A.M., and the leaflets remain open till the afternoon. The plant is so extremely sensitive to light that any slight fluctuation is immediately followed by responsive movement. Thus the transitory passage of a cloud is marked in the record by a short-lived closure movement.

Of the vast number of daily movements, perhaps the largest proportion is due to a characteristic physiological reaction which had so long remained undiscovered. Bose spent many years in an attempt to trace the unknown cause till his perseverance was crowned with success. This discovery was due to a fortunate incident. When present by the invitation of the good people of Faridpur to their celebration of the yearly *Mela* (mentioned above as established half a century ago by his father), they told him of a wondrous 'Praying Palm' growing in their neighbourhood. First then the natural history phenomenon, so far as generally observed and interpreted:

Perhaps no phenomenon is so remarkable and shrouded with greater mystery as the performances of a particular Date Palm near Faridpur in Bengal. In the evening, while the temple bells ring, calling upon people to prayer, this tree bows down as if to prostrate itself. It erects its head again in the morning, and this process is repeated every day of the year. This extraordinary phenomenon has been regarded as miraculous, and pilgrims have been attracted in large numbers. It is alleged that offerings made to the tree have been the means of effecting marvellous cures. It is not necessary to pronounce any opinion on the subject; these cures may be taken to be as genuine as other faith-cures now prevalent in the West.

This particular Date Palm, Phœnix dactylifera, is a full-grown rigid tree, its trunk being 5 metres in length and 25 cm. in diameter. It must have been displaced by storm from the

FIG. 24.—The 'Praying' Palm. The upper photograph represents the morning, and the lower photograph the afternoon position.

vertical, and is now at an inclination of about 60 degrees to the vertical. In consequence of the diurnal movement, the trunk throughout its entire length is erected in the morning, and depressed in the afternoon. The highest point of the trunk thus moves up and down through one metre; the 'neck,' above the trunk, is concave to the sky in the morning; in the afternoon the curvature disappears, or is even slightly reversed. The large leaves which point high up against the sky in the morning are thus swung round in the afternoon through a vertical distance of several metres. To the popular imagination the tree appears like a living giant, more than twice the height of a human being, which leans forward in the evening from its towering height and bends its neck till the crown of leaves presses against the ground in an apparent attitude of devotion. Two vertical stakes, each one metre high, give a general idea of the size of the tree and movements of the different parts of the trunk (Fig. 24, p. 198).

A difficulty arose at the beginning in obtaining sanction of the proprietor to attach the recorder to the tree. He was apprehensive that its miraculous power might disappear by profane contact with foreign-looking instruments. His misgivings were removed on the assurance that the instrument was made in Bose's laboratory in India, and that it would be attached to the tree by one of his assistants who was the son of a priest.

The phenomenon above described is not a marvel of the mystical East: a similar thing had happened among the prosaic surroundings of Liverpool! An English friend sent to Bose the following extract from the *Liverpool Mercury* dated December 13, 1811.

Remarkable Phenomenon.—There is at present a willow tree of considerable height and about three yards in circumference, growing on the banks of a rivulet on a farm called Yubsill, the property of the Rev. Mr. Wasney, near Shipton, which actually appears *animated*: it will, at times, prostrate itself at full length on the ground, and then rise to its original perpendicular position. Incredible as this may appear, it is a fact, and has been the astonishment of hundreds who have seen it!!!

Bose's investigation on the 'Praying Palm' is thus enunciated :

For obtaining an explanation of the phenomenon it was necessary :—

1. To obtain an accurate record of the movement of the tree day and night, and to determine the time of its maximum erection and fall.

2. To find whether this particular instance of movement was unique, or whether the phenomenon was universal.

3. To discover the cause of the periodic movement of the tree.

4. To determine the relative effects of light and temperature on the movement.

5. To demonstrate the physiological character of the movement of the tree.

6. To discover the physiological factor whose variation determines the directive movement.

For the details of this inquiry, the original paper must be referred to : enough here to summarise the main results. The curve recording the 'prostration' of the tree towards evening, with its nightly rise anew, very closely corresponds to that of the daily rise and nightly fall of temperature, though naturally lagging a little behind. This the reader will see on comparing the curves, which represent the variation of temperature and the movement of the palm (Fig. 25). Investigation on a younger and less bent palm of the same species growing in Bose's garden, down-stream from Calcutta, 200 miles from Faridpur, showed an even more exact correspondence of the tree's movements with the temperature changes, the more since this smaller tree admitted of the erection of a tent over it during its observation, so as to prevent wind from disturbing the record, and also to mitigate any possible effect of the alternation of sunlight with darkness.

The objection next arises—May not this diurnal rhythm be but a physical effect of temperature, not a physiological one ? The question, however, was finally settled by the unfortunate death of the tree, which took place a year after the commencement of the investigation.

Bose was officially informed that 'the palm tree was dead, and that its movements had ceased.'

Further experiments enabled Bose to show that movements similar to that of the palm tree occur in all

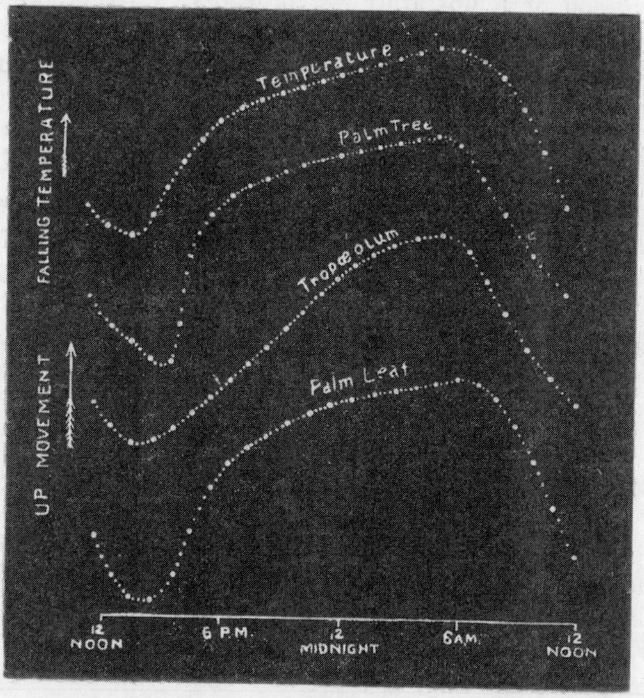

FIG. 25.—Records of the daily movement of the Palm Tree, of Tropaeolum, and of the Palm Leaf. The upper record gives the daily variation of temperature.

trees and their branches and leaves.[1] He was further able to trace the cause of the movement to the joint effects of geotropism and temperature; he designates the new phenomenon as thermo-geotropism. Under the action of the stimulus of gravity stems, branches and leaves tend to erect themselves against the force of gravity, and a

[1] *Trans. Bose Inst.*, vol. i., 1918.

curvature is thus produced. Rise of temperature reduces the geotropic effect and flattens this curvature, while fall of temperature accentuates it. Hence under the daily variation of temperature, all branches of trees and their leaves exhibit a periodic up and down movement. This is clearly seen in the records given in Fig. 25 of the diurnal movement of the palm tree, that of the procumbent stem of Tropaeolum, and of the leaf of the palm. In the tropics the thermal noon or the period of highest temperature is about 3 P.M., while the thermal dawn or temperature minimum is about 6 A.M. The different plant-organs are seen to move continually upwards from the thermal noon to the thermal dawn. The reverse movement takes place after 6 A.M., and the maximum fall is attained at the thermal noon at 3 P.M. Several hundreds of records obtained with different plants show that their daily movements—hitherto unexplained—are brought about by thermo-geotropic action.

An animal experiences a daily cycle of change passing through the stages of what we know as sleeping and waking. The fanciful name of sleep has been given to the closure of the leaflets of certain plants at night. Bose has shown how these opening and closure movements are brought about, these being in no way related to true sleep. The question as to whether plants sleep or not can be put in the form of a definite inquiry: Is the plant equally excitable throughout the day and night? If not, is there any period at which it practically loses its sensibility? Is there again another period at which it wakes up, as it were, to a condition of maximum excitability?

This problem was solved by Bose by means of a specially invented apparatus which delivers a questioning shock to the Mimosa plant every hour of the day and night, and records automatically the answering response of the plant. The size of the answering twitch gives a measure of the 'wakefulness' of the plant during twenty-four hours. In this way it was found (Fig. 26) that the plant is a late riser, waking up very gradually and very slowly; it becomes fully alert by noon, remaining so until evening. It is, however, quite awake until midnight. It then begins to grow somewhat lethargic, but does not lose its sensibility until the early hours of the morning, when its excitability disappears, and the plant ceases to give any answer.

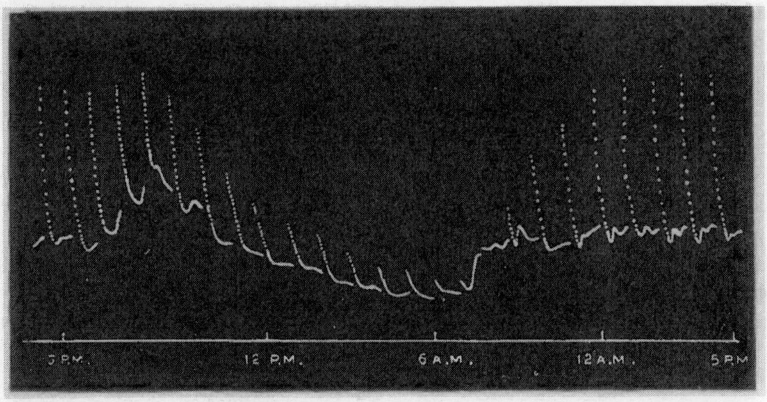

FIG. 26.—Diurnal record showing variation of sensibility of Mimosa from 5 P.M. to 5 P.M. next day.

The anomalies and intricacies of plant-movements, though so baffling, served only, as we have seen, to spur Bose to renewed efforts. As regards the possibility of unravelling the complexity, he spoke with confidence :

The extent of our range of investigation is limited ultimately by our power of detecting movement and measuring the rate of movement, that is to say in measurements of length and time. I have shown elsewhere how the employment of my Resonant Recorder enables us to measure time within a thousandth part of a second. We are, on the other hand, able by means of the Crescographic amplification to obtain records of movements magnified a million times. These possibilities and increasing refinement in our experimental methods cannot but lead to important advances towards a deeper understanding of the physiological reactions in living organisms.

His confidence has been fully justified. The varied phenomena of life-movements in plants, apparently so capricious, had hitherto been regarded as incapable of any rational generalisation. Bose, however, has succeeded in showing that all these diverse movements—the complex variations of growth, the twining of tendrils, the curvature towards or away from light, and even the diametrically opposite movements of root and shoot under the identical stimulus of gravity—result from two fundamental reactions: that of Direct Stimulus inducing contraction, and Indirect Stimulus, expansion. Few contributions to vegetable physiology can be of wider application and significance than this great generalisation, which in the phenomenon of life will rank as high as the universal theory of gravitation in the world of matter.

CHAPTER XVI

PSYCHO-PHYSICS

BOSE, as we have seen, had gone to England in 1900 in hopes of making over his researches on the borderland of physics and physiology to the physiologists; and he expected to return to continue his physical work, with its many opening perspectives. But the opposition of the physiologists challenged him to his new course of investigations. His physical turn of thinking had always repelled him from metaphysical speculation; and he had not taken much, if any, interest in experimental psychology. But unexpected results in his investigations made him realise that there were important analogies even in the field of psycho-physics, and these parallels increasingly compelled attention, though for a long time with some reluctance.

Bose's attention was first attracted to the responsive peculiarities of various forms of 'artificial retina' which he had constructed. He found that the stimulus of light has not only an immediate effect but also an after-effect; and that the after-effect of a strong stimulus persists for a longer time than that of a feeble one. He describes very interesting visual analogues where he was actually able to see better when the eyes were shut. He had been observing an experiment of Sir William Roberts-Austen on the quick fusion of metals, where owing to the glare and dense fumes it was impossible to see what happened in the crucible; but on quickly closing the eyes the visual after-effect of the smoke, being of less luminescence, cleared away first, leaving the after-image of the molten and boiling metal growing clearer on the retina.

Under continuous action of light the artificial retina exhibited periodic fluctuations in response. In trying to determine the corresponding phenomenon in human vision, he discovered 'the curious fact that in normal eyes the two do not see equally well at a given instant, but the visual effect in each eye undergoes fluctuation from moment to moment, in such a way that the sensation in the one is complementary to that in the other, the sum of the two sensations remaining approximately constant. Thus they take up the work of seeing, and then, relatively speaking, resting, alternately.' This division of labour, in binocular vision, must be of obvious advantage.

For demonstration he uses a stereoscope carrying, instead of stereo-photographs, an incised plate, through which we look at the light. The design consists of two slanting cuts, one eye looking at one and the second at the other. In this way not only is the different binocular alternation of vision demonstrated, but also the after-effects. When the design is looked at through the stereoscope, the right eye will see the right slanting cut R, and the left the other incised cut L; the two images will appear superimposed, and we see an inclined cross. When the stereoscope is turned towards the sky, and the cross looked at steadily for some time, it will be found, owing to the alternation already referred to, that while one arm of the cross begins to be dim, the other becomes bright, and *vice versa*. The alternate fluctuations become far more conspicuous when the eyes are closed; the pure oscillatory after-effects are then obtained in a most vivid manner. After looking through the stereoscope for ten seconds or more, the eyes are closed. The first effect observed is one of darkness, due to the rebound. Then *one* luminous arm of the cross first projects aslant the dark field, and then slowly disappears, after which the second (perceived by the other eye) shoots out suddenly in a direction athwart the first. This alternation proceeds for a long time, and produces the curious effect of two luminous blades crossing and recrossing each other. These alternating after-images persist for a very long period. The recurrent after-image is very distinct at the beginning, and becomes fainter at each repetition; a time comes when it is difficult to tell whether the image seen is the objective after-effect due to strain caused by stimulus or merely an after-effect of memory. In fact there is no line of demarcation between the two. One simply merges into the other.

The visual impressions and their recurrence often persist for a very long time. It usually happens that owing to weariness the recurrent images disappear; but in some instances, long after this apparent disappearance, they will spontaneously reappear at the most unexpected moments. In one instance the recurrence was observed in a dream about three weeks after the impression was made. It thus appears that in addition to the images impressed on the retina of which we are conscious, there are many others which are imprinted without our knowledge. We fail to notice them because our attention is directed to something else. But at a subsequent period, when the mind is in a passive state, these impressions may suddenly revive owing to the phenomenon of recurrence. This observation may afford an explanation of some of the phenomena connected with ocular phantoms and hallucinations.'

He then investigates certain other phenomena connected with 'Memory.'

Of that mental revival of past experience which we call memory, we may notice two different types. One is the spontaneous and recurrent revival of some strong impression from which we cannot escape: in the second case the primary impression has faded away, and it is only after an effort that we succeed in reviving the latent image. As regards spontaneous or recurrent revival of impression, I have shown elsewhere that in living tissues a very intense stimulus gives rise not to a single, but to multiple or repeated responses. Since an intense excitation is liable to recur spontaneously, without the action of the will or even in spite of it, it follows that any single impression, when very intense, may become dominant and persist in automatic recurrence. Instances of this are only too familiar.

A more interesting form of memory is the revival of an impression, the after-effect of which has faded out. Here we find that when no tangible effect of the impression remains, it may still be recalled by an effort or impulse of the will. It is clear that such a revival of impression can only take place by bringing about the original condition of excitation; in other words repeating the effect of original stimulus in its complete absence.

As a concrete example we may take the visual impression of a bright cross against a dark background. Under primary stimulus, it is clear that we have in the sensory field two areas under differential excitation. The one—the excited area—in the form of a cross; the other outside this, remaining unexcited. The image of the cross is therefore due to the differential excitation of a definite region in the sensory field. It is therefore obvious that in order to revive the picture we have to reproduce, in the absence of the primary stimulus, the same state of differential excitation as was originally induced.

Bose next shows that by the shock of stimulus, the surface acted on undergoes a molecular distortion from which there is slow recovery; but the recovery is never quite complete. Traces are left of the impression made by the stimulus. These, though invisible, remain latent, and beyond ordinary means of detection. Under certain conditions, however, this invisible script could once more be rendered conspicuous. Bose was able to form impressions on metallic surfaces, of which no sign whatever was visible even under the microscope. But when the plate was subjected to a diffused shock, these latent images were found revived. Similarly all the impressions made on the sensory surface by the localised action of stimulus remain dormant as a latent memory-image. The localised effect of this primary stimulus is to render the affected part of the tissue more excitable or a better conductor of excitation. Under the action of any form of diffuse stimulation these potentially more excitable areas become more intensely stimulated than their less active background, thus reproducing the original picture. Ordinarily such memory-revival takes place under the diffuse stimulus of the effort of the will. Here then is a wide range of inquiry, its subjects ranging from metal to plants, and lastly to man himself. And Bose concludes that 'in this demonstration of continuity, it has been found that the dividing frontiers between physics, physiology, and psychology have disappeared.'

This of course means the older conventional frontiers, and does not deny to each view-point such reasonable distinctness as may be. And while the physicists were sympathetic to these inquiries from the first, and the physiologists, though slower to convince, have come from these volumes and their successors essentially to accept them, it would seem that the psychologists are as yet insufficiently in touch with the results. Yet there are notable exceptions, President Stanley Hall of Clark University, for example, having been so interested as to have introduced the books into his syllabus for workers in psychology.

Bergson's and others' interpretations of 'Memory' need to take note of this differing one; and Bergson and Bose alike have also to discuss interpretations like those of Semon's. The psychologist, the physiologist, and the physicist have here peculiarly to collaborate in a most important field of investigation; while, as has once and again been pointed out, the mystery of Heredity is also correlated; for is not this the organic race-memory?

As psychological reaction must be related to underlying physiological change, Bose next investigated the effect of increasing stimulus from the sub-minimal to maximal. From his results there arises a fresh consideration of that famous 'Weber-Fechner's Law' which to so many has long seemed the very foundation of psycho-physiological inquiry, though to others less satisfactory. According to this, the strength of stimulus must be increased in geometrical ratio, in order that the intensity of psycho-physiological reaction may increase arithmetically. According to Weber's Law the relation between stimulus and response is quantitative; it does not take into account that the quality or *sign* of response is also liable to change. But Bose's experiments have here yielded significant results. Their many records of living tissues bring out the striking fact that the sign of response is modified by the strength of stimulus. Hence the relation between stimulus and response is by no means so simple as Weber, Fechner, and their successors have assumed; for tracings obtained with Bose's finer recording instruments show that what seemed formerly a subminimal stimulus may really produce appreciable effects. Moreover, a very feeble stimulus gives a distinct response of positive sign, i.e. expansion—the very opposite to the contractile response under usual stimulation. The continuance or even moderate increase of the feeble stimulus shows a diminishing result, going back to a point of no apparent response at all. Yet this is not a true zero, but a balance of opposite responses; for with a continued increase of stimulus the opposite and usual response begins, and increases to its maximum, as Weber observes. The fresh observation just noted introduces an element of qualitative transformation previously unsuspected, and in fact overlooked.

By employing very delicate methods of mechanical and electrical response, Bose discovered two distinct impulses of opposite signs which occur in the conducting nerve according to whether the stimulation be feeble or intense. A feeble stimulus applied at some distance from the responding pulvinus of Mimosa (which acts like contractile muscle) gives rise to an impulse which causes a positive or expansive reaction, by which the leaf becomes erected. A strong stimulus, on the other hand, gives rise to an impulse which induces precisely the opposite reaction

—namely, that of contraction and fall of the leaf. The effects of feeble and strong stimulus are therefore not merely quantitatively different but qualitatively, being of different signs, positive and negative. He obtained identical results from his electric mode of investigation, feeble stimulus causing a positive and strong stimulus a negative electric change.

Moderately feeble stimulation brings about an increase of energy; excessive stimulation, on the other hand, causes a run-down of energy; and between these extreme cases is a long range of variation in which either may predominate. But anything which raises the tonic condition is for the well-being and health of the organism, and is associated with positivity; and so of course conversely. Of the two tones of sensation the *positive* is associated with what may be regarded as pleasant or *not-painful*, and the *negative* with the unpleasant or the *painful*. Various experiments lent support to this conclusion, at least in typical cases, and with 'grounds of reconciliation to those who hold on the one hand that the motor reaction is secondary to the mental, and on the other that sensation is merely an accompaniment of movements reflexly induced,'—in fact between the common view and the Lange-James theory.

That the different sensation-tones have their physical concomitants of opposite characters is also supported by Münsterberg, who holds that 'the feeling of agreeableness is the mental accompaniment and the outcome of reflexly-produced movements of extension, and disagreeableness of the movement of flexion.' An ordinary observer is familiar with the expanded and rounded outline of the kitten purring with delight under gentle caresses, and the sudden change of its attitude and aspect in contraction and flexion, with the accompanying jump, under a pinch or a blow.

Bose next employed his very delicate method of experimentation to determine the characteristics of the nervous impulse, which is the basis of sensation. He begins with the simplest type of nervous tissue in plants like Mimosa. He uses his Resonant Recorder for determination of speed of nervous impulse and its variation—the Automatic Recorder enabling him to measure accurately to the thousandth part of a second. He shows that there is no physiological characteristic of the animal nerve which is not also to be found in the plant nerve. The various physiological 'blocks' which arrest the nervous impulse in the animal are shown to arrest the corresponding impulse in the plant. Agents which accelerate the nervous impulse in the animal are shown to exalt the impulse in the plant. Thus within the normal range, a rise of temperature of about 9° C. doubles the speed in animal nerve; this is also found to be the case in the plant.

He next determines the latent period or the perception-time of contractile tissue in Mimosa. This latent period in Mimosa, as previously stated, is 0·076 sec., or one-eighth the value in an energetic frog. We are of course prepared for slower reaction in plants, the difference between the plant and animal being one of degree and not of kind. Our perception-time is slowed down under fatigue; exactly parallel is the effect on plants.

Bose's further investigations give again very significant results as regards the power of stimulus to fashion its own conducting path. Thus a plant carefully protected under glass from the stimulating buffets of the elements looks sleek and flourishing, yet in reality it is flabby. Its conducting power is found to be in abeyance. But when a succession of blows rain on this effete and bloated specimen, the shocks themselves create nervous channels and arouse anew its deteriorated nature. 'And is it not shocks of adversity, and not cotton-wool protection, that evolve true manhood? Thus we see how organism is modified by its environment, and how an organ is, as it were, created by the cumulative effect of stimulus.' These discoveries show that the nervous impulse in plants has the same characteristics as that of animals; they also demonstrate how the inquiry into the simpler life helps towards the understanding of the more complex.

Since the tone of sensation is dependent on the intensity of transmitted excitation, Bose next asks himself whether it be possible to control the intensity of nervous impulse at will. He now enters into a new field of inquiry perhaps his most daring. In regard to sensation two extreme cases may be considered: in the first the external stimulus is too feeble for the resulting impulse to cause perception; here we would desire to exalt the conducting power of the message-bearing vehicle, the nerve, so that what was subliminal shall become perceptible. Excessively strong external stimulus, on the other hand, on account of its character or intensity causes sensation which is intolerably painful. Could such a message be altogether blocked by arresting the nervous impulse during transit? The problem is thus stated by Bose:

There is an apparent resemblance between the conduction of electric impulse by metallic conductor, and the excitatory nervous impulse by a nerve-conductor. In metal the power of conduction is constant, and the electric impulse will depend on the intensity of electric force that is applied. If the conducting power of the nerve were constant, then the intensity of the nervous impulse and its resulting sensation will depend inevitably on the intensity of shock which starts the impulse. In that case modification of our sensation would be an impossibility. But there may be a likelihood that the power of conduction possessed by a nerve is not constant, but capable of change. Should this surmise prove to be correct, then we arrive at the momentous conclusion that sensation itself is modifiable, whatever be the external stimulus, For the modification of nervous impulse there remains only one alternative, namely, some power to render the vehicle a very much better conductor or a non-conductor according to particular requirements. We require the nervous path to become supra-conducting in order that the impulse due to sub-minimal stimulus might be brought to sensory prominence. When the external blow, on the other hand, is too violent we would block the pain-causing impulse by rendering the nerve a non-conductor.

Under narcotic the nerve becomes paralysed, and we can thus by its use save ourselves from pain. But such heroic measures are to be resorted to only in extreme cases, as when we are under the surgeon's knife. In actual life we are confronted with unpleasantness without notice. A telephone subscriber has the evident advantage, for he can switch off the connection when the message begins to be unpleasant. But it is not every-one that has the courage of Mr. Herbert Spencer, who openly resorted to his ear-plugs when his visitor became tedious.

Bose then proceeds to consider the characteristics of nervous impulse. Stimulus causes a molecular upset in the excitable living tissue, and the propagation of nervous impulse is a phenomenon of the transmission of molecular disturbance from point to point. This molecular upset and propagation of disturbance may be pictured simply by means of a row of standing books. A certain intensity of blow applied, say, to the book on the extreme right would cause it to fall to the left, hitting its neighbour, and making the other books topple over in rapid succession. If the books have previously been tilted towards the left, a disposition would have been given to them which would bring about an upset under a feebler blow and accelerate the speed of transmission of disturbance. A tilt in the opposite direction would, on the other hand, be a pre-disposition to retard or inhibit this. Thus, by means of a directive force, we may induce a predisposition in the system which would enhance or retard the transmitted impulse. In a similar manner Bose imagined that opposite reactions of a polar character might be discovered by which molecular dispositions of opposite character could be induced in a nerve so as to enhance or to retard the conduction of nervous impulse.

The possibility of such a control of nervous impulse at will must be tested by experiment. Can opposite molecular dispositions be induced in the nerve, in consequence of which its conducting power would be appropriately enhanced or inhibited?

Bose was able to realise his theoretical anticipations in a striking manner, by application of electric force of a polar character. By conferring on the plant nerve a favourable molecular disposition, a feeble stimulus, previously below the threshold of perception, now produced an extraordinarily large response. Conversely, an intense excitation was arrested during transit by inducing opposite molecular disposition on the nervous tissue. A climax was reached when Bose was able by similar methods to confer on the same nerve of an animal a supra-conducting or non-conducting property at will. Thus, under a particular molecular disposition of the nerve, the experimental frog responded to stimulus which had hitherto been below its threshold of perception. Under the opposite disposition the violent spasm under salt-tetanus was at once quelled. On the cessation of the directive force the nerve immediately regained its normal property.

Bose was thus able to demonstrate experimentally the possibility of conferring two opposite 'molecular dispositions' to the nerve by which the nervous impulse could be accentuated or inhibited. And we are now able to obtain a true insight of various phenomena within our experience—the effect of attention, for example, in increasing the power of perception. The influence of suggestion, moreover, now becomes understood. The most important to us is the power of auto-suggestion or the power of Will. Who can define this power of Will intensified by practice and concentration? In the concluding portion of a recent address there occurs the following passage on the potentiality that is in man to rise victorious over circumstances:

> In the determination of sensation, then, the internal stimulus of Will may play as important a part as the shock from outside. And thus through the inner control of the molecular disposition of the nerve, the character of the resulting sensation may become profoundly modified. The external then is not so

overwhelmingly dominant, and man is no longer passive in the hands of destiny. There is a latent power which would raise him above the terrors of his inimical surroundings. It remains with him that the channels through which the outside world reaches him should at his command be widened or become closed. It would thus be possible for him to catch those indistinct messages that have hitherto passed by him unperceived; or he may withdraw within himself, so that in his inner realm, the jarring notes and the din of the world should no longer affect him.

CHAPTER XVII

FRIENDSHIPS AND PERSONALITY

THOUGH parents, kindred, and home surroundings cannot but count for much in every life, Eastern and Western, it is an old and standard observation of comparative psychology that these influences are even deeper and more enduring in the communal family systems of the Orient than in the smaller and more individualistic family systems of the West, with their greater dispersiveness. Hence, though every happily educated and productive life must rightly and gratefully recognise its early and formative influences, these tend in the East to be more frequently and clearly remembered, indeed more enduringly in evidence. Thus Bose's father's character and example, so full of varied activities and bold initiatives, has been a great impulse and continual inspiration throughout his son's life; while only second to this has been the deep affection of his mother, strongly returned, while her settlement of her son's studies in England, in spite of the decision of the family council on them, seems to have been the emphatic incident of her gentle, purposive guidance. Both parents, too, lived with the Boses after their retirement, and to the last—the father dying at sixty-two, when Bose was thirty-two, and the mother at about the same age two years later.

Bose's eldest sister, later Mrs. A. M. Bose, was his constant friend and companion in childhood, and that her influence too must have been helpful is evidenced not only from her own literary power in later life, but by her keen observation of nature. At her country house, Fairy Hall, at Dumdum, outside Calcutta, she drew her brother's attention to the peculiar movements of leaflets of Biophytum, which led to his discovery of multiple response, and its continuity with the automatic response of the Telegraph-plant.

Her husband, Ananda Mohun Bose, also affected his life deeply. A. M. Bose was one of the earliest batch of students from India to Cambridge in 1870, and was the first Indian Wrangler. His oratorical power was of the highest order. Professor Fawcett asked him to address his constituents, and declared that he could not have produced such an influence as had his young Indian friend. After his return to India he became one of the leaders of his countrymen, alike by his ability and by his saintly character. He was one of the founders of the Indian Association, and was President of the National Congress at Madras in 1902. He was a member of the Educational Commission, and founded in Calcutta the City College which has since been one of the most important in the University. He was also one of the founders of an Institution for the Higher Education of Indian Women. Bose's younger sisters have also, each in her own way, followed lives of intellectual activity; and one has trained a son to follow the footsteps of his uncle, as already an active investigator of radio-activity.

Most important, however, of all these influences from youth onwards has of course been that of his life companion of now some thirty-three years. She had an education in science, having been a medical student for four years. Fortunately too for her, in view of long-continued scanty means and strenuous saving to pay off family debts, she had been trained to skilled and thrifty house-keeping: yet here has been no simple housewife's life, but one full of active culture-interests also, not only appreciating her husband's many scientific problems and tasks, and hospitality to his students and friends, but sharing all his cares and difficulties, and so lightening them not a little. For his impassioned temperament—in younger days doubtless fiery, and still excitable enough—her strong serenity and persistently cheerful courage have been an invaluable and ever active support, like the fly-wheel steadily maintaining and regulating the throbbing energies of the steam-engine. Pilgrimages in India and visits to Europe and America have been made always together, and their one great common sorrow—the loss of their only babe in early infancy—has made them more completely at one. Alike for physical health, on the whole well maintained, yet once and again nursed back from danger, and for steadiness of intellectual output, for consolation in times of trial, difficulty and depression, as well as cheerful acceptance and constant lightening of long years of poverty and self-denial—which cannot but press more closely upon a wife than on a husband —Bose has indeed been rarely fortunate in such a helpmeet ; and no friend or biographer could fail to recognise the greatness of her share in his life's productivity and success.

The advantages of celibacy to the intellectual life have so long been urged and acted on in East and West alike that it is as well that those whose experience and career have had the yet higher advantages of wedlock at its best should also bear their testimony. And that even such devoted companionship may be fully compatible for the wife as well as for the husband with cultural usefulness and influence beyond the home is demonstrated by a life like that of Lady Bose, whose leadership in administration of the highly efficient Girls' High School opposite her Calcutta home is the fit pendant to her husband's activities in his Institute beside it.

Before we pass to his other enduring friendships, we must understand his outlook on life and immediate duties. His early childhood was, as we have seen, deeply impressed by the traditions of the heroic epoch of ancient India, and he had the unshaken belief 'that the past shall yet be reborn in a nobler future through the efforts of their lives.'

He had no patience with the easy talk about internationalism or about the virtues of renunciation. For about the former they had no right to talk of internationalism *until* their own country had won recognition as a nation; and of the latter he thought 'the weakling who has refused the conflict has acquired nothing, and has nothing to renounce; only he who has striven and won can enrich the world by giving away the fruits of his victorious experience.' He felt that the strong must bear the burden and deliberately choose the difficult in preference to the easy path; to him this was the true function of nationality. With this conviction there mingled another no less imperative. His studies had revealed to him the workings of a strange Cyclic Law—how inertness passed into climax of activity and how that climax was perilously near its antithetic decline. When we have raised ourselves to the highest pinnacle, through some oversight we fall over the precipice. Men have offered their lives for the establishment of truth; a climax is reached after which the custodians of knowledge themselves bar further advance. Those who have fought for liberty impose on others and on themselves the bond of slavery, and patriotism often degenerates into the worst form of tyranny. He resolved that his love for India should never stand in the way of his wider love for humanity; and two great friendships came to him at this phase of life which laid his misgiving to rest, and enabled him to realise fully the unity of all human efforts.

In 1899 Mrs. Ole Bull and Miss Margaret Noble (Sister Nivedita), having heard much of Bose's discoveries, came to see him in his Calcutta laboratory and to learn what they could. The mutual interest awakened that day ripened into a deep friendship only interrupted by death. Mrs. Ole Bull, an American, was the widow of the great Norse violinist who inspired a generation of writers and musicians—Ibsen, Björnson, Grieg and others—to win European eminence for their country as well as for themselves. The acquaintance ripened quickly during her short stay in Calcutta in 1899, and Mrs. Bull urged on the Boses to visit her some day in America. After Bose's attendance at the International Science Congress at Paris in 1900 and subsequent cares, his health broke down, and he was in imminent danger, when Mrs. Bull, hearing of this, came over from the Continent, found him an expert surgeon, and helped to nurse him back to health. From this time a deep friendship grew up, and Bose found in her anew the great qualities of his own mother. When the Boses went to America in 1907 her home was theirs, and headquarters for his visits to different Universities. They also came to know Mrs. Bull's brother, Mr. J. G. Thorp, a very influential and honoured citizen of Boston, and his wife, the poet Longfellow's daughter; and on a second visit in 1914, after Mrs. Ole Bull's death, Mr. Thorp's house was their home and centre for making new contacts with leading minds of Boston and Harvard.

Latest among these friendships, but in some ways of the very highest importance, came that with Margaret Noble—better known as Sister Nivedita after her dedication to the Order of Ramakrishna, which the great personality and teaching of Swami Vivekananda had launched upon its career of varied usefulness, educational and social. Nivedita's interests were too large and varied and eager to be confined within any single round of duties or system of doctrine; and she keenly realised the importance of Bose's work at once for science in general and for the fuller arousal of scientific activities in India in particular. After his serious illness, and while convalescing, Bose found a home with Nivedita's mother at Wimbledon; and later Mrs. Bose during an illness found the same hospitality, so that the two families were intimately and permanently drawn together even for the young and rising generation.

Nivedita's combination of intellectual and personal idealism was fully aroused by Bose's discoveries and his difficulties in those days in convincing others of them.

Her fervid faith in the long-dreamed-of Research Institute, its possibilities for science and its promise for India, was no small impulse and encouragement towards its realisation; and thus is explained the memorial fountain with its bas-relief of 'Woman carrying Light to the Temple' which adorns the entrance of his Institute.

Nivedita did not live to see the foundation of the Institute, for her over-strenuous efforts on behalf of those amongst whom she dwelt caused her untimely death in 1911. In the memorial volume which he prepared, Mr. S. K. Ratcliffe wrote of Nivedita: 'Those to whom she gave the ennobling gift of her friendship hold the memory of that gift as this world's highest benediction.' Lady Bose, who felt deeply the loss of her friend, wrote: 'As a woman, I knew her in everyday life, full of austerity and possessed with a longing for righteousness which shone round her like a pure flame. Others will know her as the great moral and intellectual force which came to us in time of great national need.'

Turning now to Bose's friendships among men, foremost and greatest (appropriately first also for their present order of treatment) has been that with the poet Rabindranath Tagore. On the occasion of Bose's return from his successful visit to Europe in 1896, Tagore called to congratulate him and, not finding him at home, left on his work-table a great blossom of magnolia, as a fitting and characteristic message of regard. Since that time the two have been increasingly together, each complementing and thereby widening and deepening the other's characteristic outlook on nature and life, and stimulating to his expression accordingly. Once, on receiving an invitation from the poet to stay with him at his house at Silaida on the river Padma, Bose accepted it with the demand of the fullest and highest hospitality his friend could render him—that of a new story to be written every day, and read to him every evening! It was in this fashion that one of the most beautiful series of Tagore's short stories came to be written.

Tagore, though occupying the foremost literary position in India, was not at that time known in Europe, and Bose felt keenly that the West had not the opportunity of realising his friend's greatness. So during his second visit to England, in 1900, he had one of his stories, 'The Kabuliwalla,' translated into English. Prince Kropotkin—a good critic in letters as well as science—declared it to be the most pathetic story he had ever heard, reminding him of the greatest writers among his countrymen; and Bose submitted it to *Harper's Magazine*. It was declined, because the West was not sufficiently interested in Oriental life! The time had not yet come: but Bose during his last visit to America in 1915, when Tagore's fame was reaching its meridian, did not fail to utilise the opportunity to rub this in when Harper was publishing one of his own articles.

Though Bengali literature has as yet culminated in Tagore, he had had predecessors; he has contemporaries and promising writers among the young generation. With these active groups of men of letters, Bose has had most cordial relations; and one of his activities has been in connection with the *Parishad*, the Academy of Bengali Literature, of which he was the President for several years. There is another important institution, the Ram Mohan Library, of which he is the President; this Institution organises regular lectures for popular diffusion of knowledge. With the now increasingly successful and appreciated group of painters—Gaganendra Nath and Abanindra Nath Tagore and their pupils—who are carrying their part in the contemporary Bengali renaissance, and making Calcutta more and more correspond in such activities to one of the greater culture-cities of the West, Bose has long been in closest sympathy. His Calcutta drawing-room contains a striking frieze from the 'Mahabharata' by Nanda Lal Bose, and now the adjacent lecture-hall of the Institute has a large symbolic painting, 'The Quest,' by the same hand.

Among scientific friends may be specially mentioned

Sir P. C. Ray, the chemist. On his return from his Edinburgh studies he found welcome and a home at Bose's. The spirit of departmental trade unionism which stood in the way of Indians securing responsible positions in education was, as usual, fully active. But Bose—who can be tactful for his friends, as well as combative in defence of principles—managed to disarm the reluctance of the Education Department to appoint another Indian in the Science professoriate of the Presidency College, and with long colleagueship a very close friendship has grown up between them. Bose's active championship of Ray's promise and powers has long been amply justified by the high appreciation of brother chemists and the success of his pupils.

Bose has also been on terms of closest friendship with the leaders of educational, social, and political movements. Among these may be mentioned the late G. K. Gokhale and Mr. M. K. Gandhi. Special mention must be made here of his medical adviser and friend, Sir Nilratan Sircar, the leading physician of Calcutta, who in addition to his professional work has rendered such services in the cause of higher education as to make the Indian Government select him for the Vice-Chancellorship of the Calcutta University. Fairly near neighbours in Calcutta, he and Bose are next door in Darjeeling, and to Sir Nilratan's promptitude and skill Bose has on more than one occasion already owed his life, while his fairly continued health depends much on his old friend's vigilance.

Reference may here be made to his numerous students, of whom he thus spoke in one of his addresses: 'Perhaps as a reward for years of effort, I find all over India those who have been my pupils occupying positions of the highest trust and responsibility in different walks of life. I do not merely count those who have won fame and success, but I also claim many others who have taken up the burden of life manfully and whose life of purity and unselfishness has brought gleams of joy into suffering lives.'

Of friends both in Europe and in America much might

be said, for they have been many; and it must be a matter of satisfaction that even out of his past fights he has won some of his staunchest friends.

In recognition of the unique services rendered to the cause of science, the Imperial Government has conferred on him honours on successive occasions. This recognition for the first time by the State of the importance of Indian contributions for the advancement of world's science was received with satisfaction by his countrymen. With Bose's fully developed Indian personality, yet with the best of world culture fully incorporated in his own, and high humanistic views, one can wish for no better link between East and West, of interchange and ever increasing understanding.

Bose was to have retired in 1913, on the completion of his fifty-fifth year; but the Bengal Government, in recognition of his services to the Presidency College and of his great influence over students, extended his period of service for two years, so that he retired in November 1915. As a further acknowledgment the Government gazetted him as Professor Emeritus, on full pay instead of pension—a distinction so far unique in the Education Service of India. Thus was secured his permanent connection with the Presidency College, whose renown he had so largely enhanced. Further than this, he received a knighthood and the Companionship of the Star of India.

Most men, under such gratifying conditions, would accept their honours and emoluments as their due reward for strenuous effort and would feel justified in seeking the ease of retirement; but such was not Bose's attitude, for his goal was not yet reached.

One need only recall how his life-long efforts for the establishment of a laboratory for research had so often seemed on the point of realisation only to be thwarted each time, to appreciate the irony of the fact that when eventually the properly equipped physical laboratory of his college was built, it was only on the eve of his retirement, and hence too late for the continuation of his researches. All these disappointments only made Bose more resolved to carry out his own project ; so that he worked with tireless energy, during the two years subsequent to his retirement, at the final planning, building and organisation of the Research Institute. His own researches were not, however, interrupted, for he continued to carry them out at his summer home at Darjiling and at Sijberia on the Ganges, some twenty miles down stream from Calcutta, with its pleasant little bungalow and tree-bordered grounds quietly and picturesquely situated at the junction of a minor stream with the great river. But such centres of personal activity made all the more imperative the creation of the long-dreamed-of Research Institute.

This he at length opened, on his fifty-ninth birthday, November 30, 1917, in commemoration and repetition of his vow to research twenty-three years before. Though his oft-repeated journeys to England and other countries of the West had made Bose a citizen of the world in an unusual degree, yet his fundamental attitude to life and knowledge was primarily Indian, with its ideality which embraced the service of humanity. His object and outlook will be best understood from the inaugural address, reproduced in the next chapter.

CHAPTER XVIII

THE DEDICATION[1]

I DEDICATE to-day this Institute—not merely a Laboratory but a Temple.

The power of physical methods applies to the establishment of that truth which can be realised directly through our senses, or through the vast expansion of the perceptive range by means of artificially created organs. We still gather the tremulous message when the note of the audible reaches the unheard. When human sight fails, we continue to explore the region of the invisible. The little that we can see is as nothing compared to the vastness of that which we cannot. Out of the very imperfection of his senses man has built himself a raft of thought by which he makes daring adventures on the great seas of the Unknown. But there are other truths which will remain beyond even the super-sensitive methods known to science. For these we require faith, tested not in a few years but by an entire life. And a temple is erected as a fit memorial for the establishment of that truth for which faith was needed. The personal, yet general, truth and faith whose establishment this Institute commemorates is this: that when one has gained the vision of a purpose to which he can and must dedicate himself fully, then the closed doors will be opened and the seemingly impossible become fully attainable.

[1] Sir J. C. Bose's inaugural address in dedication of the Bose Institute, November 30, 1917.

Thirty-two years ago I chose the teaching of science as my vocation. It was held that by its very peculiar constitution, the Indian mind would always turn away from the study of Nature to metaphysical speculations. Even had the capacity for inquiry and accurate observation been assumed to be present, there were no opportunities for their employment; there were neither well-equipped laboratories nor skilled mechanicians. This was all too true. It is not for man to complain of circumstances, but bravely to accept, to confront and to dominate them; and we belong to that race which has accomplished great things with simple means.

Failure and Success

This day twenty-three years ago, I resolved that as far as the whole-hearted devotion and faith of one man counted, that would not be wanting, and within six months it came about that some of the most difficult problems connected with Electric Waves found their solution in my laboratory, and received high appreciation from Lord Kelvin, Lord Rayleigh, and other leading physicists. The Royal Society honoured me by publishing my discoveries and offering of their own accord an appropriation from the special Parliamentary Grant for the advancement of knowledge. That day the closed gates suddenly opened, and I hoped that the torch that was then lighted would continue to burn brighter and brighter. But man's faith and hope require repeated testing. For five years after this the progress was uninterrupted; yet when the most generous and wide appreciation of my work had reached almost the highest point there came a sudden and unexpected change.

Living and Non-Living

In the pursuit of my investigations I was unconsciously led into the border region of physics and physiology and was amazed to find boundary lines vanishing and points of contact emerge between the realms of the Living and Non-living. Inorganic matter was found anything but inert; it also was athrill under the action of multitudinous forces that played on it. A common reaction seemed to bring together metal, plant and animal under a general law. They all exhibited essentially the same phenomena of fatigue and depression, together with possibilities of recovery and of exaltation, yet also that of permanent irresponsiveness which is associated with death. I was filled with wonder at this great generalisation; and it was with great hope that I announced my results before the Royal Society—results demonstrated by experiments. But the physiologists present advised me, after my address, to confine myself to physical investigations in which my success had been assured, rather than encroach on their preserve. I had thus unwittingly strayed into the domain of a new and unfamiliar caste system and so offended its etiquette. An unconscious theological bias was also present which confounds ignorance with faith. It is forgotten that He, who surrounded us with this ever-evolving mystery of creation, the ineffable wonder that lies hidden in the microcosm of the dust particle, enclosing within the intricacies of its atomic form the mystery of the cosmos, has also implanted in us the desire to question and understand. To the theological bias was added the misgivings about the inherent bent of the Indian mind towards mysticism and unchecked imagination. But in India this burning imagination which can extort new order out of a mass of apparently contradictory facts, is also held in check by the habit of meditation. It is this restraint which confers the power to hold the mind in pursuit of truth in infinite patience, to wait, and reconsider, to experimentally test and repeatedly verify.

It is but natural that there should be prejudice, even in science, against all innovations; and I was prepared to wait till the first incredulity could be overcome by further cumulative evidence. Unfortunately there were other incidents, which need not be dwelt on; and there were misrepresentations which it was impossible to remove from this isolating distance. Thus no conditions could have been more desperately hopeless than those which confronted me for the next twelve years. It is necessary to make brief reference to this period of my life; for one who would devote himself to the search for truth must realise that for him there awaits no easy life, but one of unending struggle. It is for him to cast his life as an offering, regarding gain and loss, success and failure, as one. Yet in my case this long persisting gloom was suddenly lifted. My scientific deputation in 1914, from the Government of India, gave the opportunity of giving demonstrations of my discoveries before the leading scientific societies of the world. This led to the acceptance of my results, and the recognition of the importance of the Indian contribution to the advancement of the world's science. My own experience told me how heavy, sometimes even crushing, are the difficulties which confront an inquirer here in India; yet it made me stronger in my determination, that I should make the path of those who would follow me less arduous, and that India should never relinquish what has been won for her after years of struggle.

The Two Ideals

What is it that India is to win and maintain? Can anything small or circumscribed ever satisfy the mind of India? Has her own history and the teaching of the past prepared her for some temporary and quite subordinate gain? There are at this moment two complementary and not antagonistic ideals before the country. India is drawn into the vortex of international competition. She has to become efficient in every way—through the spread of education, through performance of civic duties and responsibilities, through activities both industrial and commercial. Neglect of these essentials of national duty will imperil her very existence ; and sufficient stimulus for these will be found in success and satisfaction of personal ambition.

But these alone do not ensure the life of a nation. Such material activities have brought in the West their fruit, in accession of power and wealth. There has been a feverish rush even in the realm of science, for exploiting applications of knowledge, not so often for saving as for destruction. In the absence of some power of restraint, civilisation is trembling in an unstable poise on the brink of ruin. Some complementary ideal there must be to save man from that mad rush which must end in disaster. He has followed the lure and excitement of some insatiable ambition, not pausing for a moment to think of the ultimate object for which success was to serve as a temporary incentive. He has forgotten that far more potent than competition are mutual help and co-operation in the scheme of life. And in this country through millenniums, there always have been some who, beyond the immediate and absorbing prize of the hour, sought for the realisation of the highest ideal of life—not through passive renunciation, but through active struggle. The weakling who has refused the conflict, having acquired nothing, has nothing to renounce. He alone who has striven and conquered can enrich the world by the generous bestowing of the fruits of his victorious experience. In India such examples of constant realisation of ideals through work have resulted in the formation of a continuous living tradition. And by her latent power of rejuvenescence she has readjusted herself through infinite transformations. Thus while the soul of Babylon and the Nile Valley has transmigrated, ours still remains vital and with capacity of absorbing what the time has brought, and making it one with itself.

The ideal of giving, of enriching, in fine, of self-renunciation in response to the highest call of humanity is the other and complementary ideal. The motive power for this is not to be found in personal ambition but in the effacement of all littlenesses, and in the uprooting of that ignorance which regards anything as gain which is to be purchased at others' loss. This I know, that no vision of truth can come except in the absence of all sources of distraction, and when the mind has reached the point of rest.

Public life, and the various professions will be the appropriate spheres of activity for many aspiring young men. But for my disciples, I call on those very few, who, realising some inner call, will devote their whole life with strengthened character and determined purpose to take part in that infinite struggle to win knowledge for its own sake and see truth face to face.

Advancement and Diffusion of Knowledge

The work already carried out in my laboratory on the response of matter, and the unexpected revelations in plant life, foreshadowing the wonders of the highest animal life, have opened out very extended regions of inquiry in Physics, in Physiology, in Medicine, in Agriculture and even in Psychology. Problems, hitherto regarded as insoluble, have now been brought within the sphere of experimental investigation. These inquiries are obviously more extensive than those customary either among physicists or physiologists, since demanding interests and aptitudes hitherto more or less divided between them. In the study of Nature, there is a necessity of the dual view-point, this alternating yet rhythmically unified interaction of biological thought with physical studies, and physical thought with biological studies. The future worker with his freshened grasp of physics, his fuller conception of the inorganic world, as indeed thrilling with 'the promise and potency of life' will redouble his former energies of work and thought. Thus he will be in a position to winnow the old knowledge with finer sieves, to re-search it with new enthusiasm and subtler instruments. And thus with thought and toil and time he may hope to bring fresher views into the old problems. His handling of these will be at once more vital and more kinetic, more comprehensive and unified.

The further and fuller investigation of the many and ever-opening problems of the nascent science which includes both Life and Non-Life are among the main purposes of the Institute I am opening to-day; in these fields I am already fortunate in having a devoted band of disciples, whom I have been training for the last ten years. Their number is very limited, but means may perhaps be forthcoming in the future to increase them. An enlarging field of young ability may thus be available, from which will emerge, with time and labour, individual originality of research, productive invention and some day even creative genius.

But high success is not to be obtained without corresponding experimental exactitude, and this is needed to-day more than ever, and to-morrow yet more again. Hence the long battery of the highly sensitive instruments and apparatus, designed here, which stands before you in the cases in our entrance hall. They will tell you of the protracted struggle to get behind the deceptive seeming into the reality that remained unseen;—of the continuous toil and persistence called forth for overcoming human limitations. In these directions through the ever-increasing ingenuity of device for advancing science, I see at no distant future an enhancement of skill and of invention among our workers; and if this skill be assured, practical applications will not fail to follow in many fields of human activity.

The advance of science is the principal object of this Institute and also the diffusion of knowledge. We are here in the largest of all the many chambers of this House of Knowledge—its Lecture Room. In adding this feature, and on a scale hitherto unusual in a Research Institute, I have sought permanently to associate the advancement of knowledge with the widest possible civic and public diffusion of it; and this without any academic limitations, henceforth to all races and languages, to both men and women alike, and for all time coming.

The lectures given here will not be mere repetitions of second-hand knowledge. They will announce, to an audience of some fifteen hundred people, the discoveries made here, which will be demonstrated for the first time before the public. We shall thus maintain continuously the highest aim of a great Seat of Learning by taking active part in the advancement and diffusion of knowledge. Through the regular publication of the Transactions of the Institute, these Indian contributions will reach the whole world. The discoveries made will thus become public property. Besides the regular staff there will be a selected number of scholars, who by their work have shown special aptitude, and who would devote their whole life to the pursuit of research. They will require personal training and their number must necessarily be limited. But it is not the quantity but quality that is of essential importance.

It is my further wish that, as far as the limited accommodation would permit, the facilities of this Institute should be available to workers from all countries. In this I am attempting to carry out the traditions of my country, which, so far back as twenty-five centuries ago, welcomed all scholars from different parts of the world within the precincts of its ancient seats of learning at Nalanda and at Taxila.

The Surge of Life

With this widened outlook, we shall not only maintain the highest traditions of the past but also serve the world in nobler ways. We shall be at one with it in feeling the common surgings of life, the common love for the good, the true and the beautiful. In this Institute, this Study and Garden of Life, the claim of art has not been forgotten, for the artist has been working with us, from foundation to pinnacle, and from floor to ceiling of this very Hall. And beyond that arch, the Laboratory merges imperceptibly into the garden, which is the true laboratory for the study of Life. There the creepers, the plants and the trees are played upon by their natural environments—sunlight and wind, and the chill at midnight under the vault of starry space. There are other surroundings also, where they will be subjected to chromatic action of different lights, to invisible rays, to galvanic current or electrically-charged atmosphere. Everywhere they will transcribe in their own script the history of their experience. From this lofty point of observation, sheltered by the trees, the student will watch this panorama of life. Isolated from all distractions, he will learn to attune himself with Nature ; the obscuring veil will be lifted and he will gradually come to see how community throughout the great ocean of life outweighs apparent dissimilarity. Out of discord he will realise the great harmony.

The Outlook

These are the dreams that wove a network round my wakeful life for many years past. The outlook is endless, for the goal is at infinity. The realisation cannot be through one life or one fortune but through the co-operation of many lives and many fortunes. The possibility of a fuller expansion will depend on very large endowments. But a beginning must be made, and this is the genesis of the foundation of the Institute. I came with nothing and shall return as I came ; if something is accomplished in the interval, that would indeed be a privilege. What I have I will offer, and one who has shared with me the struggles and hardships that had to be faced, has wished to bequeath all that is hers for the same object. In all my struggling efforts I have not been altogether solitary ; while the world doubted, there had been a few. now in the City of Silence, who never wavered in their trust.

Till a few weeks ago it seemed that I should have to look to the future for securing the necessary expansion of scope and for permanence of the Institute. But response is being slowly awakened in answer to the need. The Government have intimated their desire to sanction grants towards placing the Institute on a permanent basis, the extent of which will be proportionate to the public interest in this undertaking. Out of those who would feel an interest in securing adequate endowment, the very first contributions have come from two from a distant province, to whom I had been personally unknown.

India's Special Aptitudes in Contribution to Science

The excessive specialisation of modern science in the West has led to the danger of losing sight of the fundamental fact that there can be but one truth, one science which includes all the branches of knowledge. How chaotic appear the happenings in Nature! Is Nature a Cosmos, in which the human mind is some day to realise the uniform march of sequence, order and law? India through her habit of mind is peculiarly fitted to realise the idea of unity, and to see in the phenomenal world an orderly universe. This trend of thought led me unconsciously to the dividing frontiers of different sciences and shaped the course of my work in its constant alternations between the theoretical and the practical, from the investigation of the inorganic world to that of organised life and its multifarious activities of growth, of movement, and even of sensation. On looking over the different lines of investigations carried on during the last twenty-three years, I now discover in them a natural sequence. The study of Electric Waves led to the devising of methods for the production of the shortest electric waves and these bridged over the gulf between visible and invisible light; from this followed accurate investigation on the optical properties of invisible waves, the determination of the refractive powers of various substances opaque to light, the discovery of the effect of air film on total reflection and the polarising properties of strained rocks and of electric tourmalines. The invention of a new type of self-recovering electric receiver made of galena was the forerunner of the application of crystal detectors for extending the range of wireless signals. In physical chemistry the detection of molecular change in matter under electric stimulation led to a new theory of photographic action. The fruitful theory of stereo-chemistry was strengthened by the production of two kinds of artificial molecules, which like the two kinds of sugar, rotated the polarised electric wave either to the right or to the left. Again the 'fatigue' of my receivers led to the discovery of universal sensitiveness inherent in matter as shown by its electric response. It was next possible to study this response in its modification under changing environment, of which its exaltation under stimulants and its abolition under poisons are among the most astonishing outward manifestations. And as a single example of the many applications of this fruitful discovery, the characteristics of an artificial retina gave a clue to the unexpected discovery of 'binocular alternation of vision' in man;—each eye thus supplements its fellow by turns, instead of acting as a continuously yoked pair, as hitherto believed.

Plant Life and Animal Life

In natural sequence to the investigation of the response in 'inorganic' matter, has followed a prolonged study of the activities of plant-life as compared with the corresponding functioning of animal life. But since plants for the most part seem motionless and passive, and are indeed limited in their range of movement, special apparatus of extreme delicacy had to be invented, which should magnify the tremor of excitation and also measure the perception period of a plant to a thousandth part of a second. Ultra-microscopic movements were measured and recorded; the length measured being often smaller than a fraction of a single wave-length of light. The secret of plant-life was thus for the first time revealed by the autographs of the plant itself. This evidence of the plant's own script removed the long-standing error which divided the vegetable world into sensitive and insensitive. The remarkable performance of the 'Praying' Palm Tree of Faridpore, which bows, as if to prostrate itself, every evening, is only one of the latest instances which show that the supposed insensibility of plants and still more of rigid trees is to be ascribed to wrong theory and defective observation. My investigations show that all plants, even the trees, are fully alive to changes of environment; they respond visibly to all stimuli, even to the slight fluctuations of light caused by a drifting cloud. This series of investigations has completely established the fundamental unity of life-reactions in plant and animal, as seen in a similar periodic insensibility in both, corresponding to what we call sleep; as seen in the death-spasm, which takes place in the plant as in the animal. This unity in organic life is also exhibited in that spontaneous pulsation which in the animal is heart beat; it appears in the identical effects of stimulants, anæsthetics and of poisons in vegetable and animal tissues. This physiological identity in the effect of drugs is regarded by leading physicians as of great significance in the scientific advance of Medicine; since here we have a means of testing the effect of drugs under conditions far simpler than those presented by the patient, far subtler too, as well as more humane than those of experiments on animals.

Growth of plants and its variations under different treatment is instantly recorded by my Crescograph. Authorities expect this method of investigation will advance practical agriculture; since for the first time we are able to analyse and study separately the conditions which modify the rate of growth. Experiments which would have taken months, their results vitiated by unknown changes, can now be carried out in a few minutes.

Returning to pure science, no phenomena in plant-life are so extremely varied or have yet been more incapable of generalisation than the 'tropic movements, such as the twining of tendrils, the heliotropic movements of some towards and of others away from light, and the opposite geotropic movements of the root and shoot, in the direction of gravitation or away from it. My latest investigations have established a single fundamental reaction which underlies effects so extremely diverse.

Finally, I may say a word of that other new and unexpected chapter which is opening out from my demonstration of 'nervous' impulse in plants. The speed with which the nervous impulse courses through the plant has been determined; its nervous excitability and the variation of that excitability have likewise been measured. The nervous impulse in plant and in man is found exalted or inhibited under identical conditions. We may even follow this parallelism in what seem extreme cases. A plant carefully protected under glass from outside shocks, looks sleek and flourishing; but its higher nervous function is then found to be atrophied. But when a succession of blows is rained on this effete and bloated specimen, the shocks themselves create nervous channels and arouse anew the deteriorated nature.

A question long perplexing physiologists and psychologists alike is that concerned with the mystery that underlies memory. But now, through certain experiments I carried out here, it is possible to trace 'memory impressions' backwards even in inorganic matter, such latent impressions being capable of subsequent revival. Again the tone of our sensation is determined by the intensity of nervous excitation that reaches the central perceiving organ. It would theoretically be possible to change the tone or quality of our sensation, if means could be discovered by which the nervous impulse would become modified during transit. Investigation on nervous impulse in plants has led to the discovery of a controlling method, which was found equally effective in regard to the nervous impulse in animal.

Thus the lines of physics, of physiology and of psychology

converge and meet. And here will assemble those who would seek oneness amidst the manifold. Here it is that the genius of India should find its true blossoming.

The thrill in matter, the throb of life, the pulse of growth, the impulse coursing through the nerve and the resulting sensations, how diverse are these, and yet so unified! How strange it is that the tremor of excitation in nervous matter should not merely be transmitted but transmuted and reflected like the image on a mirror from a different plane of life in sensation and in affection, in thought and in emotion. Of these which is more real, the material body or the image which is independent of it? Which of those is undecaying, and which of these is beyond the reach of death?

It was a woman in the Vedic times, who when asked to take her choice of the wealth that would be hers for the asking, inquired whether that would win for her deathlessness. What would she do with it, if it did not raise her above death? This has always been the cry of the soul of India, not for addition of material bondage, but to work out through struggle her self-chosen destiny and win immortality. Many a nation had risen in the past and won the empire of the world. A few buried fragments are all that remain as memorials of the great dynasties that wielded the temporal power. There is, however, another element which finds its incarnation in matter, yet transcends its transmutation and apparent destruction: that is the burning flame born of thought which has been handed down through fleeting generations.

Not in matter but in thought, not in possessions nor even in attainments but in ideals, is to be found the seed of immortality. Not through material acquisition but in generous diffusion of ideas and ideals can the true empire of humanity be established. Thus to Asoka, to whom belonged this vast empire, bounded by the inviolate seas, after he had tried to ransom the world by giving away to the utmost, there came a time when he had nothing more to give, except one half of an *Amlaki* fruit. This was his last possession, and his anguished cry was that since he had nothing more to give, let the half of the *Amlaki* be accepted as his final gift.

Asoka's emblem of the *Amlaki* will be seen on the cornices of the Institute, and towering above all is the symbol of the thunderbolt. It was the Rishi Dadhichi, the pure and blameless, who offered his life that the divine weapon, the thunderbolt, might be fashioned out of his bones to smite evil and exalt righteousness. It is but half of the *Amlaki* that we can offer now. But the past shall be reborn in a yet nobler future. We stand here to-day and resume work to-morrow, so that by the efforts of our lives and our unshaken faith in the future we may all help to build the greater India yet to be.

CHAPTER XIX

THE BOSE INSTITUTE

WE have given in Bose's own words the ideals that animated him in the foundations of his Institute, and his inaugural address produced a profound impression not only in India but also in the West. We may in this connection quote the following passage from a leading article in *The Times* :

When Sir Jagadis chose the teaching of Science as his vocation a generation back, it was generally held that by its very constitution the Indian mind would always turn away from the study of Nature to metaphysical speculation. At that time, even had the capacity for enquiry and accurate observation been assumed, there were no opportunities for their employment; neither well-equipped laboratories nor skilled mechanicians existed. Little or nothing had then been done to break the almost exclusively literary mould into which higher Indian education had been directed. To bringing abcut the scientific renaissance Sir Jagadis has influentially contributed. Indians are justly proud of the possession of a few men who have gained world-wide reputation in their particular fields of activity, and this pride reacts strongly on public opinion. At the Research Institute a group of Indian post-graduate students devote their lives to research. The published Transactions of the Institute show that under the leadership of this eminent Bengali, Indian research is making substantial contribution to scientific knowledge; that in this field there is no fundamental difference between the Western and the Eastern mind, as was assumed when Sir Jagadis began his work. It may be, as one writer said, that the bent of research and the colour of theories will take something from the inherent qualities of the Indian mind; but the faith in ascertainable truths and the appeal to facts can

The Bose Institute.

underlie that research and those theories equally well in India and in Europe. In this no less than in other fields of knowledge India has her special contributions to make. Sir J. C. Bose's work has shown that through her meditative habit of mind she is peculiarly fitted to realise the idea of unity and to see in the phenomenal world an orderly universe, and this habit confers the power to hold the mind in pursuit of truth in infinite patience.

The *Athenæum* wrote :

The foundation of an Institute for research in pure science is an event in the history of India. The publication of the Transactions, the firstfruits of its activity, shows that it is an event also in the history of science.

We may now describe the Institute with its great scheme of continuing the researches of its founder, and of carrying on his large conceptions of the investigation of the processes of life with the help of all the resources and refinements of the physical sciences.

The building stands conveniently central for the intellectual activities and for the public of Calcutta. The building is of striking and dignified design, constructed of fine greyish purple sandstone, in Indian style of the pre-Mahommedan period, with symbolic ornament and details throughout. In front is a small garden, appropriately of sensitive plants, in which are a fountain and pool, and a sun-dial and an electrically controlled clock-dial for mutual comparison. A distinctive sign of the Institute and its work is a large double tracing, being automatically made in two parallel curves before the eyes of the observer. One of these curves records the result of the essential changes of the atmospheric environments—temperature, light, etc.—while the other summarises the responses of a large tree to those changing conditions for every minute of the twenty-four hours. This autograph of the tree gives striking and vivid demonstration that all plants, including even rigid trees, are fully sensitive to the changes around them. Even the passage of a drifting cloud is perceived and recorded by the tree in its own peculiar script and by an instrument devised for the purpose. Here, too, we have an illustration of the significance of the Institute as no mere laboratory of this or that peculiar line of physical or physiological research, but as from the first aiming at the concentration of the main resources and methods of the physical sciences, and their bearing upon the central problem of all the biological sciences—the problem of the essential processes of life itself.

The spacious Entrance Hall has a long series of glass cases which at once exhibit and preserve the essential apparatus of many past years of inquiry, from physical researches on electric waves to physiological researches on life. These are arranged in sequence of increasing perfection in observation and record. Step by step one passes from instruments direct and simple, sometimes rough and ready, to the present wellnigh magical elaboration of delicacy and exactitude. Here we have Bose's first apparatus for space signalling so far back as 1895. Recent instruments record the hitherto imperceptible pulsation of a plant's growth, marking perception-time within the thousandth part of a second and measuring ultra-microscopic movements. Thus the significance of the Institute as a centre of new invention of the most delicate apparatus, and as a centre of exceptional skill in construction, with the importance of these to science and eventually to industry, becomes apparent. For it is here worth noting that most of the great physical discoverers and inventors, as from Watt to Kelvin, or back to Galileo and Leonardo da Vinci, or onwards to Bell and Edison, and now to Bose himself, have been their own instrument-makers. For hand and brain alternately stimulate each other, to the complemental advances we call respectively 'discovery' and 'invention.'

Passing by the great Lecture Hall, we may look into the actual Laboratories, where researches are in progress. These are partly in the main building, but in greater number in the annex; and indeed primarily in the Garden around, with which we may therefore best begin. Here sensitive and other moving plants preponderate, like twiners and climbers, which cover a long and shady pergola ready to serve as a college cloister with its 'Philosophers' Way.' The nearer ground is laid out with pleasant lawns, fountain and tank for water-plants, and a group of trees, some old inmates of the Garden, others lately transplanted hither, at full size, under anæsthetics. Under these trees is a variety of apparatus, and above is perched an open platform for observation and thought by turns, since this alternation of keen outlook and meditative interpretation is the very process of science, the rhythm of its intellectual life.

From these and other beginnings of the Bio-physical Garden we enter the Laboratories. Here beyond the small marble entrance porch, again kept free for observation and meditation, are glass-houses—white, red and blue—for the study of the growth and behaviour of plants under light from opposite ends of the spectrum, as compared with normal conditions. Beyond are the larger laboratories —electrical, chemical, mechanical, microscopical, and physiological.

Having thus broadly surveyed the new Institute, and seen, or foreseen, something of its working, we may now enter the great Lecture Hall, which is seated for some 1500 auditors. Here the inauguration of the Institute took place, and courses of lectures by the Director and others are regularly given embodying the main results of the work of the Institute.

As the laboratories and grounds of the Institute afford various departures from conventional design, so too does this Hall, perhaps as yet the very best of environments for scientific exposition. It is of simple, efficient and beautiful plan, in which a large audience can at once see and hear without the visual interruption and the acoustic defects too common in auditoria designed without the collaboration of the physicist. Its purpose is neither restrictedly scientific, as its magnitude shows, nor yet simply popular. The essential idea is that of providing for the scientific exposition of new knowledge, and this at its highest appeals to the intelligent public.

The ornamentation of the hall appeals alike to scholar, artist, and the student of science. The ceiling design, with its great radiating lotus, is freely adapted from one of the cathedral caverns of Ajanta, and is bordered with the sensitive plants so specially connected with the work of the Institute. The body of the Hall is left quiet and plain, as befits its purpose of attention; but above the lantern screen an allegorical frieze has been painted—'The Quest,' by Nandalal Bose, a well-known member of that little group of Calcutta artists who are recovering the traditions of Indian painting, and adapting them to modern interest and to individual expression. Starting from the sacred river at dawn, strides forth the tall and keen-braced figure of Intellect, feeling the sword-edge with which he has to cleave his way, and companioned in his adventurous journey by his bride Imagination, who inspires him with her magic flute. The final and focal ornament of the Hall is a great relief in bronze, silver and gold, of the sun-god rising in his chariot to the daily cosmic strife of light with darkness.

How this new Institute may act and react with Indian thought and life, as well as with the world's science, and how also it may advance here industry, there agriculture, there again medicine, and above all the needed emancipation and renewal of higher education, it is too soon to predict. Enough for the present that this flowering of a creative life should now fully be opened. Its fruits will ere long be maturing, and its seeds of new activities spreading throughout India and flying over the world.

The substance of the foregoing description was written immediately after the opening of the Institute. Two years have since elapsed, and already the hopes then entertained are in the way of ample fulfilment. Two large volumes of 'Transactions' of the Institute have so far been published. They contain more than two score of papers, which embody many of Bose's initiatives, worked out under his continual direction and with the help of the research scholars and assistants, who by this means are brought into closest contact with their leader and enabled to catch his spirit and enthusiasm.

There remain, however, many needs to be provided for, if the enterprise is to be prepared for covering the vast fields of clearly conceived research. Much is still wanting before space and equipment can be deemed adequate; much before such provision can be made for the scholars that they may continue their work unhampered by anxiety for the future. In this service they can look for no worldly advantage, nor is any honour likely to be conferred on them by the University. For the test applied in the examinations of the Indian Universities is that of knowledge thoroughly accepted and established in the West; and it cannot be until after the passage of many years that Bose's discoveries will reach the academic centres through the medium of standard text-books.

Hence the permanence of the Institute, and the continuance and progressive expansion of its activity, were realised as a matter of great urgency. Bose, it is true, has made over all his fortune to the Trustees; but an international Institute of Science cannot be built up on an endowment of necessity so inadequate. And it will be obvious that for such a man as Bose to be beset by business and financial anxieties could not fail to be disastrous. His one consuming desire is and must be to concentrate the whole of his powers upon his work, in order to secure the full initiative, and wherever possible the completion, of the many fresh lines of discovery to which his researches incessantly lead—lines which, it would appear, no other has so clearly discerned, if indeed conceived at all.

But this necessary quiet and leisure for the pursuit of work is plainly not yet to be his for several years. He has had to train his successors for the administration of the Institute. He had the initial good fortune to secure as Assistant Director an old pupil who proved his ability and his devotion in the pursuit of research. To those who are working under him Bose has given every opportunity of developing their individuality.

It was towards the end of 1919 that Bose felt impelled, in the interests of his Institute, to visit England—there to convince, fully and finally, the scientific public of the importance of the modern Indian contribution to science.

But the time chosen for this purpose did not at all seem promising. Bose's English friends uttered abundant warning as to the distracted political and social conditions of England. The national affairs, the national temper, had made little apparent progress, in the first year of nominal peace, towards a recovery of the normal. He would find it impossible, they said, to arouse any interest in such scientific work as his, still less in such a scheme as the Calcutta Institute. The discouragement was powerful and various; but in spite of it Bose persisted in his plans and reached London in the middle of November.

His reception was extraordinarily different from what he had been led, by friendly voices in England and India, to expect. It was as though the entire British world had been prepared, by every sort of experience, to receive and acclaim the discoveries which, in previous years, had seemed to be problematical and remote. It was as though all doors were flung wide open.

What may be described as the authentic recognition by leading thinkers came in December, in the form of a meeting at the India Office, arranged by Mr. Montagu, the Secretary of State for India, who had been deeply interested in Bose's work ever since, a good many years before, during his tour as Under Secretary, he had met with it in Calcutta. Bose was invited to give a lecture and demonstration, with Mr. Arthur Balfour in the chair. There can be no exaggeration in saying that the occasion was without parallel in the records of the India Office, and we may take it as a fine and peculiarly agreeable promise of a new spirit in the governmental conception of India. The lecture-room was filled with a distinguished and highly representative audience, whose response was immediate and enthusiastic. They were shown a typical series of results, and were given a demonstration of the powers of the Magnetic Crescograph, which was doubtless for those present a startling revelation of the widening world of experimental knowledge.

So great was the interest excited that full summaries of the lecture were cabled to the Continent and to America, while the British Press accorded to the discourse an amount of space, and to the Indian savant a warmth of appreciation, which is unusual in newspaper treatment of scientific events. A leading article in *The Times* contained the following passage :

> Sir Jagadis Chunder Bose is a fine example of the fertile union between the immemorial mysticism of Indian philosophy, and the experimental methods of Western science. Whilst we in Europe were still steeped in the rude empiricism of barbaric life, the subtle Eastern had swept the whole universe into a synthesis and had seen the *one* in all its changing manifestations. . . . He is pursuing science not only for itself but for its application to the benefit of mankind. We welcome the additions to knowledge which he has made, but most of all we welcome in him the evidence that India and Great Britain can unite their genius to mutual advantage.

Professor J. Arthur Thomson wrote in the course of an article in the *New Statesman*:

> It is in accordance with the genius of India that the investigator should press further towards unity than we have yet hinted at; should seek to correlate responses and memory impressions in the living with their analogues in inorganic matter, and should see in anticipation the lines of physics, of physiology and of psychology converging and meeting. (These are) questionings of a prince of experimenters whom we are proud to welcome in our midst to-day.

Within a month, therefore, of his arrival in London Bose had overflowing evidence of the most eager and widespread interest in his work and its significance for the world. As regards his fellow-investigators and the educated public in general, this interest is not to be wondered at. The years of the war, the years since his last visit to England, have been a period of unexampled mental upheaval and, in the sphere of applied science, of experiment and achievement surpassing everything hitherto known. With this there has come an intense stimulus to all inquiry and discussion relating to the mysterious activities of life, and more particularly to the phenomena in the borderland between the animate and the so-called inanimate. In that curiosity to-day the average person shares as never before.

As regards the interest of the leaders in thought and scientific inquiry, Bose has fully secured it in recent years. When, before the war, he set up a temporary laboratory in Maida Vale, he was continually called upon by men distinguished in many walks of life. During the spring of 1920 his laboratory in Bloomsbury Square was visited by almost all the leading men of science. He was invited by both the Universities of Oxford and Cambridge, and gave his addresses and demonstrations before highly appreciative audiences. The Vice-Chancellor of Leeds University sent him a most cordial invitation to lecture. In offering him the welcome of the University, Sir Michael Sadler, who had recently been in India as Chairman of the Commission for the Reform of Calcutta University, spoke with the authority of personal knowledge of Bose's work in India as University teacher as well as original investigator. 'India,' he said, 'needed more science in her secondary and higher education, and needed to be delivered from the tyranny of excessive examinations. When he and his colleagues were inquiring into the educational work in the Presidency of Bengal, he realised more vividly than before what Sir Jagadis's work meant not only to Bengal but to India. It was the genius of the Indian and the genius of the Englishman to do the finest work under conditions of freedom and under the stimulus of a master mind. The great work in science and in arts would be done not under the punctual and meritorious preparation for an examination, under a syllabus designed by a Sanhedrin, but in institutes devoted to the free investigation of some great problem. Sir Jagadis Bose's name, and the name of the Research Institute he founded in Calcutta, acted to thousands in India as a beacon light, because science was studied for the love of science, and with freedom and zeal.'

There followed an honour from the University of Aberdeen, which awarded Sir Jagadis Bose the honorary degree of LL.D., in recognition of the important contributions which he had made for the advance of general physiology and for his investigations on the Irritability of Plants.

Finally, in relation to this matter of formal acceptance and recognition by his European peers, a word remains to be said touching the most significant incident of all. The honour recognised by men of science throughout the British Dominions as the proudest of all is the award of the Fellowship of the Royal Society. That is being conferred upon Bose as this volume goes to press (May 1920), in recognition of his contributions, not only in physics, but in physiology also. It comes to him as the culmination of a series of discussions and incidents spread over two decades, and at the last in a collective decision which had in it something of dramatic unanimity and completeness. In May 1901 Bose had communicated to the Royal Society his first results in plant response; and, as has been recorded in this narrative, his paper was rejected. It took almost twenty years for the truth to make its way completely into the light—twenty years of persistent and unswerving labour devoted to the working out of new methods of inquiry; the victorious following out of the experiments which, questioned and belittled in the first stage, have since added a marvellous new province to the empire of human knowledge. What was deemed, in 1901, to be dubious and obscure was, in 1920, acknowledged and acclaimed. Bose's former opponents had now become his warmest and staunchest friends; and in the Royal Society, physicists, physiologists, and psychologists united in according the honour of the Fellowship to their fellow-worker and revealer from the East.

Two things in particular seem worthy of clear statement in this connection. The first is that among men of science full recognition comes earliest to those whose labours lie in clearly defined paths and well within the frontiers laid down by the orthodox classification of the sciences. It comes last and most hardly to men like Bose, who find themselves impelled over the frontiers as drawn, moving among the conceptions of different sciences and pursuing experiments in territory where, inevitably, they are looked upon as intruders.

The second thing is this. There are some who regarded the prolonged delay in the grant of official recognition by the high court of scientific judgment as due to prejudice against a stranger. In Bose's case any such hypothesis would be absurd. From beginning to end he has stood among his fellows simply as a man of science. In the discussions over the nature and final value of the extraordinary results with which his name and fame are identified, there has never been any hint of misunderstanding, or collision between East and West. His great work has won for him the enthusiastic admiration of scientific men all over the world; and this became strikingly evident on a recent occasion. A persistent opponent of his wrote to *The Times* questioning the reliability of the crescograph and suggesting that a demonstration should be given at a physiological laboratory before leading experts. Bose accepted the challenge, and the result of his demonstration was the occasion of a conjoint tribute so remarkable that it probably stands by itself in recent science. The following appeared in *Nature*, May 6, 1920:

Sir Jagadis Bose's crescograph is so remarkably sensitive that doubt was recently expressed as to the reality of its indications as regards plant growth: and the suggestion was made that the effects shown by it were due to physical changes. A demonstration in University College, London, on April 23, has however led Lord Rayleigh and Professors Bayliss, V. H. Blackman, A. J. Clark, W. C. Clinton, and F. G. Donnan to state in *The Times* of May 4: 'We are satisfied that the growth of plant tissues is correctly recorded by this instrument, and at a magnification of from one million to ten million times.' Sir W. H. Bragg and Professor F. W. Oliver, who have seen similar demonstrations elsewhere, give like testimony that the crescograph shows actual response of living plant tissues to stimulus.

The following extract is reproduced from Bose's dignified letter to *The Times*, May 5:

Criticism which transgresses the limit of fairness must inevitably hinder the advance of knowledge. My special investigations have by their very nature presented extraordinary difficulties. I regret to say that during a period of 20 years these difficulties have been greatly aggravated by misrepresentations and worse. . . . The obstacles deliberately placed in my path I can now ignore and forget. If the result of my work, by upsetting any particular theory, has roused the hostility here and there of an individual, I can the more take comfort in the warm welcome which has been extended to me by the great body of scientific men of this country.

The difficulty among the orthodox, in science as in religion, is the relation of new truth to old theory. The innovator whose word or work cannot be accepted without the modification or rejection of established dogma knows of a surety what his destiny is. He must fight his way. The kingdom of knowledge is taken by storm. In the case of J. C. Bose, the Royal Society has admitted the innovator and crowned his work.

The life-story of Jagadis Bose is worthy of close and ardent consideration by all young Indians whose purpose is shaping itself towards the service of science or other high cause of the intelligence or the social spirit. It is possible that, looking upon the triumph of the end and knowing nothing of the long uphill road, the slow costly attainment of ends, they may think that a fine laboratory or other material endowment the antecedent condition of successful achievement in intellectual creation. The truth, indeed, is far otherwise. The countless obstacles which had to be surmounted only called forth in Bose all the endurance and all the effort which are latent in manly natures, welding them to the fullest strength of character and intensity of thought by which alone a great life-task can be accomplished. In contemplating the great career of his countryman, the young Indian will be stimulated to put brain and hand to fine tasks, nothing fearing. Thus will he be inspired not only to recover the noble intellectual traditions of the Indian past, but to restate these traditions in modern terms, and find the greatest challenge for mind and soul in achieving their vital relation with the coming age. By impassioned inquiry and research, by resolute and unfearing work, by direct and personal action on positive lines and in the constructive spirit—by these things, and by nothing short of these, can India or Europe or the vast enduring brotherhood of mankind be carried further along the road to their deeply needed and long awaited reconstruction.

But now the question may be asked—many indeed will find themselves impelled to ask it—What of the teeming and toiling millions of India : what part have they in these great schemes of science, and what can such schemes do for them ? Of course, with only too great readiness the same question may be asked in respect of the millions of Europe and America—for it is clear that their full awakening to science is still far off, their incorporation into the best that civilisation has to offer. The answer in both cases must be essentially the same : the arousal and incorporation must in the end come, unless our modern world of knowledge and society is to go down in tragic failure.

As regards India, it is profoundly true, as it is still true of the European multitudes, that illiteracy does not necessarily connote darkness. The Indian villager is not nearly so ignorant as by the average of literates he is judged to be. The needed popularisation of science is commonly thought of by us as a matter of definite exposition to the untaught; but that is only part of it. In the meantime, and continuously, the traditional life of the people, with its spiritual roots in the organic being of Society and its folk-knowledge linking the generations, enables the people to get at something of the greater knowledge in their own fashion. The story of a Moslem villager who invited Bose to enter his house so that his women-folk might see him is delightfully to the point. It was soon after the Indian Press had spread the news that the Bengal wonder-worker had been received with acclamation in every country he visited during his tour round the world. 'But am I not a stranger?' Bose asked, 'and do you not maintain the seclusion of your zenana?' 'You,' replied the Moslem triumphantly, 'are no stranger. You are one of us. Has not your voice reached everywhere?' So, too, with Bose's village neighbours at Sijberia. Of his experimental garden there they say, 'That is where, at night, the plants talk to him!'

In their own way then—a very real way—the simple labouring folk may be, and even now are being reached by such vital movements of quickening and renewing literature and advancing knowledge as their poets and men of letters, headed by Rabindranath Tagore, their men of science headed by Jagadis Bose, are opening out to them—to them, and above all to their children; for manifestly it is only with the coming generations that such sowings can be brought to harvest, and thence again to fresh sowings on ever widening fields.

It is here, perhaps, in the quietude of his village that we might have left him at the close of this record. But I seem to hear his words of protest: 'No, it is not in the village that my work is to end ; from the village I came out, to discover a larger world. Like that of my boyhood's hero, Karna, my life has been ever one of combat, and must be to the last. It is not for man to complain of circumstances, but bravely to accept, to confront, and to dominate them. The faith in which my long-dreamed-of Temple of Science has been at last brought within reach of fulfilment, is the faith that when one has gained the vision of a purpose to which he can and must dedicate himself wholly, then the closed doors will be opened and the seemingly impossible become attainable.'

Hence, accordingly, the symbol of Bose's life, struggle, and achievement is to be found less in the village that nourished his childhood and provides the periodic retreat for his maturity, than in the abounding energy of the great city, in which, of necessity, his Institute is placed and from which it draws its power and inspiration. He alone who has striven and conquered can enrich the world by a generous bestowing of the fruits of his victorious experience.

INDEX